GIVE THEM WHAT YOU HAVE

D1411823

GIVE THEM WHAT YOU HAVE

Interpreting the New Testament for Today

John J. Denniston

Liguori
<small>LIGUORI, MISSOURI</small>

Imprimi Potest: Thomas D. Picton, C.Ss.R.
Provincial, Denver Province • The Redemptorists

Published by Liguori Publications • Liguori, Missouri
www.liguori.org

Library of Congress Cataloging-in-Publication Data
Denniston, John J.
   Give them what you have : interpreting the New Testament for today /
John J. Denniston.
      p. cm.
   ISBN 978-0-7648-1620-8
   1. Bible. N.T.—Criticism, interpretation, etc. 2. Bible. N.T.
Gospels—Criticism, interpretation, etc. I. Title.

BS2361.3.D46 2008
225.6—dc22   2008003348

Liguori Publications, a nonprofit corporation, is an apostolate of the Redemptorists. To learn more about the Redemptorists, visit *Redemptorists.com.*

Printed in the United States of America
12 11 10 09 08   5 4 3 2 1
First edition

To my nephew,
JOSEPH A. WALLACE
Even if autism keeps you from reading the Word of God,
may you sense it each day in our family's love for you.

With my love
and my prayers we all
live each day generously
and with laughter

love
Father John

Contents

Introduction   ix

Acknowledgments   xi

1. Learning to Drive   1

2. Beginning to Interpret the Bible   15

3. The Bible Before Jesus   29

4. The History of Israel   37

5. Paul and the New "Way"   69

6. The Gospel According to Mark   93

7. The Gospel According to Matthew   121

8. The Gospel According to Luke   141

9. The Gospel According to John   167

Epilogue   191

Introduction

G ive them what you have...
    They say beginnings and endings are the easiest to endure. We do them only once. The span between those markers—the great middle—is where we more often confront complexity, even weariness. In response to our confusion, a Scripture scholar and popular Church leader on Long Island, New York, once offered a homily that concluded with a paraphrase of Jesus' words to his bewildered apostles when they tried to feed five thousand people with only a few loaves of bread: *Give them what you have...I will take care of whatever else is needed* (see Mark 6:37). In the end, the mission of the Lord's closest followers is to share the bits and pieces they have come to believe about God's presence, despite personal failings and blindness, and then allow God to complete it.

Those familiar with the New Testament will recognize the feeding of the multitudes as one miracle story repeated in each of the four canonical (authorized) Gospels. Mark has two versions (6:31–44; 8:1–10), so does Matthew (14:13–21; 15:32–39). It is found once in John (6:1–15) and once in Luke (9:10–17). Some scholars think the story was popular in the early community celebrations of the Eucharist, especially with its call for the active participation of Jesus' friends in his mission. In any event, the paraphrase of the Gospel text is an example of a traditional and ancient way of understanding Scripture, a practice often used in homilies. That is, the paraphrase arises from a so-called spiritual reading of the Gospels with an application to everyday life (what theologians refer to as *tropology*). Such spiritual reading (often used in preaching) can make a Gospel theme "come alive" for listeners, putting Jesus into our streets, and hopefully into our hearts. This book uses the same hermeneutic tools, that is, the devices that help us build our understanding of Scripture with respect to our world. At times, there is a "homiletic," sometimes "spiritual," tone in the essays—a ring no different from what echoes throughout the Scriptures. As we will see, the final versions of the New Testament as we know it arose from a time when theologians, philosophers, scientists, artists, and preachers alike applied the Word of God to everyday life, making clear that Scripture is not static. The Scriptures, they say, are dynamic, empowering us to live every aspect of our life with respect to revelation. The issues, problems, and hopes the New Testament addresses are painfully similar to the ones we experience today. In the study that follows, attention is paid to the way some contemporary people feel and behave, and the unfinished work of biblical scholarship.

I am grateful to the undergraduate students at Fordham University. It was the experience of listening to their requests for a simple resource to use before reading the biblical text—a first for many—that planted the seeds for the essays. It seems to me, when the ordinary experiences of people are brought near to the word of God, light is thrown not only on their experiences, but on the Word of God as well. We give "what we have"; sometimes, we give a few reasons to believe. And the most promising question we can ask as we read the New Testament is: What kind of God is presented? Images of God, like self-images, never exhaust the reality in question; they remain as unfinished as the mission Jesus gave his friends or the expectations we make about ourselves—others are needed to complete them. My hope is that these essays will encourage people, especially beginners, to explore the New Testament with thoughtfulness and excitement, and to recognize along the way the debt we owe to those who have made generous, lifelong commitments to biblical scholarship and to the mission of the Lord's church to feed and to be fed by his words.

Acknowledgments

Who can decide where indebtedness begins, especially when influence on your thinking is in question? I recall with gratitude my teachers and mentors, especially those whose influence I feel even after more than twenty-five years of teaching and ministry. I am grateful to scholars such as the late Myles Bourke, Madeline Boucher, and Homer Giblin, S.J., for their extraordinary commitments to biblical scholarship and to service in the academic and church communities. So, too, I received numerous formative ideas from Bishop Emil Wcela, William Marin, and George McCauley, S.J. Their writings and unpublished lecture notes remain resources I continue to consult and form the bedrock on which the following chapters rely. I am grateful to my friends Bill Wrensen and Jesuit Fathers Joseph Lienhard and Ned Mattimoe for reading various drafts of essays in the volume and for their judicious comments. Finally, I thank Daniel Michaels of Ligouri Publications, for his support and enthusiasm for the project, and for the many conversations wherein we shared the distress and humor of proofreading as well as of life.

John J. Denniston

Proceeds from the sales of this volume will be donated by the author to the "Dean of Fordham College 'Agape' Fund" to assist students who lose a parent during their college studies. Agape is used in the New Testament more than 250 times. It is sometimes translated as "selfless giving," "charity," or less accurately as "love." It comes from a verse in Saint Paul's First Letter to the Corinthians (13:13): "And now faith, hope, and love abide, these three; and the greatest of these is love."

1

Learning to Drive

The Bible is a complex book. If the Bible were a car, most of us couldn't identify the make, model, or power of the engine, and we would have difficulty discerning whether or not we should drive or be passengers. In fact, we may not even recognize it as a mode of transportation. A few passages of the Bible are immediately understandable, but anyone looking for more than a superficial knowledge must puzzle over its obscure genealogies and place names, archaic rituals, unfamiliar ideas, and apparent contradictions. Students soon learn that the Bible is a collection of letters, poetry, histories, and narratives. These materials were preached, edited, liturgically prayed, translated, and laboriously recopied centuries before the translations available to us today were printed.

Some of us know people who attempt to read the entire Bible from Genesis to the end of the New Testament but stop exhausted at the Book of Exodus or soon thereafter. Frustrated and no wiser, they settle for more entertaining and less venturesome interpretations from media documentaries, family, friends, the Internet, or Sunday sermons. Others honor their version of the Bible to the letter and without gloss as God's word. Still others are so deeply committed to confessional allegiances (for example, Catholic versus Protestant or believer versus atheist), they sometimes ignore even their intellectual integrity to defend their community.

Ultimately, we must learn how to assimilate the various components of the Bible—structure, authorship, history, style, and so forth—before we can move our faith forward. This book is a Bible driver's manual, a simple introduction to the key concepts that shape our understanding of God's word.

EXTREMES OF BIBLICAL INTERPRETATION

Isn't it amazing how extremes teach us about life? Our first experience behind the wheel of a car, for example, teaches us that the gas pedal moves us forward and the brake pedal brings us to a stop—it takes some skill before we find the happy medium between fast and slow (some never do)—not to mention the fact that we have to steer the wheel and shift gears at the same time. The brake pedal, we quickly learn, is diametrically opposed to the gas pedal, but we must learn to operate them in harmony before we can arrive at our destination. Similarly, two popular forms of biblical interpretation today espouse radically different viewpoints and require unique skill sets: one of blind acceptance ("literal fundamentalism") and one of complete suspicion ("secular postmodernism"). Navigating our way between these extremes will help us get a feel for the wheel—and hopefully discover the richness of the Bible.

Literal Fundamentalism

A popular biblical theme park in Texas depicts dinosaurs and people living together in the Garden of Eden. The creators and enthusiastic visitors revere the Bible as, quite literally, "words from God." Scripture, they say, is exempt from contemporary archaeology, linguistics, science, history, and cultural studies. In fact, for them, the trajectory of knowledge is opposite—the Bible teaches us about contemporary science (which may explain why one can find Deuteronomy and dinosaurs in the same space). If the Bible says that God made the world in six days or that Jonah lived in a fish's stomach, then that is what happened and no further discussion is needed. Christians who subscribe to this view are known as *literal fundamentalists*. Most will stop at nothing to reconstruct their existence with respect to the Bible, and they are bold enough to assume that they have the signature (original) version of God's word. Unfortunately, their all-gas-and-no-brake interpretation of the word can sometimes crash them head-on into the historical inaccuracies and inconsistencies within the Bible. They often speed by the rich nuances and healing power of the Gospels in favor of black-and-white answers. Christians are not alone in this regard.

An equivalent view is found in Islamic fundamentalism. The Qur'an (meaning "recitation") is revered as a miracle. According to fundamentalist Muslims, the Qur'an is *the* direct and final divine revelation given to Muhammad (ca. 571–632) in Arabia during the seventh century. So, too, the Church of Jesus Christ, Latter-Day Saints (the Mormons) records that its founder, Joseph Smith (1805–1844), received a series of private revelations from God delivered by the angel Moroni, son of the prophet Mormon, near Binghamton, New York, in 1830. The angel presented golden tablets to Smith and provided him with spectacles to translate its writings. The Book of Mormon is revered, among other things, as a sequel to the New Testament. In fact, Mormons are still waiting for an unspecified date when God's revelation will be finished, perhaps through another prophet. In most fundamentalist traditions, God's "literal" authorship of the Bible makes every word sacred for its adherents.

Secular Postmodernism

On the opposite end of the spectrum, if not in another sphere altogether, stand secular postmodernists. Secular postmodernism, like biblical fundamentalism, has many varieties. However, the term typically refers to thinkers who have a profound skepticism toward the assumptions people make about knowledge, truth, reason, and religious faith. Some advocates question the validity of any claim to absolute truth (such as the "absolute" existence of a transcendent God or the Trinity). They understand the basis of "truth" as a story (sometimes referred to as a "narrative") that privileges certain groups and marginalizes others. The "truth" of the Bible, they claim, is no exception. Some postmodernists evaluate claims to absolute truths, such as one might experience in the Bible, as either myths or a power plays to impose an overarching story (or "meta-narrative") on the vulnerable and voiceless. They are particularly cautious of religious metanarratives. Common to those who share these sympathies is the fear of any person or system of people that claims to understand ultimate truth. Thus, according to a secular postmodernist, any dogmatist (a person who defines beliefs for a particular church) or absolutist (one who sees the world as black and white, such as a fundamentalist) is particularly naïve, reactionary, and dangerous. In contrast to the all-or-nothing literal fundamentalist, secular postmodernists have their feet firmly against the brake, refusing to acknowledge anything that has to do with faith. As anyone has witnessed when driving behind a garbage truck, it's hard to get to your destination when your foot is on the brake. Similarly, it is difficult to discover the heart of Jesus' message when stopping short of the transcendent and universal elements of faith that prompted the writing of the Bible in the first place.

This synopsis of fundamentalist and postmodernist viewpoints is not meant to deny their prevalence, complexity, and relevance or to wish them away. To the contrary, they each provide a partial description of the ways in which contemporary Western thought and opinion unfolds, and they offer a corrective to our sometimes lazy interpretations of Scripture. They are moods that seem to represent deep preconceptual attitudes toward the meaning of existence and thus are worthy of consideration. They are the ways in which people characteristically apprehend the world and their place in it. Langdon Gilkey once explained that these moods are not philosophies as much as they are backgrounds for specific philosophies of life. They are presuppositions of thought, sometimes unconscious or unreflective, that form part of the cultural life of an epoch. In the following chapters, we will evaluate these descriptions, especially as they inform and explain the current atmosphere in which people approach the Bible, if not life itself.

DIVINE INSPIRATION

Is it any surprise that many who plunge unguarded into the Bible drown in the minutiae of laws, prophecies, historical anomalies, and thousands of unfamiliar names, places, and events? From dry and bewildered lips, unprepared readers utter a universal plea for help—who is God? How does God speak to us? And, unfortunately, after several strokes into the Book of Genesis, many either discard the credibility of the Bible altogether or they rely solely on the teaching of others, particularly our mentors in Hollywood. For many Christians, then, the Bible appears not to speak directly to us but sneaks into our lives by way of an end around. The millennia that separate us from the writers of the Bible compound the mystery. We not only question how God speaks to us, but we wonder how God spoke to the writers of the Bible in the first place. This fundamental question—how God spoke to biblical authors or "divine inspiration"—has been proposed again and again (with varying results) by the many "moods" of history. The dialogue is our starting point for discovering an appropriate method of interpreting Scripture.

Most Christians have a relationship with the Bible that resembles a prearranged marriage—we've inherited our faith from our parents and we've been told to love God through a book that we've never met. Our first task, it seems, is to figure out how God spoke to our new friends (the characters in the Bible), and from there we can learn how God might be speaking to us. This courtship with God has challenged scholars for centuries. Consider the most popular translation of the Bible (from Hebrew and Greek to Latin) prepared in the fifth century by Jerome and used throughout Christianity for more than one thousand years. His translation is known as the *Vulgate*, the "public" Bible, and it has shaped most of the theology in the Western Church. A painting by Simon Vouet (1625) depicts Jerome in an ecstatic trance with an angel holding a trumpet near his ear. According to Vouet, Jerome's angelic iPod blasted words of centuries past directly into his ear and onto the parchment. The idea that inspiration means listening to an angel or taking divine dictation has been rejected by scholars and church leaders, as we will see, from the earliest times, yet Christians have always recognized the Scriptures as somehow containing God's revelation. Despite countless accounts to the contrary, including that of Jerome and the biblical authors themselves, the angelic trumpet version of divine inspiration keeps playing into our culture and understanding of the Bible.

Luke eliminates the idea of trance-induced dictation in the opening sentences of his Gospel. He acknowledges the great personal labor he put into the work of gathering information and writing the narrative. "Since many [Mark and perhaps Matthew or others he relied on] have undertaken to set down an orderly account of the events [in Jesus' life] that have been fulfilled among us…I too decided, after investigating everything carefully from the very first, to write an orderly account for you…" (Luke 1:1–3). No iPods, no trumpets—just the Holy Spirit and honest research.

The most remarkable biblical statement on the subject is found in the Old Testament Book of Second Maccabees:

> [A]ll this, which has been set forth by Jason of Cyrene in five volumes, we shall attempt to condense into a single book….For us who have undertaken the toil of abbreviating, it is no light matter but calls for sweat and loss of sleep, just as it is not easy for one who prepares a banquet and seeks the benefit of others. Nevertheless, to secure the gratitude of many we will gladly endure the uncomfortable toil, leaving the responsibility for exact details to the compiler, while devoting our effort to arriving at the outlines of the condensation.
>
> 2 Maccabees 2:23, 26–28

In other words, the inspired writers worked without any direct awareness that God participated as they wrote. The author concludes by saying "So I will here end my story. If it is well told and to the point, that is what I myself desired; if it is poorly done and mediocre, that was the best I could do" (2 Maccabees 15:37–38). It seems the literal fundamentalists must overlook these admissions before plugging in their angelic headsets.

The Catholic Church acknowledged that the Bible is the word of God, and God himself is the author and the ultimate source of its teachings, but the Church asserts that the text was composed by people, working as people do. An example might clarify the point. Not long ago a friend was ordained a priest in the Episcopal church. At her ordination, her daughter said to me, "God made my Mom a priest." Her mother, no doubt, has a profound sense of gratitude to God for the call to ministry in her denomination. The fact of God's call did not eliminate any of the struggles, the doubts, the questioning of fitness or motives, the examination of other alternatives. My friend had to decide to ask for ordination. It was a free choice.

We can learn from the teaching of Christianity that God's freedom does not compete or interfere with human freedom. Otherwise, it would be very difficult for us (God and humanity) to love each other. With love as our litmus test, we know that God will never force us to do anything. A person can make a free choice, wrestling with all the possibilities and responsibilities, yet the choice that follows can be understood as God's choice, too. This is one of the puzzling mysteries in Christianity. Another example may help to clarify the teaching.

When we struggle to accomplish something and succeed, some people feel the need to thank God. Even if it was a personal success, believers give God credit, too. When God acts in (or through) us, God doesn't make us less human, like robots, but more human. God's activity in our life (when we allow it) helps us to embrace our humanness as it was meant to be—in love with others and with God. When one is effectively doing God's will, the believer might say, "I am the most free."

A similar idea takes place with inspiration. When God "guides" the composition of a particular writing and makes it speak his own word, the writer remains thoroughly human and free, usually unaware of any divine presence and assistance. This is why, when we want to know the fullest meaning of a Scripture passage, we use all the available resources of historical and literary study to learn what the human authors meant to say to their audiences long ago. The Second Vatican Council in the 1960s recommended to Catholics: "Seeing that, in sacred scripture, God speaks through human beings in human fashion, it follows that the interpreters of sacred scripture, if they are to ascertain what God has wished to communicate to us, should carefully search out the meaning which the sacred writers really had in mind, that meaning which God had thought well to manifest through the medium of their words" (Dogmatic Constitution on Divine Revelation [*Dei Verbum*] 12).

FAITH AND REASON

We should use caution when we examine history to understand divine inspiration. Historians sometimes are required to separate the meaning of the Bible from its literary form, and the facts become set within a new interpretative framework that is defined by the scholar, and thus not by the Bible. Analogously, it would be like a modern critique of the U.S. Constitution drawn solely from the perspective of historians who specialize in the original authors of the document, without accounting for its dynamic, amendable character, and/or the government that it continues to shape today. Such methods would freeze the Constitution in time and disregard the good (and bad) that has come from our courts and political offices. Accordingly, we must beware that a static, history-only account of the Bible will limit our perspective to the assumptions held by biblical historians alone.

In May 1996, Joseph Cardinal Ratzinger, now Pope Benedict XVI, analyzed this concern in a speech titled "Relativism: The Central Problem for Faith Today." He presented it to the doctrinal commissions of the Bishops' Conferences of Latin America in Guadalajara, Mexico.

...The historical-critical method is an excellent instrument for reading historical sources and interpreting texts. But it contains its own philosophy...if it is applied to the Bible, two factors come clearly to light...First, the method wants to find about the past as something past. It wants to grasp with the greatest precision what happened at a past moment, closed in its past situation, at the point where it was found in time. Furthermore, it supposes that history is, in principle, uniform; therefore, man with all his differences and the world with all its distinctions are determined by the same laws and limitations so that I can eliminate whatever is impossible. What cannot happen today in any way could not happen yesterday nor will it happen tomorrow.

If we apply this to the Bible, it means the following: A text, a happening, a person will be strictly fixed in his or her past. There is the desire to verify what the past author said at that time and what he could have said or thought. This is what is "historical" about the "past." Therefore, historical-critical exegesis does not bring the Bible to today, to my current life. This is impossible. On the contrary, it separates it from me and shows it strictly fixed in the past....

Such exegesis, by definition, expresses reality, not today's or mine, but yesterday's, another's reality. Therefore, it can never show the Christ of today, tomorrow and always, but only—if it remains faithful to itself— the Christ of yesterday.

The pope's cautions relate to a mistaken idea of the sufficiency of a strictly historical method used by biblical scholars. Note that the pope does not discourage historical critique; he merely cautions against making history the *only* basis of study. Despite his caution (and many others scholars of faith), in a desire to be scientific and objective, some scholars (even some Catholic scholars) consider the religious dimension of the Bible's origins, its compilation, and usage as unreliable details in a scientific method. Not surprisingly, these scholars are the same ones who reject anyone who claims to know about an absolute truth or "metanarrative," those I have named *secular postmodernists*. As a result of these scholars, the reigning paradigm in postmodern academic biblical studies focuses solely on the human character of the writers with no value or attention given to the question of divine authorship. The Bible, they say, is best understood as a human invention, rather than, in any sense, a divine revelation.

Strict objectivity may be essential to the scientific method, but in the humanities—the study of "human," creative, often faith-filled existence— it is necessary to evaluate the subjective assumptions scholars use in their interpretations. Subjective elements of interpretation are not usually self-evident or explained by the so-called experts who write about the Bible. As a result, students may not understand the worldview of the scholar much less the world-view of the Bible, and these voids lead to disastrous interpretations.

Pope Benedict XVI recommends a reorientation of biblical scholarship to include the religious presuppositions of faith that inspire the writing of bibli-cal resources. He does not counsel abandoning the exacting science of bibli-cal exegesis as it seeks to understand them in their proper historical contexts, or the disciplined interrogation of biblical sources to gain the most verified information possible. Instead, he recommends the revival of a third arena of biblical methodology: Christian tradition or Christian life and practice. The conclusions offered by exegetes and historians are valuable—they need to be re-spected and utilized even as they remain unfinished when they avoid the Bible's religious context—but they must always be interpreted within the framework of a dynamic, faith-filled community of believers, which sometimes requires more than empirical evidence.

Competent and complete biblical reading requires openness to the possibility of new interpretations and the religious dimensions of the word. Faith was part of the context in which the biblical authors wrote as well as how their writings were received, and contemporary explanations of this reality and the meaning of God's authorship need to be deciphered. Contemporary Bible readers need assistance to evaluate the faith of the biblical authors as well as their own. Thus the pope encourages a refoundation of biblical theology, rather than a continu-ing uncritical acceptance or rejection of current biblical studies methods.

How can this be accomplished? Scholarship needs to criticize its own sci-entific methods, especially those unstated attachments to philosophical pre-suppositions rooted, for example, in the eighteenth- and nineteenth-century Enlightenment rejection of metaphysics (the study of things beyond or above ["meta"] the physical) in which the possibility of humans hearing (being in-spired by) anything from God is denied. When these presuppositions reveal the human dimensions of the Bible only, according to Benedict, "the Word's genuine author, God, is removed from reach." Catholic theology is in particular need of a renewed unity between its biblical specialists and other branches in its theol-ogy, especially between dogmatic (the study of doctrine) or systematic (how we organize our faith) theology and biblical theology. A more critical criticism of biblical methods is essential along with a revival of an ecclesial exegesis—that is, an interpretation of the Bible (exegesis) from the perspective of the universal Church (*Ecclesia*)—to assist contemporary believers. If biblical interpretation is to offer more than academic insights, abstractions, or conclusions, the role of religious faith must not be excluded from the act of interpretation.

The American biblical scholar, Raymond Brown, shortly before his death in 1998, warned: "For their part scholars would do well to avoid a rhetoric whereby their discoveries are presented as certain, making the discoverers the infallible arbiters of Christian faith." Brown, who dedicated his life to the technical and critical study of the Bible as a distinct scientific discipline, recognized that a much more comprehensive interpretative process includes Christian tradition and practice. "Biblical books are documents written by those who believed in the God of Abraham and the Father of Jesus Christ: good sense suggests that communities sharing that faith have an authority in dealing with those books."

The above is not a call to some sort of ecclesial fundamentalism; rather it is a caution to keep in mind. Certain methods are incapable of providing a comprehensive account of the spiritual, faith-filled realities that are also the subject matter of the Bible. Discipleship, tradition, and faith are necessary elements of interpretation. Benedict wants a method that begins with the best scientific tools available in order to gain the literal, historical, and cultural meaning of the Scriptures, as well as a method that searches out the deeper spiritual implications of the Bible. Benedict's reorientation to Scripture is actually a call to return to our roots. Literal and spiritual modes of interpretation have existed for centuries, but we have only recently begun to tap these vital resources once again. We will return to these ideas in the pages ahead.

DISCIPLESHIP

The term *disciple* is central to any biblical interpretative method, and it plays a critical role in the upcoming text. Discipleship is where the rubber meets the road; where we practice what we preach; where we experience what we truly believe about the Bible. When push comes to shove, we may discover that we are more fundamentalist or postmodern than we suspected, and we may realize that we're better for it. Perhaps we are parallelized between extremes, caught with road rage that prevents us from learning from either side. At the very least, heavy gas pedal or not, we will soon learn that if we really want to know Jesus, we will always be students of Scripture. We are, after all, commissioned as disciples and in the New Testament, the word disciple *(mathetes)* means "pupil." It is used two hundred fifty times with respect to those who follow Jesus. We cannot explore them all in detail, but the identification of a few nuances of its use will help us shift into gear and we'll be on our way through the Bible.

The Call

Discipleship often begins with a "call" in which the initiative is taken by Jesus (see Matthew 4:19; Mark 1:17; Luke 5:9–11; and John 1:35–42). This seems to imply that we should be on guard, watching and listening for the moment when we can take Jesus' hand. We probably shouldn't expect it to be as obvious as a message through an iPod, nor should we expect it to be so cryptic that we need a doctorate in theology to decipher it. Fortunately, according to Scripture, Jesus will meet us where we are, just as he met the apostles. In fact, Jesus seems willing to accept a person who has a readiness to follow him without his personal invitation (see Luke 9:57, 61). Thus our exploration in the pages ahead will require openness, attentiveness, and responsiveness.

Qualifications

Jesus calls people who seem to lack the necessary qualifications (see Mark 2:13). How many of us have felt completely unworthy and unqualified when we enter a sacred space or attempt to read a sacred text? Jesus does not seem to care. All are welcome. Whether your foot is on the gas or the brake, Jesus invites us into his way, and he is willing to catch up to us if we drive too fast, slow down if we tap the brake, or heal us if we crash exhausted.

The Word Among Us

Some followers of Jesus are part of a wider circle of associates, having no personal call from him, but moved by his message nonetheless (see the case of Cleophas in Luke 24:18). Modern-day counterparts might include friends and family who claim no institutional church but are attracted to the love that they know comes from Jesus (through us). Don't be surprised if your understanding of the Bible begins to attract some sympathetic listeners. Jesus might speak through you.

The Call to Action

A great number of people are near Jesus, interested in his message, but are not fully committed to him (see John 6:60 and 66). To this day, for example, many followers of Jesus sit idle while atrocities against our neighbors (close and far away) rip through their lives—worship-filled Sundays come and go, but destruction moves forward in the shadows every day. Our exploration of Scripture should show us how to be "on the Way" instead of "beside the Way." We are called to action!

The Living Lord

Jesus is called *rabbi* ("teacher") by Peter, Judas, and the Pharisees, yet the term *Kyrios* ("Lord") is used more often in the Gospels than *rabbi*. In John's Gospel there is a special use of the term *rabbi* that is explained. It means "giving witness to Jesus in the Christian community" as opposed to the more traditional meaning of transmitting special teachings. In other words, according to the Gospel of John, Jesus is *not* the head of a rabbinic school; he is the living Lord. Thus the Bible is not meant to be a textbook in the traditional sense. Rather, the Bible is a living document that proclaims a living Lord—it will require engagement with real life.

Partnership With Jesus

Among other things, the call to discipleship is a call to partnership with Jesus (see Luke 5:1ff). This is verified in the sayings of Jesus (see especially Matthew 5:13; John 17:13; and Matthew 25:14). Luke's Gospel has one distinctive qualification: Jesus' teachings have power or are effective only when there is first a personal commitment to him. In various ways, Luke develops this theme throughout his Gospel and the Acts of the Apostles. Although crudely analogous, our reception of Jesus' call to discipleship is like our reception of an advertisement on the radio; unless we personally commit to the product or the cause, we will not spend any money or time to make it part of our lives. Of course, before we hear the solicitation, we must listen to the radio in the first place and tune into the proper station. As disciples, we must be dialed into the word of God and be committed to Jesus before we will be able to follow his way as prescribed in the Bible.

Eternal Genesis

Jesus used a variety of images to speak about his closest followers. It has been said that he had the ability to make words "dance." His followers were to be salt of the earth, a light to the world, a bit of yeast in a batch of bread dough that expands everywhere. They were not to work for money or acclaim, but silently, unnoticed like a seed that grows while we sleep. To those who endure unbearable sorrows and sufferings in this world, they were to bring forgiveness. Into whatever darkness they entered, they were to know that they carried within the light of the world. The New Testament is the testimony of his followers that there is an eternal genesis: God is always offering a new beginning.

The interpretive tools in the following chapters should help us discover how God speaks to us through Scripture—again and again and again. For now, be assured that confusion and misunderstanding are part of the process. Move forward with an open mind, attentive to the many moods of history and the variety of interpretations today. Fear not, for we do not walk alone.

REVIEW QUESTIONS

1. Define the following terms: literal fundamentalism, inspiration, synoptic Gospels, disciples, historical critical method, mystery, and *eikons*.
2. Benedict XVI has called for a renewal of biblical scholarship. Explain his suggestions.
3. Secular postmodernists and biblical fundamentalists seem to hold opposite opinions. Describe the opinions each group values.

FOR FURTHER STUDY

1. Web sites are unreliable. When operable they may offer easy access to primary source materials and the work of scholars. Many of Pope Benedict XVI's addresses and lectures are available in full on the Web.
2. See also Benedict XVI, *Jesus of Nazareth* (New York: Doubleday, 2007). The volume is an excellent example of how Benedict envisions a "canonical exegesis," that is, an exegesis that cooperates with faith and interprets passages from the Bible connecting them with other biblical verses. Benedict never condemns other methods that rely on archaeology or other sciences. In fact, he respects various research sciences, especially sociological ones from which he hopes more information will illuminate contemporary interpretations of the biblical period.
3. Charlesworth, Max. *Religious Inventions: Four Essays* (Cambridge: Cambridge University Press, 1997). The author illustrates the diversities found within all denominations and their use of symbols and texts. The plural character of a religion prohibits use of one interpretative method.
4. Murphy, Nancey. "Bodies and Souls, or Spirited Bodies?" *Current Issues in Theology* Series (Cambridge: Cambridge University Press, 2006). She reviews perceptions of God, the human being, and morality from ancient times to developments today in science and biblical theology. She assesses contemporary attitudes toward God and the survival of dualism and other views in a scientific era.
5. Pelikan, Jaroslav. *Whose Bible Is It? A History of the Scriptures Through the Ages* (New York: Viking, 2005). A distinguished historian of religion examines the development of the Hebrew and Christian Bibles. His method is sensitive to the reality that neither community would be anything without

their Scriptures. The Scriptures depend on communities in every generation to interpret and reinterpret biblical themes.

6. Van Voorst, Robert E. *Reading the New Testament Today* (Belmont, CA:
   Wadsworth, 2005). Includes a template of contemporary methods of bibli-
   cal interpretation and provides concrete applications for students to use.
   No evaluation of the Bible's use in the Christian churches.

7. Brown, Raymond. *An Introduction to the New Testament,* The Anchor Bible
   Reference Library (New York: Doubleday, 1997). Careful, clearly written
   text in which the historical critical method of biblical interpretation is
   outlined and applied to the analysis of the New Testament.

8. Delsol, Chantal. *The Unlearned Lessons of the 20th Century: An Essay on
   Late Modernity* (Wilmington, DE: Intercollegiate Studies Institute, 2006).
   This French philosopher offers an overview of failed Utopian hopes. She
   labels the present time as "late modernity" rather than postmodern. An
   excellent resource to research themes suggested in Review Question 3.

2

Beginning to Interpret the Bible

To begin the analysis of any biblical passage, we should *not* ask "Is it true?" but rather "*What* is true?" or "What does it *intend* to say?" Focusing on subject matter (as opposed to the truth of the matter) upholds the long-standing teaching of the Western Christian church, going back as far as Athanasius (296–373), Jerome (347–419), and Augustine (354–430). The idea is this: The inspired truth—that which God intends to communicate to us—of a biblical passage is usually not the "obvious," modern-day interpretation that comes to mind in the reader. Rather, God's truth is shrouded in the idioms and thought patterns of the original human authors and it is up to us—with some help from the Holy Spirit and much diligent research—to bring the word alive today. The original authors did not intend to write a static history of Jesus. The dynamic structure of the Bible demands our active participation, translation, interpretation, and appropriation into our lives.

This interpretative principle is guided by the fact that we have unprecedented resources today for knowing the past. Techniques for uncovering, classifying and reconstructing the ancient world are scientific and extensive. For example, we know the history of Israel far better than the apostles Peter or Paul could have, and specialists have more data about Peter and Paul than their ancient contemporaries. Scholars tell us that the churches existed before one line of the New Testament was ever actually recorded in text. Twenty years separates the lifetime of Jesus from the oldest book in the New Testament, Paul's First Letter to the Thessalonians (ca. 49).

A COMMUNITY RECORD OF FAITH

Preaching and worship preceded writing about the risen Christ, and a number of biblical writings sometimes developed in response to controversies in and around the emerging Christian communities. Believers gathered in groups to pray and to celebrate a common developing faith. Their faith, we are told, rested on the testimony of eyewitnesses and others. They claimed to share a personal relationship with Jesus, interacting with him as we would our neighbors, friends, and family. Thus the Bible is *NOT* a history book or news commentary, but a communal record of faith. As such, it requires unique rules of engagement.

Not surprisingly, then, a number of problems with the Bible are resolved when we utilize a variety of methods to assess biblical religious teachings and spiritual messages. Without assistance from several types of research, for example, our contemporary way of reading news reports, novels, or histories may cause us to overlook and/or discern the subtle, allegorical, and/or the direct, literal meanings of Scripture. We are often caught between the brake pedal (suspicion) and the gas (blind acceptance), and thus we tend to fall short—or overshoot—our destination. By studying history and language, culture and society, and anything else that pertains to a given era, we try to establish what the authors meant. In the process, we may come to know people of great religious faith and complexity, not unlike some people of our day. We learn more about their choice of analogies and metaphors, and we learn the strategies that they used to communicate of the reality of Jesus, his mission, and discipleship. In the end, of course, our nuanced understanding of biblical authors frees us to bring the Word to life in the metaphors, symbols, and actual events of our own age.

METAPHOR

Metaphor may be described as a kind of verbal dare. Someone interprets one reality using terms borrowed from a different reality. For example, a term or phrase from one context (such as an apple falling close to its tree) is related to another term or phrase from a different context (such as a child who looks or acts like a parent). A "child" (the *subject*) relates to "apple" (the *vehicle*) while "tree" (subject) relates to "parent" (vehicle). In logical terms, "A is *like* B." Metaphor, however, can take several forms: (1) a standard *metaphor*—"A is B"; (2) *simile*—A is *like* B; or (3) *synecdoche*—"A is used in the place of B," where A is part of B or vice versa (for example, "His parents bought him a new set of wheels [car]"). In short, metaphors stir attention and facilitate understanding, particularly when directed toward someone who is familiar with one context but unfamiliar with another. The results can be quite powerful.

The Problem of Metaphor

Some metaphors are well known in contemporary English: *wallflower* (a shy or unpopular person who does not participate in events), *cold fish* (an aloof person), or *wet blanket* (one who discourages enthusiasm or enjoyment). Other metaphors, however, are far more complex, particularly those from Scripture that are derived from other languages and cultures (such as Greek or Aramaic), or if the context is based on unfamiliar historical settings (such as the Hellenistic world of the New Testament). Even modern English metaphors do not translate well into other modern languages. Consider the following example: *"Andrew is like a sheep."*

When translated to or from other modern languages, this sentence can take on the following meanings:

"Andrew has long hair."
"Andrew is a drunkard."
"Andrew does not answer back."
"Andrew follows without thinking."
"Andrew is a young fellow waiting for girls to follow him."

We can't easily bridge the gap between modern metaphors, much less discern the meaning of ancient metaphors. We need proper tools, symbols, and ways of reading that help us understand other cultures.

Fortunately, Jesus was a champion of metaphors, and he left us with some tools that will help. We'll learn more about his technique later. For now, we must recognize that it is critical to understand Jesus' worldview before we can understand his metaphors or his message. He knew the value of daring images to keep his audience interested, and he knew that his creativity would keep his mission alive in the hearts of later generations. It's up to us to learn how and why he said what he said to the people he encountered in the context of his day, and then we can begin to bring his Spirit into modern translations of the word.

Jesus often used parables to deliver his metaphors. A parable has been variously described as a story with a scene from everyday life, or imaginary ones. A parable must tell a brief story with several levels of meaning: one meaning is clear from the story line; the other is on a deeper level that lures people toward other, more significant interpretations. In the pages ahead, we'll learn some techniques that can help us peel away the various layers of interpretation contained within Jesus' parables.

SYMBOL

Another term used in biblical scholarship is *symbol*. Like metaphor, there is a spectrum of definitions and implications associated with the word. In fact, symbol is a type of metaphor—where one term relates to another. Some claim that symbols such as earth, wind, and fire, for example, automatically touch nerves in people. They stir folks to feeling, even to thinking. Sometimes symbols remind us of something unfinished, of possibilities or needs to be filled. Symbols may express personal or collective histories in enigmatic ways. If I participate in symbolic gestures, such as staring into a fire, letting water wash over me, running with the wind at my back, or feeling for the density of a massive rock, some suggest that I will experience deeper levels of my inner life that otherwise are seldom considered.

Others suggest that symbols contain uncertain and shifting meanings. Symbols are ambiguous and conflicting references to reality. For example, water, on one level gives a sense of refreshment, but it may also be dangerous, especially if one cannot swim. The wind may be brisk, but it also can barrel in at lethal speeds, as in a hurricane or tornado. Others describe symbols as things that must be deciphered. That is, there is something more to understand about them than is available from a spontaneous, everyday, or natural level of understanding. So, too, symbols may mean different things to different people. We learn what a symbol is by asking the person using it what specifically they intend to say by it. When contemporary advertising recognized that symbols are ambiguous, they harnessed them to sell all sorts of commodities.

Symbols are part of the language of religious faith. They are a representation that goes beyond a simple image or a sign. In religion, they are a means by which religious faith expresses its interpretations of the holy, the sacred, the "Other." In other words, they have the power to express how the invisible, transcendent, or divine communicates to creatures. Symbols are created by and for people, which means that they are adaptable and can be created with anything. Many use these human symbols to help make intelligible the meaning and existence of God. They may be visual, conceptual, or expressed in everyday language. We will discuss them throughout this book.

DEEPER LEVELS OF MEANING

Studying the Bible as an academic exercise, of course, differs from reading or praying with it as a part of church worship or in private meditation. Although the Bible deals with personal and communal symbols of religious faith, many people today use scholarly methods to assess ranges of its significance other than in theology. Even so, the discoveries made by scholars with no explicit religious beliefs may offer those of us who share religious faith further insights. It is important, at the start, to recognize that scholarship is not faith-based instruction or catechism, but for people of faith, every truthful discovery that helps to unlock the mysteries of the Bible needs to be acknowledged and utilized.

WHAT'S IMPORTANT AND WHAT'S NOT?

The older we get, the more we realize that we simply cannot fit every piece of information into our brain at one time. Despite our best efforts, we must choose what to save and what to throw away. Our understanding of history—which affects how we interpret our life today—is limited to the fragments that have been chosen to survive. An example will illustrate the point.

I have an interest in American history. Some years ago I visited the grave of Thomas Jefferson located on his estate in Monticello, Virginia. The grave marker reads: "Here was buried Thomas Jefferson," then the dates of his life. The inscription continues with: "Author of the Declaration of Independence and of the Virginia statute for religious freedom, and the Father of the University of Virginia." There is no mention of the fact that Jefferson was elected president of the United States. Since I am a descendent of his vice president, George Clinton, a number of questions immediately came to mind. Why no mention of his presidency? Who wrote the text on the headstone? Does the inscription suggest that he was disappointed by his presidency? To discover answers, I searched the works of historians and uncovered several conflicting interpretations. The short answers to each, for those interested, are: it was his choice not to mention the presidency; he authorized the headstone inscription ahead of time; and his opinion of being president continues to be debated. The point is that we can't know everything about Jefferson because we are *not* Jefferson. We cannot rely on reality TV, iPhones, iPods, or other mass communication devices to interpret the deeper meanings of Jefferson's final wishes.

The same type of confusion surrounds interpretations of Jesus. We only have secondhand accounts of his life, each of which portrays Jesus in a different way with different evidence. From the earliest days of Christianity, believers have questioned the meaning of certain biblical passages, and wondered, in the absence of more evidence, whether or not the various parts of the New Testament were literally true or part of some larger story. Although unaware of it at the time, early Christians were setting the stage for our contemporary debates about the meaning of Scripture. Even Jesus' contemporaries had trouble deciphering Jesus' message. Paul spent most of his career defending Christianity to the communities that never met Jesus firsthand, and he admitted that his interpretation was limited by what he had learned through faith (see 1 Corinthians 15).

Ultimately, the essential questions of interpretation about what to keep and what to throw away—what to believe by faith and what to know as fact—involve levels of interpretation that stretch us from the physical (that which we see, hear, feel, remember, and so forth) to the metaphysical (that which is above our reason, such as faith, hope, or love). If we want to know the heart of Jefferson, we need to look beyond his gravestone. Similarly, if we want to know Jesus, we have to read between the lines of Scripture, thereby letting our faith (and the faith of many others) speak God's Word. This revelation has led us to study the Bible in various ways or "senses."

The Four Senses of Interpretation

The famous theologian Origen (ca. 182–253/254) proposed that there are different levels of meaning in the Bible. If a particular passage seems "repugnant" to reason, that is, the *literal sense*, he suggests that interpreters look for the *spiritual sense* or deeper meaning of the word of God.

In the centuries that followed, a specific method of interpretation developed that considered something other than the literal sense of a biblical passage. For example, John Cassian (ca. 360–435) proposed that the Bible has four levels of meaning. Every biblical passage, says Cassian, may be interpreted in four ways: a "literal" or "historical" sense, and three "spiritual" senses—an *allegorical* sense (something that pertains to faith, such as a passage in the Old Testament that prefigures our faith in Christ and his mission of salvation continuing now in the church), a *tropological* or moral sense (a biblical phrase that gives wisdom or advice for virtuous or moral living), and an *anagogical* or eternal sense (a passage that is considered to have eternal or heavenly references). For example, when a Bible passage speaks about Jerusalem, it may refer to the city (the literal sense), the church on earth (the allegorical sense), the soul of the believer (the tropological sense), the heavenly Jerusalem (the anagogical sense), all four senses, or a combination of them. The *Catechism of the Catholic Church* (109–119) explains that the Church has always concentrated on both the literal and spiritual senses of the Bible. Although *allegory* is still a popular term among biblical exegetes and preachers, we don't often hear about the other senses when we learn about Scripture. Nevertheless, as the *Catechism* attests, the four senses of Scripture have existed for centuries and they permeate the many different methods of interpretation in continued use today.

Making Sense of the Senses

Amazingly, the four senses of Scripture—history, tropology, allegory, and anagogy—account for the broad spectrum of ways that we communicate with God through the word. History tells us the literal story, tropology helps understand how to act, allegory helps our belief or faith, and anagogy leads us to God. For many centuries, scholars were able to interpret the four senses of Scripture from the Bible, applying their knowledge of the tradition and their understanding of science. We use similar techniques today, but our understanding of science has changed so much that we have developed a variety of techniques that allow us to dig even deeper than our ancestors.

For example, feminist interpretation seeks to do justice to the claims of those whom the dominant culture has excluded, not least of all rhetorically. Social scientists and cultural historians also probe the Bible for social patterns and associations that allow us to enhance and interpret God's word.

Literary analysis proposes techniques to evaluate genres that preceded the written books of the Bible and they are able to analyze its final form, content, and structure. Anthropologists and archeologists use their scientific skills to challenge the assumptions we make about the people and places of the Bible. These scholars assume that respect for the Bible and the findings from critical study are not incompatible. Analytical thinking is a means to understand its complexity and value. Some scholars avoid making connections between their scholarship and religious commitments, but even they cannot deny that their findings have an impact on the historical, moral, faithful, and spiritual dimensions of the Bible.

The Bible is more than one more example of great classic literature. God is not merely a character in a narrative. For the Christian, the Bible is a witness to, and the story of, God's interactions with the human family. The text of the Bible, as many medieval exegetes popularized, contains both letter and spirit. The biblical text has a number of possible meanings in the encounter between author and reader. The intention of the biblical author is one aspect, not always the central one, in the complex phenomena of the multiple levels of meaning in the biblical text.

It may be helpful to map out a few popular types of biblical research, charting in outline form what contemporary Bible scholarship values and emphasizes.

Diachronic Interpretation

Diachronic interpretation pertains to the changes in a linguistic system between successive points in time. On its most basic level, diachronic interpretation is like putting together the frames of a movie—one image or frame depends on the frame before it—in order to understand the story that emerges when viewed as a whole. Diachronic interpreters are more concerned about the movie itself than the effects the movie may have on the viewer. Since the story of faith has spanned many centuries and many different genres (from speech to images to text), diachronic biblical interpretation is more like putting together the pieces of many movies, with various pieces of film cut up and overlapping others. Thus before we can understand the Bible, it is essential for us to assemble the order, form, and context of each frame.

Not surprisingly then, diachronic methods of biblical scholarship are interested in how the books in the Bible came to exist and how they were put together. Sometimes referred to as *critical* methods (as in "rational analysis"), these techniques are usually not well received by either literal fundamentalists or secular postmodernists (the two extremes identified in the Introduction). Literal fundamentalists accept Bible interpretations only from those who profess a specific type of religious faith (as opposed to objective scientific opinion). Fearful that scholarship will be agnostic or areligious, fundamentalists often misunderstand critical methods as condescending to people of faith. Many postmodernists, on the other hand, are suspicious of our ability to understand anything that occurs in other cultures or time periods. They warn us not to assume anything about the past, especially if our information pertains to matters of faith or comes from those who have power. If you are a strict literal fundamentalist or secular postmodernist, you will need to be aware that this book is indebted to several scientific *and* faith-based methods of biblical criticism as well as to the Bible's function and place in the life of the church. Relying on God as the ultimate arbiter of truth, we must not fear the contradictions that may arise through our limited, human pursuit of understanding in the Bible.

Criticism is a term with a Greek origin. It implies the rational exercise of analysis. It is not the same term used in everyday language that implies a negative evaluation. Instead, modern criticism investigates the Bible with techniques aimed to unravel the history of the Bible's development by studying the cultural, social, and literary elements it contains. Such "criticism" will help us to find the balance between the gas and brake—between an overly simplistic, blind-faith reading of Scripture and an overly suspicious rejection of faith-based inquiry. The following diachronic methods of historical-criticism are the basis of most mainstream diachronic interpretation of the Bible. It would take years to unpack the details of each method. This summary, along with the suggestions for further reading at the end of the chapter, should be enough to get us started.

Source criticism (sometimes called *literary criticism*) seeks to establish a trustworthy text of the Bible using available manuscripts. In short, it tries to identify the written sources behind a particular text. Source critics search for authorship, contradictions between texts, multiple versions of narrative within the same story, and different literary styles. One of the most famous examples of source criticism is the Four-Source Hypothesis, which attempts to explain why Matthew, Mark, and Luke share so much of the same material.

Form criticism is a complex cataloging of how the various traditions in the Bible took shape. Form critics examine narratives, legal documents, poetry, historical materials, and other forms of writing in ancient texts and compare them with the forms found in the Bible. True to its name, form criticism identifies the proper "form" of each part of the Bible (for example, legends, laws, prophecy, hymns, laments, narratives, parables, and more).

Redaction criticism analyzes the work of editors who are thought to have shaped traditions or texts that they received into continuous story forms. In other words, redaction critics not only look at the form and sources of the

Bible, but they try to determine why it was shaped into its final version(s). The editorial results of their labor are what we now have in the Bible. Ultimately, redaction critics try to identify how the writers and editors of the Bible used their sources when composing the final edition.

Tradition criticism analyzes how various authors of the Bible used or understood "traditions" different from their own. For example, how did the apostles understand the Book of Exodus? How did the prophets view the creation account? Tradition critics identify how the authors of the Bible understood the traditions of Israel.

Rhetorical criticism can take many different forms, but two are dominant in biblical studies. The first approach pays attention to a text's unique stylistic or aesthetic qualities (and thus is a corrective to form criticism's focus on the "typical" or "conventional"); the second approach, by contrast, combines many different disciplines—such as literary criticism, hermeneutics, structuralism, semantics, and so forth—with classic rhetoric in order to uncover the social underpinnings of the language used in the Bible. Although it is ultimately a form of social research—and as such it is sometimes classified as a synchronic discipline—its main focus is the use of language and thus it is also a historical discipline.

There are literally hundreds of other historical-critical approaches to the Bible—as many as there are scientific disciplines. Archeology, ethnography, and anthropology, for example, are other popular forms of diachronic biblical study. Understanding all of them is not as important as knowing that they are all important components of biblical interpretation. These are the tools that will help us accelerate or apply the brakes so that we can achieve an accurate, balanced interpretation of the Bible.

Synchronic Interpretation

Synchronic methods of biblical interpretation are interested in what the passages of the Bible meant to people outside the biblical period, including modern-day interpretation. If we return to our movie analogy, we can say that synchronic interpreters are not as interested in the frames of the film as they are in the places and people who actually view them. A synchronic interpreter would much rather analyze the reactions of the people in the movie theater than provide an analysis of the movie. In the world of biblical interpretation, synchronic interpretation often looks at the genres of the Bible without examining the people who wrote it or how the Bible once functioned for them. Such methodology, as a result, sometimes has little or no interest in what the authors of the Bible intended. The primary questions, they say, must pertain to the reader, or how the meaning of a passage emerges from the interaction be-tween reader and text. In the end, synchronic methods have interests governed by the desire to understand the Bible at the present time (for the reader today). A few examples should help us discern the difference between diachronic and synchronic interpretation.

Literary criticism is the study of the principal themes and concerns in a text. Although there are many different forms of literary criticism, and the term itself *(literary)* can be understood as category for interpretation, it typi-cally refers to the Bible as literature. For example, does the text include literary devices, such as, repetition, word play, irony, and parallelism?

Literary context tries to answer questions about the relationship of a pas-sage to the entire work—how do the characters, plot, location of the passage in a chapter or book, and story line contribute to readers' reception of the text?

Semiotics identifies the notable signs that the reader sees in the text; that is, it identifies particular words and gestures used between characters (characters understood as "people" and characters in the sense of "letters of the alphabet"). How do these reveal particular cultural codes?

Reader response criticism assesses facts that impact the reader's interpre-tative activity and help to determine meanings derived from the text. The pri-mary focus, not surprisingly, is on the active role of the reader (or community of readers). Due to the wide variety of biblical readers—enthusiasts, academ-ics, uneducated, and everyone in between—there are many different forms of reader response criticism.

Sociological criticism, or social-scientific criticism, analyzes the social and cultural dimensions of the Bible and the environment from which it came. It presupposes that the intentions of the biblical authors are directly linked to their historical and social setting. Although sociological criticism is, strictly speaking, a historical discipline, it is more synchronic than diachronic. In other words, it is not as much concerned with sources, dating, authorship, language, or other historical things, but with the social conditions that existed apart from the biblical text itself. This social information is then used to reorient modern interpretation of the Bible.

Gender studies investigate what supports or undermines patriarchal (male) structures contained in the Bible and how to recover the rightful place of all readers (women and others) in the development and reception of the Bible.

Ideological criticism identifies "class" distinctions from the perspective of the Bible and its interpreters. Some of these scholars move beyond traditional criticism and try to relate the Bible to non-Western cultures and minorities.

INSPIRATION

Students of the Bible must not become so obsessed with diachronic and synchronic methods of interpretation that they overlook the role of the Spirit. The Bible is, after all, a record of faith, not science or even pure history. All Christians agree that God must have revealed something to the authors of the Bible. We often refer to this as biblical *inspiration,* taken from the Latin verb *inspirare,* meaning "to blow into or upon; to breathe into." There are several technical meanings for the term *inspiration* and numerous ways of applying it to God's word, so a few distinctions will help us navigate our journey.

Scholars often distinguish between the role of inspiration as it relates to the *writings* of the Bible from inspiration upon the *authors* of the Bible, but sometimes the term applies to both author and writings. Ultimately, as noted, inspiration implies that God communicates with us and our job is to figure out how. Since the question has challenged humanity for centuries, there are numerous theories to explain it—far too many to explore here. For the sake of simplicity, we start with four categories: mechanical inspiration, verbal inspiration, dynamic inspiration, and human inspiration.

Mechanical Inspiration or Dictation

As the name implies, *mechanical inspiration* presupposes that God "mechanically" guides the authors of the Bible to record his exact words (much like Vouet's portrayal of the angel trumpeting the words of Scripture into Saint Jerome's ear). This type of inspiration is often referred to as *prophetic,* particularly since it bears a likeness to the type of communication that many ascribe to the Old Testament prophets. Many of the Fathers of the Church claimed that inspiration was an ecstatic phenomenon whereby biblical authors were possessed by the Holy Spirit.

Verbal Inspiration

Most biblical scholars recognize the prophetic nature of inspiration, but not all agree that it is (or was) purely ecstatic. The Bible has its origins in God, but we must acknowledge that human authors played a role in the process of writing it down. We learn from the famous Catholic theologian Thomas Aquinas, for example, that biblical "prophets" (authors of the Bible) did not necessarily have immediate or direct contact with God (such as one might have with a fellow human), but they know God through a "likeness" (see *Summa Theologica* II:2.173). In other words, God did not dictate the words of the Bible but guided authors to choose the appropriate words. Either way, all of the Bible is considered to be the word of God.

Dynamic Inspiration

Proponents of *dynamic inspiration* assert that the Bible has a divine origin and is the end product of God self-accommodation in a mediated revelation to people who wrote the Bible over centuries. In light of the historical reality of the Bible's formation, there are many versions of dynamic inspiration and thus it is very difficult to summarize or characterize as one theory. In general, dynamic inspiration accounts for the social, historical, and scientific dimension of authorship. It examines Scripture with an appreciation for the human quality of the text, particularly the social and psychological settings from which it was born, and the literary implications of the words that were chosen. Insofar as possible, dynamic inspiration uses the synchronic and diachronic tools of biblical interpretation to interpret the relationship among the authors of the Bible, God, and the text that we have today. Although sometimes scientific in structure, dynamic inspiration assumes that the Bible is God's word.

Human Inspiration

A minority of biblical scholars consider the Bible to be merely a book of great literature or byproduct of ordinary human inspiration and creativity—a method devoid of divine authorship. This viewpoint is sometimes taken by contemporary interpreters who use diachronic and synchronic methods of interpretation but who do not assign any authorship to God.

MOVING FORWARD

Thus far we have raised more questions than answers, and we've encountered a lot more theory than actual data about the Bible. However, as we begin to dig into the actual stories in the Bible, we will discover that the complex questions in this chapter will help us unravel the riches of the word of God. The sources for further study at the end of this chapter are invaluable in locating the deeper meanings of Scripture.

REVIEW QUESTIONS

1. Define the following terms: *symbol, metaphor, biblical criticism, diachronic, synchronic.*
2. Explain the "method" of biblical study used in this book and offer an evaluation.
3. Is there a method of biblical interpretation you prefer? What are its strengths and limitations?

FOR FURTHER STUDY

1. See Felix Just's Web site (http://catholic-resources.org/Bible/) for articles on biblical methods as well as his terse and readable profiles for many New Testament books from a Roman Catholic and a biblical critical point of view.

2. See also the American Theological Library Association and its Selected Religion Web site, edited by Mahlon H. Smith, for a variety of biblical study themes and full Scripture citations (http://www.atla.com//atlahome. html).

3. Robert, Mark D. *Can We Trust the Gospels? Investigating the Reliability of Matthew, Mark, Luke and John* (Wheaton, IL: Crossway Books, 2007). A scholar within the Evangelical Christian tradition, Robert argues the canonical Gospels predate those referred to as *gnostic* Gospels.

4. Several American biblical scholars and educators (Paul Achtemeier, Daniel J. Harrington, Robert J. Karris, George W. MacRae, and Lawrence Boadt) in the Roman Catholic tradition contributed to *Invitation to the Gospels* (Mahwah, NJ: Paulist Press, 1997). The text is written in a popular style and useful for general readers.

5. Berlin, Adele, Marc Zvi Brettler, and Michael Fishbane. *The Jewish Study Bible* (Oxford, Oxford University Press, 2003). These authors offer a modern Jewish English translation and commentaries of their sacred texts. Of interest is their use of modern critical theories of various kinds without reference or guide to Jewish practices and liturgy. Numerous articles survey critical scholarship, especially linguistic and archeological findings. Conservative, Orthodox, and Reform scholars contributed to the translation and commentaries.

6. Wcela, Emil. *The Story of Israel: God's People through the Years* (Collegeville, MN: Pueblo, 1977). The published and unpublished works of several theologians are resources used throughout this text. It includes lecture notes on the Old Testament offered thirty years ago by Bishop Emil Wcela at Immaculate Conception Seminary in Huntington, New York. Wcela offers a survey of Israel's development, crises endured, liturgical developments, and sectarian divisions that I utilize and amend in this volume.

7. Jasper, David. *A Short Introduction to Hermeneutics* (Louisville, KY: Westminster, 2004). A readable survey of the complex history of biblical interpretation from patristic to postmodern scholarship. A useful development of methods to answer Review Question 2.

3

The Bible Before Jesus

I once wished that I had lived in biblical times because it seemed that God was so much more recognizable and active long ago. I thought it would give me the opportunity to understand why the Bible sometimes uses such obscure language and imagery. Belief in God should have been easier, I thought, especially if fire was falling on evil people and seas divided to let good people escape slavery. Today everything seems so far from God, so far from anything that allows the divine to touch our physical lives. Our scientific search for clarity seems to have obscured our vision of God and our modern presuppositions have altered the way we understand the Bible. In a world of digital databases and high-speed processors, it's difficult to avoid the "logic" of faith. Although we don't live in biblical times and we cannot podcast interviews from the original apostles, we can use the sources of our ancestors and modern technology to understand how the Bible became a formal collection of books, and then we can begin to understand what it means for us today.

Even expert biblical scholars will admit that the Bible can be very difficult to interpret. For example, it sometimes includes competing accounts of the same events—some told from a logical, human point of view and others from a more transcendent, spiritual point of view. For example, to this day many assume that Moses literally parted walls of water for escape from Egypt in Exodus 14—much like Charlton Heston in the *Ten Commandments*. Their filter of interpretation, perhaps, is Psalm 78:13: "He [Moses] divided the sea and let them pass through it, / and made the waters stand like a heap." Others postulate that the Israelites crossed the water in a particular location to take advantage of a driving wind that caused an extremely low tide: "The LORD drove the sea back by a strong east wind all night, and turned the sea into dry land; and the waters were divided" (Exodus 14:21). Two accounts of the same event, yet two very different approaches.

Regardless of the vehicle for the event (walls of water versus wind and low tide), we can still assume that Moses and God played a role in the event and that the passing was equally miraculous. The point of these stories is to celebrate

God's care for his people in two different contexts. Neither story was inserted as a rejection of the other; rather, these competing accounts were meant for different audiences, situations, and many other factors. As we begin to decipher thousands of stories in the Bible—its people, places, and events—we will discover many contradictions, awkward wording, and numerous other semantic challenges. Regardless of these discrepancies, we will also discover that each story reveals important things about our relationship with God.

WHY WAS THE BIBLE WRITTEN?

Each semester I ask students to evaluate various interpretations of the Bible's origin and the reason for its existence and compare them to their own understanding of the Bible. It is important for students to be familiar with their biases as they study and interpret the biblical texts, and they need to appreciate my own position on these issues. We (all of us) are children of the times in which we live, and several factors influence the context in which we pursue knowledge. Understanding our presuppositions helps us unlock the universal message of Scripture.

I study the Bible with a Christian viewpoint and an explicit faith commitment. I approach the New Testament, as mentioned previously, as created by the community and written for insiders; it is a church document. I accept the Christian designation for the Hebrew Scriptures as the "Old Testament." There are other approaches, such as studying the Bible as literature or analyzing the Bible as a compendium of mythic folklores, that augment my understanding of my faith.

Most mainline interpreters of the Bible also accept that Christian Scripture was meant to strengthen and deepen personal and communal faith in the risen Christ. A collection of texts—what would later become the Bible—were read and adapted in worship services or liturgies. They were not composed as presentations for unbelievers or cultural historians. Local communities of faith were the intended audiences, and Jesus was the subject.

Most early communities, say scholars, repeated what had been preached to them, added further interpretations to it, and enshrined some of it in worship ceremonies. Eventually (decades after the first eyewitnesses to Jesus) the words of the Bible were collected, recorded, and organized for use in various communities—particularly for liturgical purposes.

The trajectory or development of the books that were included in the Bible was influenced by politics, heresies, and calls for order and uniformity as new situations arose. Eyewitnesses of Jesus' life died and new members sometimes proposed interpretations that would not have been recognized by the original community of believers. Some early writings were never included in the official list of books (often referred to as the "canon"). These books, letters, and other writings were consciously rejected for a variety of reasons—questionable authorship, inaccuracies, forgery, and much more. In the end, however, each book of the Bible—indeed, every word of the Bible—addresses the needs of faith-based communities that emerged in the wake of God's covenant with the people of Israel.

THE BIBLE JESUS READ

Even if the original authors and editors wrote or compiled long after the death of their subjects, the Bible was not finalized in one day, year, decade, century, or even millennium. Influenced by ongoing history, politics, war, and many other factors, the number and order of books in the Bible has varied with succeeding generations and faith communities. In fact, Christians still disagree about which books should be included in the Old Testament.

Most Protestant Bibles do not include seven books and several chapters that are included in Orthodox and Catholic Bibles: Tobit, Judith, Wisdom, Sirach (also known as Ecclesiastes), and Baruch, First and Second Maccabees, three chapters from Daniel, and six chapters from Esther. As a result, Protestants have sixty-six books in their Old Testament, while Orthodox and Roman Catholics have seventy three.

The official list of the Old Testament books used by Orthodox and Catholics is based on Scripture texts from the Jewish community in Alexandria, Egypt. This version is known as the *Septuagint* or *LXX,* both of which mean "seventy" in honor of the number of copyists (or translators) who transformed the Hebrew books into Greek books. It came into being for the Alexandrian Jewish community about two hundred eighty years before Jesus.

In order to evangelize and communicate with the Gentile (non-Jewish) world, the Greek Septuagint (LXX) became the standard version of the Old Testament used by the writers of the New Testament. It was the most widely circulated version of the Bible that circulated during apostolic times. It remains the text used by millions of Eastern and Western Christians. Some scholars suggest that the Bible references found in the New Testament refer to the Septuagint translation more than to any other Hebrew translations. In short, the Old Testament references cited by Matthew, Mark, Luke, John, Paul, and several others was the two-hundred-year-old Greek Septuagint translation.

Fragments of the Septuagint (LXX) and several other important writings were uncovered in the last century among the collection known as the Dead Sea Scrolls of the Qumran region. Apparently, this dissident Jewish settlement, who some believe to be the Essenes, the separatist Jewish sect from the late Second Temple Period (200 BCE to 70 CE), read the Septuagint and Hebrew translations of the Bible. In other words, there is evidence that the final books and translations of the Old Testament took several centuries to be finalized. Scholars contend that the number of sacred books among the Jews was not agreed upon until about the year 200 CE, two centuries after the birth of Jesus.

Although both Hebrew and Greek versions of the Old Testament were used during the lifetime of Jesus, it is clear that the Greek edition was preferred by the writers of the New Testament, who were predominantly Greek- and Aramaic-speaking Jews.

THE CHANGING FACE OF THE OLD TESTAMENT

I once had a student who, after reading the Old Testament for the first time, told me that it disturbed her. Reading it through, she had the impression that God was gradually becoming more mature. In the earlier stories, she said, God appears arbitrary and violent, destroying the human race in a flood or commanding the slaughter of entire villages. Later God grows more reliable, patient, willing to forgive, and seems more reasonable in his demands.

The discovery shook her faith because she had never thought that the word of God was written by people with human limitations, in particular historical circumstances, as she had been led to understand that the Bible was revealed by God. But the shock gave her a new insight: "What happened in the Old Testament books was not that God became more mature but that the people who wrote about him did."

Her insight is shared by most biblical scholars—that is, our understanding of God developed over the course of many centuries and it continues to grow, forcing us to reinterpret and refine our theology. Although the slow and dynamic development of the Bible makes it increasingly difficult to decipher, it is evidence for the increasing bond between God and humanity. For example, the development of monotheism—a concept that we now take for granted—and the notion of personhood show how our understanding of God emerged from our cultural and historical circumstances.

From Polytheism to Monotheism

Monotheism, the central teaching of Judaism, was not imagined overnight. Moses, thirteen centuries before Jesus, at first seemed comfortable with the presumption that other gods existed. He sang, "Who is like you, O LORD, among the gods?" (Exodus 15:11) The first commandment of the Decalogue shows the same way of thinking. Scholars call it *henotheism:* although other gods might exist, the Israelites worship only one (read Judges 11:23 below). The one God brought them out from Egypt into a promised land. He is their God and they are his people.

*So now the LORD, the God of Israel, has conquered the Amorites for
the benefit of his people Israel. Do you intend to take their place?
Should you not possess what your god Chemosh gives you to possess?
And should we not be the ones to possess everything that the LORD
our God has conquered for our benefit?*

Judges 11:23–24

Before long, their faith expanded to the point that God was known as the
one who made all things. By the seventh century before Christ, the prophets
were ridiculing foreign gods as powerless.

*Their idols are like scarecrows in a cucumber field,
and they cannot speak;
they have to be carried,
      for they cannot walk.
Do not be afraid of them,
      for they cannot do evil,
      nor is it in them to do good.*

Jeremiah 10:5

And the experience of the Babylonian Exile in the sixth century finally crystallizes the monotheism that became the central hallmark of the
community:

*Thus says the LORD, the King of Israel,
      and his Redeemer, the LORD of hosts:
I am the first and I am the last;
      besides me there is no god.*

Isaiah 44:6

From Tribe to Tribe Member

Appreciation for the dignity of the individual person developed in a similar way.
Early writings consider the tribe, not the individual, to be the principal object
of God's concern. Rewards and punishments for moral behavior are thought
to fall upon the entire people, not merely on the individual.

*They abandoned the LORD, and worshipped Baal and the Astartes.
So the anger of the LORD was kindled against Israel, and he gave
them over to plunderers who plundered them, and he sold them into
the power of their enemies all around, so that they could no longer
withstand their enemies. Whenever they marched out, the hand of the*

Lord was against them to bring misfortune, as the Lord had warned them and swore to them; and they were in great distress.

Judges 2:13–15

During the early years of Israel's history there was no belief in personal immortality: "For in death there is no remembrance of you; / in Sheol who can give you praise?" (Psalm 6:5). "Is your steadfast love declared in the grave, / or your faithfulness in Abaddon? / Are your wonders known in the darkness, / or your saving help in the land of forgetfulness" (Psalm 88:11–12). These questions reveal that the realm of the dead is not transcendent or heavenly, but it is Abaddon, "the place of perishing," land of forgetfulness, and most especially darkness—not a word that we often associate with eternal life.

Only when the nation is destroyed as a political entity by the Babylonian armies in 587 BC do we begin to find prophets speaking of a relationship between God and individual persons. At the very end of the Old Testament period (sometime before 164 BC), Israel finally dared to believe that this relationship was stronger than death. A personal resurrection or a resurrection of the body, however, is clearly attested to only in the second century BCE by Daniel in 12:2 and 12:13. In other places, the Old Testament makes reference to life for Israel even beyond death. Christians later interpreted these as references to Christ (see, for instance, Hosea 13:14; Isaiah 25:8; 26:19; 53:10; Ezekeiel 37; Job 14:14–15; 19:27; and Psalms 16:9–11; 17:15; and 49:15).

At that time Michael, the great prince, the protector of your people, shall arise. There shall be a time of anguish, such as has never occurred since nations first came into existence. But at that time your people shall be delivered, everyone who is found written in the book. Many of those who sleep in the dust of the earth shall awake, some to everlasting life, and some to shame and everlasting contempt. Those who are wise shall shine like the brightness of the sky, and those who lead many to righteousness, like the stars forever and ever.

Daniel 12:1–3

TOWARD A GREATER UNDERSTANDING OF GOD

The development of monotheism and the dignity of the individual are just two of many things that warn us not to read everything in the Bible literally. They remind us that we are in a relationship with God that continues to evolve. We must use all of the tools of biblical interpretation to understand the diverse circumstances and people that bring us the revelation of God.

Each new insight of the Israelites in the Old Testament grew out of experience, sometimes very painful experience, confronted by a faith which trusted that whatever happened, God somehow stood behind it. And because of this, the developing thought of the Old Testament can be brought together by studying it in the framework of historical events that provoked it, an undertaking explored in the next chapter.

REVIEW QUESTIONS
1. How do Protestant and Catholic Bibles differ on the number of books they accept in their Old Testaments?
2. How would you explain this sentence: "The churches existed before one line of the New Testament was written"?
3. Monotheism is a hallmark of Judaism; however, the biblical writings indicate that monotheism developed gradually. What events in Jewish history influenced the development of monotheism?

FOR FURTHER STUDY
1. Consult a biblical commentary for articles relating to the development of Israel's writings and history.
2. See the *Anchor Bible Dictionary* (Freedman, David N., et al. New York: Doubleday, 1992, six volumes). This exhaustive resource of contemporary scholarship covers a broad range of biblical topics, including the Dead Sea Scrolls, various groups within Jewish society during the late Second Temple period, explanations of disputes between early Christians and Jewish groups, as well as use of literary, sociological, and feminist hermeneutics. Careful and clear explanations given throughout.
3. Brown, Raymond, E., J. A. Fitzmyer, and Roland E. Murphy, eds. *The New Jerome Biblical Commentary* (New York: Prentice Hall, 1999). See articles on canon and/or canonicity for the complicated story of the formation of the Jewish and Christian canons of Scripture.
4. Lienhard, Joseph, S.J. *The Bible, The Church and Authority: The Canon of the Christian Bible in History and Theology* (Collegeville, MN: Michael Glazier Books, 1995). Emphasizes the "rule of faith" as the key element in the formation of the canonical list of books accepted by the Church. This rule of faith is unknown among the historicist school of biblical interpretation. Explains clearly the differences in the number of books accepted in Protestant and Roman Catholic Bibles and permits the reader to come to their own conclusions.
5. Dalley, Stephanie. *Myths from Mesopotamia: Creation, the Flood, Gilgamesh and Others* (New York: Oxford University Press USA, 2000; revised edition). Excellent bibliography and explanatory notes for each ancient myth.

6. Collins, John J. *The Apocalyptic Imagination: An Introduction to Jewish Apocalyptic Literature* (Grand Rapids, MI: Eerdmans, 1998). Clear analysis of various groups and movements and different historical moments and situations and their influence in the development of the genre.

7. Hurtado, Larry W. *One God, One Lord: Early Christian Devotion and Ancient Jewish Monotheism* (Edinburgh: T & T Clark, 2003). A fascinating study that unpacks Christian resources for cultic practices and devotions aligned with Jewish monotheism. Scholarly treatment yet written in a clear style for all.

8. Bynum, Carolyn W. *The Resurrection of the Body* (New York: Columbia University Press, 1995). A fascinating addition to a school of interpretation in which the history of the human body is evaluated. Of special interest is the template of interpretations given to the meaning of the resurrection in art and letters from the time of the first Christians to the medieval period.

4

The History of Israel

The Jewish people trace their history back to Abraham and Sarah. First known as "Hebrews," they later came to be called "Israelites," then "Jews." Abraham and Sarah were called by God to leave their homeland and wander. This is recounted in the ancestral or patriarchal narratives in Genesis 12—50. God promises Abraham and his descendents many blessings, including children, land, and prosperity. Abraham was sometimes a doubting believer, yet God remained a covenant partner with him.

Five hundred years after the Genesis story ends, for no apparent reason, a group of slaves in Egypt is set free by Moses under the guidance of divine authority. This "new" divinity bound Moses by a covenant and led the Jews through the Sinai desert with the promise of "a land of milk and honey." Moses not only received his commission but God revealed his name. The name derives from a Hebrew verb *YHWH*, or "to be," from which the word "Yahweh" derives. In the context of the Old Testament, it is often translated "I am, who am."

After Moses' campaigns for the slaves, they are set free. This is the beginning of Israel's history as a people and the gradual formation of their nation.

The early history of the Israelites is one of repeated conflicts. God is understood primarily as a "God of hosts" (see the books of Samuel, Kings, and Chronicles)—that is, a God of armies, who destroys the Egyptians, then the Canaanites, then the Philistines with his "strong right arm." Judges chapter 5 contains an ancient poem that captures the spirit of these times, even though many of its verses are now historically obscure.

> "LORD, when you went out from Seir,
> when you marched from the region of Edom,
> the earth trembled,
> and the heavens poured,
> the clouds indeed poured water.
> The mountains quaked before the LORD, the One of Sinai,
> before the LORD, the God of Israel.

Judges 5:4–5

HISTORY BEFORE THE ISRAELITES

Although the first Israelite tribes to enter into covenant with God fought for their identity through sweat and blood, the Book of Genesis—the history before the Jewish people—contains an optimistic view of human beings. Genesis contains two different creation narratives in chapters 1 and 2, respectively. The stories do not include the same facts—actually they are contradictory at times—but they both convey the foundation of God's relationship with humanity. Literary and form criticism teaches us that each story brings forward different but equally important elements of God's creative work, and each account was developed by different editors and redactors from different historical, political, and social contexts. With such complexity, there are simply too many elements for a comprehensive overview. Instead, we'll examine two aspects of creation that dig deeper than most literal interpretations.

Co-Creators With God

The most familiar creation account is found in the first chapter of Genesis, but the second chapter includes some important events and theology. Specifically, Adam has to work in the Garden. He farms in paradise and is expected to protect the Garden from harm (see Genesis 2:5, 15). This ideal state is no endless vacation, but one in which Adam (whose name is a word play that means "humanity") must exercise responsible management of creation.

So, too, Adam seems to have been given nearly everything he could imagine, including the freedom to do anything he pleases. He has access to all the mysteries of life as symbolized in the tree of the knowledge of good and evil. The only fact he has to accept is that he is not God. He is a creature, and he has to trust that he is better off as such.

A great symbol of God's love for Adam is given in the love of a partner. "It is not good that the man should be alone," God says. "I will make him a helper as his partner" (Genesis 2:18). This passage introduces the relational structure of God's design and the role of humanity in creation itself. Not only are man and women partners (sexually and spiritually), they are co-creators (that is, partners with God) with respect to all life on earth. Thus the creation of Eve (the "mother of the living") is preceded by the naming of creatures by Adam (a.k.a., humanity). Adam seems to name the creatures in a perfunctory way and he is restless without a human partner. Adam must join in to complete the work of the Creator. The author places the creating and naming of creatures to emphasize a point: even as Adam shares much with the birds and animals, since all are formed from the earth, he is somehow different from them. He is aware that he is alone and life is incomplete without someway to express the love that he has received from God.

It is only with his partner that Adam finds a kind of sharing that makes all the work, the use of talents, and living the mystery of life meaningful and complete. With the woman, he has a counterpart, an equal, who helps him to know that he is not alone, that he is loved, and that together they can love in a new way—they can produce new life. They practice with each other the divine act of giving in anticipation of the other's needs. And the Book of Genesis says that all of this is good.

Evil

The presence of evil in the Garden is narrated in chapter three. "To know" is the Hebrew equivalent for the English word "experience." The familiar story of the talking and tempting serpent makes use of a simple argument: If one wants to be like God, one must "know" all things, which in Hebrew is not only intellectual, but also relational and experiential. The serpent implies that humans should know good *and* evil, the first and last in a series of opposites. According to the serpent, the Creator is at once the author of light and darkness, virtue and malice, beauty and its opposites. And so the serpent argues that if Eve and Adam have no "knowledge" (experience and relation) of evil, they have not mastered life.

We must realize that the serpent is *not* Satan, although many traditions have interpreted it as such. The snake is simply a mischievous creature made by God with the sole intention of tempting Eve (mother of the living), a reminder that humanity is endowed with radical free will. The serpent disappears from the narrative when his function is complete. Ultimately, the serpent claims that God has a selfish, withholding attitude, and he accuses God of not sharing the fruit of the tree of knowledge (representing the mastery of all life) for that reason. Eve is fooled by the argument, Adam falls equally hard, and they are quickly confronted by their nakedness, ignorance, and limited human condition.

Nevertheless, even when chaos falls upon the couple, hope for them is not eliminated. The Creator promises that something more will be revealed to them in the future. They are still made in the image of God, they still co-create with God, and thus they have the faculties to know (experience and relate) love. And so there is promise, hope, and optimism as the story ends.

THE FORMATION OF A KINGDOM

The lands in which the Hebrews wander are occupied by other people, and the Canaanites live in the region the Hebrews claim as their own. Joshua leads the Hebrews in a few victories, but the struggle turns into an extended conflict. Whether this period was one of assimilation rather than conquest is debated by scholars. The Hebrew people settled the land of Canaan and eventually divided the land among twelve tribes, each ruled by a judge. The judge was elected leader by the people based on personal integrity and character. There was no hereditary position, coinciding with the Hebrew theological teaching that there is only *one* king: YHWH, or Yahweh. The period of the Judges included festivals at special sites, usually on mountaintops, where storytelling of their history kept them on track. Mutual cooperation seemed to help the tribes defend themselves against invaders, but it was hard to maintain.

Pressure for a monarch becomes greater as time moved on. Samuel tried to dissuade the people with no success (see 1 Samuel 8:19–20). Saul was anointed monarch. The northern tribes continued to resist the idea of a monarchy, but Saul was a competent leader. He and his son Jonathan were eventually killed in battle, and the precedence of hereditary monarchy was short lived. This opened the door for the kingdom of David.

David was anointed king, "messiah" ("anointed one") in the year 1012 BC. He was distrusted by Saul, possibly due to his popular appeal as a poetic hero. Saul tried to have David killed. Even so, David pushed back the Philistine armies who had plagued the Israelites for nearly two centuries. The land of milk and honey was finally theirs. In the joy of victory, David was celebrated as God's "son," which in Hebrew implied that he was God's "representative." He set up Jerusalem as his political capital and was able to unite the tribes into one nation. Through God, he had the power to rule the entire world.

The LORD says to my lord,
  "Sit at my right hand
until I make your enemies your footstool."

The LORD sends out from Zion
  your mighty scepter.
  Rule in the midst of your foes.
Your people will offer themselves willingly
  on the day you lead your forces
  on the holy mountains.
From the womb of the morning,
  like dew, your youth will come to you.
The LORD has sworn and will not change his mind,
  "You are a priest forever
  according to the order of Melchizedek."

The Lord is at your right hand;
  he will shatter kings on the day of his wrath.

He will execute judgment among the nations,
filling them with corpses;
he will shatter heads
over the wide earth.
He will drink from the stream by the path;
therefore he will lift up his head.

Psalm 110

Although this psalm carries a violent undertone (shattering heads and corpses), it actually recounts the peace and prosperity that existed during David's rule. Using the tools of biblical interpretation—particularly historical and form criticism—we learn that there is much more to this history than meets the eye.

The figure of Melchizedek and his place in Hebrew history and writing is thoroughly discussed. Psalm 110:4 is arguably one of the worst-preserved passages of the Bible. We are told that it is possible that the original wording did not refer to Melchizedek at all; a possible translation is "legitimate king by God's edict." The only certain reference to Melchizedek is Genesis 14:18–20. He was king and high priest of the city of Salem at the time of Abraham. Salem may have been an early name for Jerusalem. He was one who worshipped the Canaanite deity El Elyon. Genesis states that after Abraham gathered an army and completely defeated four kings, Melchizedek came forward and tried to pay his respects to the victor. He offered Abraham bread and wine, symbols of hospitality, and blessed him. Monotheism would begin with Moses half a millennium later, so even though Abraham worshipped a god he called El Shaddai, he seems to have been pleased with favor given by whatever other divine forces there might be.

The story was ancient history by the time it was written down. Some critics argue that it is more legend than fact—even if it conveys a fundamental reality—and it is as remote today as the English tales of King Arthur and the Knights of the Roundtable. Melchizedek was a somewhat legendary ancestor in the memory of the Hebrew people. He is included in the Old Testament for political reasons. After David's conquest of Jerusalem, the city remained a stronghold of Canaanite religion, even after David made it his capital. He worked out an agreement with its people, and this fragment from Psalm 110:4 shows David's ancestor, Abraham, and Jerusalem's ancestor, Melchizedek, at peace. It is a useful scene to help justify David's action.

The rabbis of later centuries had a fascination with mysterious figures from their past, especially the ones who bridged the distance between the people and God. Books filled with revelations were written and attributed to people such as Enoch (see Genesis 5:24ff). Special attention was devoted to the speculations over what Elijah was doing (read 2 Kings 2) and as we already know, Melchizedek, the mysterious priest-king who represented Jerusalem. The Essenes in Qumran believed that Melchizedek would return with the messiah to destroy all enemies; the New Testament writer of the Book of Hebrews seems to agree, calling him the "king of peace…resembling the Son of god, he remains a priest forever"(see Hebrews 7:2–3).

After David's death, his son Solomon became king. He had a reputation as a wise man, but was overindulged. David had been reared in ordinary circumstance, while Solomon was reared as a prince. He had many ideas as to what kingship entails and began a number of building projects, including a great palace. He drafted thousands of citizens as slave laborers. He had a suspicion of northerners who continued to voice their disapproval of Solomon and the notion of monarchy.

King Solomon died sometime during the tenth century and was succeeded by a king with no tact (Rehoboam). The kingdom divided into north and south. The northern ten tribes were called *Israel*, centered in the town of Shechem, and the southern two tribes called *Judah*, centered in Jerusalem. The story of the southern two kingdoms is filled with intrigue and foreign conquests.

A KINGDOM DECLINES

At the end of Solomon's reign, the northern half of the kingdom broke away in a civil war. An endless series of military and economic disasters followed. The people abandoned belief in one God and found other, more comforting, deities. Against this, the prophets blamed their troubles on sin. "If you are willing and obedient, / you shall eat the good of the land; / but if you refuse and rebel, / you shall be devoured by the sword; / for the mouth of the LORD has spoken" (Isaiah 1:19–20). Thus they warned the people to turn back to God. Some prophets spoke in terms of a righteous and holy *messiah* who would see that God's will was carried out. "For a child has been born for us, / a son given to us; / authority rests upon his shoulders; and he is named Wonderful Counselor, Mighty God, / Everlasting Father, Prince of Peace" (Isaiah 9:6). They announced that a rich and trouble-free paradise, complete with the perfect king, would thrive on earth if only they turned from their sinful ways.

> *A shoot shall come out from the stump of Jesse,*
> *and a branch shall grow out of his roots.*
> *The spirit of the LORD shall rest on him,*
> *the spirit of wisdom and understanding,*

> *the spirit of counsel and might,*
> *the spirit of knowledge and the fear of the LORD.*
> *His delight shall be in the fear of the LORD.*
>
> *He shall not judge by what his eyes see,*
> *or decide by what his ears hear;*
> *but with righteousness he shall judge the poor,*
> *and decide with equity for the meek of the earth;*
> *he shall strike the earth with the rod of his mouth,*
> *and with the breath of his lips he shall kill the wicked.*
>
> *Righteousness shall be the belt around his waist,*
> *and faithfulness the belt around his loins.*
>
> Isaiah 11:1–5

The "branches" in Isaiah 11:1 represent the historical kings whom Isaiah had discounted in favor of a return to the source of the dynasty—David. Isaiah notes that the future king would be endowed with "Yahweh's spirit," the same force that was given to Moses, judges, prophets, David, and many others. In other words, this future king would represent a return to the charismatic leaders of centuries past. Centuries later Christians interpreted Isaiah to mean that Jesus is the "shoot" from Jesse, the fullness of Yahweh's spirit.

Another prophet, Amos, announced the judgment of God on the prosperous northern kingdom during 786–746 BC. At that time, there was a great worship center or shrine in Bethel. Amos was opposed by its chief priest, Amaziah. As a prophet, Amos combined several roles. He not only called for a change away from injustice and idolatry, he also predicted the downfall of the kingdom. Amos was the one who announced the impending "day of the Lord."

To develop a picture of the period in which he lived, imagine that the Confederate army had won the American Civil War and that the South went on to prosper. Now imagine that a northern Union person offered a series of lectures on the social and moral evils that accompany prosperity. Would the Confederate states have accepted the "wise" advice of the Union? In Amos' day it was the northern kingdom that had seceded from the union created by King David. Amos was from the south, a Judean worker who punctured the bark of sycamore trees to let the wormy pests escape. His secular job is one metaphor for his prophetic position in the north. He went there to preach social justice.

What is of interest to our study, and is evident in the case of Amos, is the dialectic that seems to be set up throughout the Jewish writings between prophets and priests. It is not an unusual type of opposition. Amos turned his diatribe against religious practices, shrines, and rituals, especially the practices that were sponsored by the northern king. According to him, people were using religion to cover up their indifference to issues of social justice.

The priest was a master of rituals; he knew the rites, words, and gestures that more or less bridged the distance between divine and the human. The priest tried to keep these realms in some sort of harmony for the people. The role of the priest was protective and conservative, offering the rituals that eased the anxieties of people, blessing their flocks and farms, offering prayers at ceremonies that kept continuity and preserved social order.

The prophet, in contrast, commented on all that was unfinished or incomplete in the religious response of leaders and people. A prophet was on a mission. The priest embodied the reassuring, humanized dimension of God's presence. The prophet represented the presence of God that is more demanding, sometimes frightening, and truly involved in any authentic religion. In Israel's earliest period, prophecy almost amounted to madness. Those who were called prophets specialized in dancing themselves into a trance (see 1 Samuel 10:5ff). When they lost control of themselves, they were considered to have been taken over by supernatural forces—"possessed by God." Their visions and sayings were thought to be divine revelations. Even when trances went out of fashion, the prophets' messages were seasoned with symbolic and mysterious visions and oracles. The connection with madness never completely faded.

Even the great prophets like Jeremiah and Isaiah, never perceived as raving dreamers or madmen, remained out of step with the times in which they lived. They were ridiculed and misunderstood, "possessed" by visions that put them beyond conventional ways of thinking. These prophets questioned what no one wanted to question. They tended to criticize the status quo in the name of what God wanted to exist. The prophets were almost the exact opposite of the priests.

Amos, for one, spoke out against the established system at Bethel. The differences, almost a chasm, that existed between the economically comfortable and the poor were an injustice. According to Amos, the king was the primary one who could change it all (see Amos 7:12ff). The priest took the side of the king and the status quo. Amaziah had enough of Amos' seditious talk and screamed at him: "O seer, go, flee away to the land of Judah, earn your bread there, and prophesy there; but never again prophesy at Bethel, for it is the king's sanctuary, and it is a temple of the kingdom" (Amos 7:12–13). Amos' answer is odd: "I am no prophet, nor a prophet's son" (v. 14). In other words, he has no association with the remaining groups of visionaries. "I am a herdsman, and a dresser of sycamore trees, and the LORD took me from following the flock, and the LORD said to me, 'Go prophesy to my people Israel'" (Amos 7:14–15).

The same argument is expressed throughout the Old Testament. It is rare to find prophets and priests on the same side of an issue. Priests speak out to remind everyone of what is already given by God and what has been achieved in the past. Prophets speak for what is unrealized and needs reform. Even if this interpretation is an oversimplification, it is a caution against the more serious oversimplification of simply siding with one group or the other. Both sides are important. Without prophets there would be no vision of the future, no direction for further growth, only the tired celebration of the present condition. Without the priests there would have been no order, no connections to the past. The result is tension, argument, and exaggerations on both sides, and this saga is told again and again in the Old Testament.

As we reflect on the rise and division of the kingdom(s) in the Old Testament, we need to look beyond the bare "historical" facts (who, what, where, and when) and focus on how the characters interact with God.

THE BABYLONIAN EXILE

The northern tribes fell to the Assyrian empire in 722 BC. In 587 BC, 135 years later, the Babylonian armies overwhelmed the southern kingdom of David. Leaders were carried away to captivity in Mesopotamia. The misery of defeat had a devastating effect on religion. Were the prophets wrong when they claimed that David's throne would stand forever (see Isaiah 37:35)? Was God powerless? Had their sins been so great as to exhaust God's patience? Either way, Israel's existence seemed doomed, its people scattered in foreign lands.

Amid this time of crisis, the prophets offered a reassuring insight: God remained loving and loyal, beyond every defeat. The people had indeed broken the covenant with their sin, but God would take them back. God would make a new covenant and put his own spirit in their hearts. "The days are surely coming, says the LORD, when I will make a new covenant with the house of Israel and the house of Judah" (Jeremiah 31:31). And from Ezekiel: "A new heart I will give you, and a new spirit I will put within you; and I will remove from your body the heart of stone and give you a heart of flesh. I will put my spirit within you, and make you follow my statutes and be careful to observe my ordinances" (Ezekiel 36:26–27). The dead bones of Israel would live again. No matter the extent of human sin, God's forgiveness is greater.

> *"They say, 'Our bones are dried up, and our hope is lost; we are cut off completely.' Therefore prophesy, and say to them, Thus says the Lord GOD: I am going to open your graves, and bring you up from your graves, O my people; and I will bring you back to the land of Israel. And you shall know that I am the LORD, when I open your graves, and bring you up from your graves, O my people. I will put my spirit*

within you, and you shall live, and I will place you on your own soil;
then you shall know that I, the LORD, have spoken and will act," says
the LORD.

Ezekiel 37:11–14

Cyrus the Persian in 538 BC announced that the Jews could return home. Nearly forty years later, about five hundred years before Christ, many had done so. Cyrus had conquered Babylon and seemed more enlightened regarding conquered peoples. Encouraged by the proclamations of the prophets, they thought they would finally see the messiah and kingdom they were promised. It is important to notice that many Jews did not return home. They had made new lives in Babylon. Those who returned found a changed environment. Jerusalem was in ruins, work was slow, times were difficult, and the glory of the old kingdom was not easily recaptured.

They were sorely disappointed. Inhabiting an impoverished land with no king of their own, they continued under foreign rulers. Their overlords taxed heavily and by the fourth century they no longer had prophets to interpret their way. God seemed absent. The heavens were sealed over. Why did God not act? "How long, O Lord?" The mood of the final centuries before Christ was one of suspense.

Earlier Nehemiah in 439 began the arduous task of rebuilding the walls of the city, and Ezra set to rebuild the religious life of the people. To help unify the community there, he developed the notion of separation from other cultures. Racial purity became idealized, and the stories of Ruth and Jonah were likely written during this period. They tried to moderate the racial purity extremists and remind the people of their calling to be a "light to all the nations." The writings of Joel and perhaps Malachi also date from this era. The Jewish faith became more codified, even as they experience further invasions and conquest.

JUDAISM AT THE TIME OF JESUS

The years before the birth of Jesus were difficult ones for the Jewish people. Scholars propose that Jesus was born sometime around the year 4 BC. For the Jewish people in the Roman province of Palestine, except for a few generations of independence won by the Maccabees, one foreign government after another controlled them for about five centuries since their return from exile in 537 BC: first the Persians, then the Greeks, and finally the Romans. There were economic restrictions and heavy taxes, infringements on religious liberty and, at times, persecution.

Priesthood

Judaism at the time of Jesus was not a monolithic religious sect. People were Jewish in a variety of ways. There were priests who managed the Temple in Jerusalem. Unlike clergy in many religions today, the Jewish priesthood was hereditary.

Some scholars suggest that there were about a half million individuals in Palestine at that time, with a few thousand priests. The priests lived in villages not far from Jerusalem. Many had obligations to work in the Temple, which included worship services—including ritual sacrifice—and maintaining the storage facilities there.

Sanhedrin

The Temple in Jerusalem was a magnificent structure for its time. During the lifetime of Jesus it was near completion and was a symbol of God's special presence to his people. The Roman occupiers permitted the priests to govern their people through the Sanhedrin, a political and religious group of leaders that resembled our modern political parties, though not all priests were members. The Sanhedrin often tried to arbitrate disputes between the occupiers (Romans during the time of Jesus) and the Jews, but there are only traces of historical evidence about the organization and their manner of proceeding.

Sadducees

Although it was primarily a lay organization, some priests were also Jewish aristocrats known as Sadducees. Again, historical evidence outside Christian writings does not yield a complete picture of their status or identity. They are remembered most for their positions of wealth and comfort through shrewd cooperation with foreign overlords. Although they often controlled the structure of worship, they were not noted for piety. Many Sadducee priests favored continuation of traditional temple rituals, reading only the first books of the Jewish Bible, denying the existence of angels, and rejecting any concept of a messiah or the advent of a new Jewish apocalyptic king. Critics of the Sadducees claimed they paid lip service to the ancient religious traditions that put them into power. From what we know, they were more secular than religious in their day-to-day interests and decisions. According to the New Testament, Jesus did not speak to these priests often.

Zealots

During the time of Jesus, there were also angry, young rebels who thought anything would be better than the present powerlessness of the Jews in the face of Roman occupation. These Zealots, as they were known, believed that

God's promises to Israel could be fulfilled through rebellion. Their assassinations and skirmishes with the Roman occupiers were rooted in religious fanaticism. Zealot leaders would sometimes, in fact, claim to be "messiahs," but the New Testament referred to them as "bandits." Barabbas may have been one of them—Mark claims that he "was in prison with the rebels who had committed murder during the insurrection" (Mark 15:7). Zealot ideology, over time, came to dominate the Jewish community, leading them into a disastrous rebellion that ended with the destruction of Jerusalem and its temple by Roman armies in the year AD 70. Still, one of the apostles selected by Jesus was Simon, a known Zealot.

Jewish Communities Disbursed

During the political and religious struggles of the first century in Palestine, many emigrants left the poverty of Palestine to seek a new life in Damascus, Antioch, or Alexandria in Egypt. Nearly every sizeable city between Babylon and Rome had its colony of expatriate Jews. In Rome, for example, one scholar estimates that at the time of Jesus there were thirteen synagogues. A number of Jews spoke Greek and, as mentioned earlier, they used a Greek Bible (LXX) rather than the Hebrew one used in Palestine. These Jews were more cosmopolitan than their provincial kinsmen in Palestine. Many of their concerns and identifications with Judaism eased as they busied themselves with life in the more prosperous and wider world of the empire.

Anawim

Back in Palestine there were masses of poor and working-class people. Known as the *anawim*, they were often too preoccupied with daily survival to take much interest in religious observances. Many in Palestine looked down on the anawim. They were identified as "sinners." Their meager economic status was thought to be a sign of God's disfavor. The words of Jesus resonated with them and, as such, they formed crowds to follow the itinerant teacher.

Essenes

One movement of Jews, the Essenes, had given up entirely on the religion of the Jerusalem priests. They are not mentioned in the Christian Bible but they are important for New Testament background. They were a radical sect, or sects, so disturbed by Sadducee control of the Temple priesthood in Jerusalem that they set up communities in the desert, most notably at Qumran near the shores of the Dead Sea. They removed themselves completely from the popular Jewish social network in Palestine. Some scholars muse that they were dissident priests of the Temple, who removed themselves from the corruptions and amusements enjoyed by the urban Temple priests. Writings from the Qumran community, the "Dead Sea Scrolls," were discovered in the last century. From recent translations of these scrolls, it seems this community lived a rigorous and highly organized life, probably in several groups spread over the wilderness. They were messianic communities in the sense that they awaited God's special agent ("messiah") to destroy the corruption they saw everywhere. Some speculate that John the Baptist may have been associated with this sect, but the New Testament is silent about this possibility.

Pharisees

The Pharisees, whose name means "separatists," were a lay movement. Although the New Testament portrays them in a negative light, the Pharisees had a major impact on devotional practice. They were primarily a voluntary organization, with no formal control of government or religious affairs. Their primary social program was to extend the priestly regulations of ritual purity mandated in the Book of Leviticus to all Jews. Thus they were obsessed with regulations about what is permitted on the Sabbath, how many times a day to pray, or how to wash hands or even dishes, and what tithes to pay the Temple. The rules had a positive side. The fact they reach into every aspect of life is proof of a genuine and pious desire to obey God's will in all things (see Psalm 119). Scholars continue to examine the place of the Pharisees in first-century Jewish life. Fragments of evidence that mention them in extrabiblical sources, such as the writings of Josephus, and brief citations in the Mishnah and Talmud, have led scholars to see the Pharisees as deeply devoted to the Torah.

While the Torah (meaning instruction, Law, or the "revealed will of God" as contained in the first five books of the Old Testament: Genesis, Exodus, Leviticus, Numbers, and Deuteronomy) had been a part of Israel's oral tradition from the start, and was recorded in written form about 450–400 BCE, it had not always been the all-embracing center of devotion. A new emphasis developed on its centrality in the time of the Babylonian exile during the sixth century BCE, especially after the Temple was destroyed. Emphasis on the Torah expanded even more during the period of their return to Palestine.

After the exile, the Jews returned to Palestine full of hope. They felt forgiven, graced, and restored. Their prophets said that all God's promises were about to be fulfilled. But nothing of the sort happened, and then there were no more prophets. Was God with them or not? Unable to see his hand at work around them, some turned to the past for security. The sacred scrolls and writings were codified and studied; sometimes its regulations were enforced with rigor.

Ezra, a scribe from about 400 BCE (see Nehemiah 8), is remembered as the great promulgator of the Torah. Over the years other great teachers and scholars (or scribes) offered further instructions, spelling out God's will in greater detail to bridge the gap between the original legislation from Moses, now centuries old, and the daily lives of the devout. By the time of Jesus, some Jews were meeting every week in village buildings to study. These places were called synagogues. These pious Jews immersed themselves in knowledge of both the written Scriptures and the traditions of their greatest scribes. Some practiced fasting on Mondays and Thursdays. Others wore clothing identifying them as "pure ones." Obedience to God's will was the sum and substance of their religion.

Devotion to the Law of Moses, the Torah, gave the Pharisees an impressive strength, a sense of identity that weathered all the political and economic storms that hit Palestine. After the tragic war with the Romans that destroyed Jerusalem in AD 70, it was the Pharisees, more than anyone else, who preserved the Jewish faith for future generations. But their strength, according to the New Testament portrayal, was also their weakness. The strong wall of tradition that sustained them tended to become, in the Christian view, a prison, trapping them in a smug and inflexible stance. They were searching so scrupulously for God in the traditions of the past that they could not see it when he stood before them in the present.

Their religious approach is remembered by Christians to have suffered from *externalism*—the substitution of outward performance for interior motivation. Along with this went a legalistic view of life, in which every possible situation was governed by rules. Every rule has exceptions, but the legalist avoids the responsibility for making them. Legalists want a rule for the exception, too. The result is a legal prison cut off from life, like a country with a constitution that never allows amendments. Scholarship seems divided today as to the depth of legalism to which the Pharisees subscribed. A more sympathetic view is that they concentrated on the observance of special rites and customs so as to preserve their religion from further dilution by gentile overlords.

According to the New Testament, the Pharisees imagined God as a distant but fair employer who rewards service with justice. These religious people wanted to be safe with God, to know where they stood, to have no surprises in the relationship. They were shocked by Jesus' ideas of a God who delights in forgiving sinners. But we should remember that they were good people, upright, dedicated, observant of their religion. Jesus excoriated them the way we do when we fight with someone we love very much.

One way to explain the excesses of the Pharisees is to say that they listened too well to the ancient prophets. In the years before the Babylonian exile, the prophets had called Israel to repentance with the explanation that the sufferings they experienced were due to sin. The prophets were ignored, but after the terrible experience of the exile, the Jews tried to prevent further disasters by purifying the people of all sin. The Pharisaic approach to the law is the end product of their anxiety.

THE REIGN OF GOD IN HEAVEN AND EARTH

By the same token, the prophets had also promised that obedience to God would bring blessings, and these blessings came to be summed up under the heading of the "kingdom," or "reign of God." Some Christians tend to presume, mistakenly, that this meant "heaven," a place of salvation for souls after death. But Judaism did not imagine a body-and-soul dichotomy in the modern Western sense. As mentioned earlier, the *reign of God* referred to a future age for Israel in this world, when God's people would enjoy all the good things described by the prophets: swords beaten into ploughshares, the lion and the lamb at peace, an outpouring of God's spirit on all flesh, an end to tears and evil, God ruling the world through a chosen king (messiah).

The prophets' descriptions of the kingdom make no mention of salvation for those already dead. Instead, the kingdom is for the living. The doctrine of the resurrection of the dead develops in Judaism only about the third century before Jesus, and only the Jewish books of Daniel and Second Maccabees refer to it.

Dualism

When belief in resurrection finally broke into Jewish thought, it was part of a new wave of religious imagery that owes something to the influence of Persian cosmic dualism. The Persians ruled Israel for two centuries after the exile. They explained the persistence of evil in the world not primarily in terms of human sinfulness, but as the consequence or effect of evil spirits. Their belief was that these forces of darkness, which dominated the world at present, would one day be defeated by the armies of light. Then people would rise from the dead and be judged by fire. Those who proved themselves good and righteous would enjoy eternal life; the others, eternal fire.

Apocalyptic Ideology

Jewish tradition emphasized human responsibility and was wedded to the reality of this world as designed by God for people. The Jews did not accept Persian ideology and cosmology easily. But as the years went on, as times became worse instead of better, as the hopes raised by the prophets remained unfulfilled, and as the sense of God's absence grew stronger, they became more convinced that their world was dominated by evil forces. Jews began to interpret the coming of

God's kingdom less in terms of their own conversion and more as God's mighty intervention. When the predestined moment arrived, they imagined God unleashing his wrath upon all evildoers in a cosmic holocaust. This would introduce a new age on earth in which the world would be returned to the paradise it knew at the beginning of creation.

This type of thinking is part of a literary "genre" or type of writing that is called *apocalyptic.* It finds its first full-fledged literary expression in the Jewish Book of Daniel. On some levels, the Jews had known harassment by foreign overlords, but it would be the Syrian king, Antiochus IV Epiphanes, who went beyond all previously known atrocities. To consolidate his power against the expanding strength of the Romans, Antiochus violated the Temple of Jerusalem. He robbed the Temple of Jerusalem and demanded that the Jews worship him as a manifestation of Zeus. The Jews were willing to die rather than conform to this decree. The Book of Second Maccabees 6:18–7:42 tells the story of torments they suffered for their faith. It was not unusual for people of this time to imagine that the end was near. God would put a stop to the many evils his people experienced. A number of authors searched the writings of their prophets for clues, trying to discover in them some sign of how long the evil age would continue before God's reign would begin. About this time, an unknown scribe composed the Book of Daniel to reassure a tortured people that the powerful enemies of God would soon meet their end and a new age on earth would begin.

From the time of Daniel until the time of Jesus, the apocalyptic mood was never far below the surface of Palestinian Judaism. There was a pervasive sense that the world was collapsing, that anything might happen, that history was coming to an explosive climax. The Jews, especially the Pharisees, begged God for that climax—only then would the world be freed from its attachments to evil and all things be made new as in the Garden of Eden. "Thy kingdom come" was not a petition prayer invented by Jesus. Rather, Jews had been expecting the coming of the kingdom for centuries.

Other apocalyptic books of the Bible were attributed to famous figures in the Jewish tradition—Enoch, Baruch, and Ezra, in particular. Each book had the same purpose: to encourage endurance in times of great stress and disorder. In special ways, these books claim that God's people had not been abandoned. Their struggle was described as part of a great, final conflict between evil and good. The evil would soon end, they claimed. This basic message usually included timetables that predicted God's plan, including predictions of angel armies prepared to do battle and other terrible punishments awaiting God's enemies. Flamboyant and bizarre imagery was meant to fill the reader's imagination to create a sense of God's transcendent power.

A Warning for Contemporary Readers of the Bible

When we read apocalyptic writings today we should be careful not to forget their historical background. Literal fundamentalists often are caught up in the apocalyptic spirit, thinking they have found secret messages and signs, hidden long ago in the biblical text, that only now are coming true. What they fail to realize is that the apocalyptic writers, with all their mysterious language, were speaking of the events in their own day. The "abomination of desolation" (see Daniel 12:11), for example, was the pagan altar erected by Antiochus Epiphanes in the sanctuary in the Jerusalem Temple. The "woman" seated on the seven mountains in Revelation 17:9 was the imperial capital city of Rome. And "the beast" of Revelation 13:18 was the Emperor Nero. Any applications to the present time have to begin from the original meaning intended by the writers.

Obviously the writers' expectations of an imminent end to evil did not come true, at least, not in the way they had envisioned. The power of evil continued to work in the world: the lion and the lamb did not learn to rest together in peace; the new creation of paradise remained in the future; even as a definitive intervention of God into human history was about to take place.

The Reign of God for Jesus

According to Mark, the first Gospel written, Jesus appeared in Galilee proclaiming, "The time is fulfilled, and the kingdom of God has come near; repent, and believe in the good news" (1:15). Mark's Jesus sounds like someone immersed in the apocalyptic themes of the Jewish tradition. In fact, Mark has a chapter that is filled with apocalyptic images. We can also look to Paul's First Letter to the Thessalonians (4:13—5:11) and the third chapter of Peter's Second Letter. Of course, the entire book of Revelation is replete with apocalyptic imagery, but it deserves a much more complete treatment than can be provided here.

The fundamental point made in all of these New Testament accounts of apocalyptic thought is that God has not abandoned his creation. The present state and condition of the world, they said, may reflect the power of sin and death more than the power of God, but the situation is temporary. Eventually— no one knows the day—God will reassert himself and intervene to purge the world of evil and make all things new (see Revelation 21:5).

The powers of evil are not going to surrender without a fight, and the apocalyptic writers outdo themselves in describing the upheaval that takes place in that final "Armageddon." Monsters, antichrists, or armies of demons embody the evil forces; armies of angels or torrents of fire from heaven combat them in God's name. Stars are swept from the sky, the earth cracks and shakes, and people die of fright. The outcome is never in doubt. Evil will be destroyed, and God's creation will be the radiant reflection of his glory as it was meant to be from the beginning.

Jesus Is the Answer

Up to this point, we have explored all biblical apocalyptic writings, whether Jewish or Christian. In the Christian writings one further element must be examined: the work of Jesus. In Jewish apocalyptic thought, the victory of God over evil is a future event. For the Christians, it began decisively in the events of Jesus' life, death, resurrection, and sending of the Spirit.

In other words, the battle of good and evil is not something Christians shudder to anticipate; it is already in progress. "Children, it is the last hour! As you have heard that antichrist is coming, so now many antichrists have come" (1 John 2:18). The fire from heaven that conquers evil is the Holy Spirit given to all Christians, as a community or as individuals. Christians are not to stand by trembling, but to join in the battle by living courageously with the confidence that the same victory we see in Jesus will also be ours. The program Jesus outlines in the Sermon on the Mount in Matthew 5—7 presumes these ideas and we will study them in depth later.

In light of popular apocalyptic thinking of the day, it is understandable why the first Christians were not concerned about a future Judgment Day. The return of Christ to judge humanity, they thought, would spell the end for evil in the world and this transition was imminent.

The final destiny of God's creation was not intended to be destruction but renewal and transformation. In chapter 21 of Revelation we find a poetic evocation of the "New Jerusalem," the symbol of a world made new by God. Risen from the dead like Jesus, people will somehow experience a creation no longer "subjected to futility" (see Romans 8:20) but perfected, a fit home for them and for God.

These New Testament apocalyptic writings teach us that the world is our home, created by God to be "very good" (see Genesis 1:31). The fact that we experience ourselves as aliens and restless creatures is due to sin, which is the human decision to exclude God. A very wise person once remarked, "God gave us a very beautiful world. The only thing that's wrong is some of the people who are in it." But sin is not an absolute like God. One day God will see his will done on earth as it is in heaven and people will finally be at home.

It should be clear by now that the coming of God's reign was the "good news" or "Gospel" that was expected by some of the Palestinian Jewish people. But why did Jesus ask for reform of life? The word for "good news" in the Greek means literally "let your awareness be transformed." Why would such a change in outlook be necessary—wasn't the kingdom of God exactly what everyone was praying for?

The Palestinian understanding of the kingdom was not what Jesus meant. Their interpretation mirrored their legalistic and apocalyptic understanding of their oppressive times. Jesus' "news" was more extensive. Without preparation and study, readers may not recognize this difference and are often stunned by what they find in the Bible. The primitive ideas of God in the early parts of the Old Testament that upset my student serve as a classic example. So, too, the stories of God's unreasonable punishments, his destruction of anyone in the way of the Chosen People, his apparent silence regarding polygamy and divorce, and so on. "Is this the God you believe in?" cries the skeptic, and the believer cringes.

The answer, of course, is a renewed understanding of the gradual development of the Old Testament—both in history and interpretation. The revelation of God to the Israelites took place slowly over thousands of years. The Old Testament records a long history of deepening insights as God's word slowly shaped Jewish morality and faith.

Resurrection From the Dead

There is a television evangelist who seems to enjoy disturbing innocent believers by telling them that the Old Testament speaks of rewards or punishments given by God in this life only. She is almost entirely correct. Belief in a life beyond death did not emerge in Judaism until the late third century before the Common Era. Previously, the Jewish people were content to see God's justice worked out through the rise and fall of the nation in history. There was little sense that God might have a lasting relationship with individuals, apart from the family or tribe. Individuals die like the grass and will be no more. Only the nation will endure forever.

Of what is now included in the Jewish Bible, the Book of Daniel (ca. 165 BCE) alone speaks of resurrection from the dead. A few earlier passages hint at the idea—notably Ezekiel 37, Isaiah 53, and several psalms—but they were speaking either collectively that the whole nation would rise again, after being apparently destroyed; or they were speaking metaphorically—God would save the holy man from an early death.

As we have seen, the books of the Maccabees were not included in the list of inspired books that the Jews finally compiled and accepted. They were written sometime near 100 BCE, and they offer clear evidence that resurrection faith was of significant importance to Jewish martyrs of the second century. An interesting point is that Maccabean books teach a resurrection of good people only; the impious presumably will remain dead. By contrast, if you read Daniel

12:2 and following, you will notice that both will rise from the dead; the good to everlasting life and the evil to everlasting disgrace. Differences like this existed because the whole concept of resurrection was still emerging.

A complete theology of resurrection was still not fully accepted or developed for nearly a century after the Maccabean books. The Sadducees, in particular, were opposed to the idea of resurrection. As noted previously, they were wealthy aristocrats, adept at maneuvering whatever political power that dominated them as foreign overlords. For the most part they are thought by scholars to have been priests, and the center of their influence was Jerusalem. Although their priesthood seems to indicate that religion was important to them, they were not particularly spiritual. In their view, God had given his Law [Torah] to the Hebrew people and then left them to more or less work things out for themselves. They saw no reason to accept innovations that lacked support in the ancient Scriptures—such as resurrection of the body.

On the other side were the Pharisees, dedicated believers to whom God was in no way remote. The idea that human knowledge of God should continue to develop was essential to their theology. Once the uniqueness of each person was understood as addressed by God, the doctrine of resurrection was considered to be a corollary of God's love. They did not pretend to know or to preach concretely how the dead would rise. They believed that in some sense there would be continuity with everything a person is in this life and that at the same time everything about the person would be transformed in the "after" life. They used imagery of dazzling light ("the brightness of the sky," Daniel 12:3), for example, or compared this risen existence to that of the angels.

When Jesus was questioned on this issue, he sided with the Pharisees (see Luke 20:27–38). The particular challenge brought by the Sadducees was based on Deuteronomy 25:5, and the force of Jesus' reply is obscure to people today. Jesus' point is this: you must allow God to meet you where you are. In other words, we shouldn't try to contain God to the formulations of a dead past because he is the living God of living people. His love far surpasses our imagination and neat calculations. What God has in store for us, even after death, is far beyond our petty objections and comfortable lifestyles. "And the fact that the dead are raised Moses himself showed, in the story about the bush, where he speaks of the Lord as the God of Abraham, the God of Isaac, and the God of Jacob. Now he is God not of the dead, but of the living; for to him all of them are alive" (Luke 20:37–38).

✳

In most of the Old Testament, and probably most of the world, this is too much to imagine or to expect. But to those who dare to believe it, according to the Christian viewpoint, it means the discovery of an astounding truth: It is not the precise nature of what lies beyond death for "what we will be has not yet been revealed" (1 John 3:2)—but the unspeakable depth of God's love, eternally pledged to all and whose kingdom is now breaking into everyone's life.

TOWARD A NEW TESTAMENT UNDERSTANDING OF THE KINGDOM

As I see it, claiming that there is no God is equivalent to claiming that all creation is random and has no great purpose. One child grows up healthy and strong, well loved, and taught to live a full and creative life; another, like my nephew, is autistic and may never clearly understand the world that surrounds him. When life is over, what difference does any of this make?

If there is a God, it does make a difference. The principal way that the biblical world articulates this conviction is with the concept of a future—the world has a future. Someday all things will be right; what is now broken will be made whole, what is now distorted by indifference and exploitation will be established in love and with justice. Someday the world will live up to its promise, glimpsed at the beginning of creation when God pronounced it "very good."

The Bible speaks of yearning, longing, hoping for, "the age to come," and the "kingdom of God." If people were less conditioned by modern Western philosophies, they might even hear the Bible speak of God's yearning for this future. Our contemporary line of thinking about God pictures him above all time, all change, all past and future—essentially uninvolved in creaturely matters such as dreams or hopes. This standard line of thought is forced to bend a bit when it meets the idea of "God with us." In other words, God longs for a future with people. The language is inadequate, for God must also be the future; if we reduce God entirely to waiting and hoping with us then he would no longer be God, and we would have contradicted the hope we started with. Yet, having acknowledged this, there are in the biblical tradition ample grounds for saying that in some true sense God waits and hopes with us, and what does he hope for? That his creation might reach its completion, that his own infinite richness might show forth in a world worthy of him; that his kingdom might finally come, his will be done as on earth as it is in heaven.

What were the elements of Jesus' teaching on this kingdom? First, with regard to the Law of Moses: The Pharisaic mentality, as mentioned, suffered in the New Testament estimation from externalism, legalism, and a distorted idea of God. Externalism receives scathing words from Jesus in Matthew 23: "[W]oe to you, scribes and Pharisees, hypocrites! For you lock people out of the kingdom of heaven. For you do not go in yourselves, and when others are going in, you stop them. Woe to you, scribes and Pharisees, hypocrites! For you cross sea and land to make a single convert, and you make the new convert twice as much a child of hell [Gehenna] as yourselves" (vv. 13–15). This type of attack was not unique to Jesus. Long before Jesus was born, Israel's prophets had a long tradition of similar words for those whose religion was merely external performance (see Amos 5 and Isaiah 58).

Legalism was a subtle issue, particularly since it involved good, pious people. But it was just as serious. Looking for a refuge from ambiguity in an age when so much was going wrong, people had reduced God's will to a set of rules that was sometimes cumbersome but not deeply challenging. It took no greatness of spirit to avoid, for example, the thirty-nine forbidden activities on the Sabbath. Decent people were able to say, "All these commandments I have kept since my youth" and this became the basis for their security and self-satisfaction: "God, I thank you that I am not like other people" (Luke 18:11).

These people must have had good intentions, but they were missing the point of their religious inheritance. By settling into a smug structure of rules, they cut themselves off from the commandments. Rules are necessary. They offer guidance as we learn what should be done or avoided, but they go only so far. Laws cannot protect us from wasting our lives in the wrong vocation, for example, or from marrying the wrong person, or from missing an opportunity to grow in love. Even the best series of laws and regulations will not in themselves make people moral.

To wake people up, Jesus frequently compared the upright with those who had led disreputable lives. He told the upright that they were second best, "tax collectors and prostitutes are going into the kingdom of God ahead of you" (Matthew 21:31). The story of the Pharisee and the tax collector in Luke 18:9–14, the saying about ninety-nine just men and one sinner in Luke 15:7, and the parable of the prodigal son—each makes the same point. We will study these teachings in the text to come.

Jesus did not praise sinners for their sins, but he praised their willingness to change. "But why should we change?" asked the upright. Jesus adjusted the demands of the Law:

> *"You have heard that it was said to those of ancient times, 'You shall not murder'; and 'whoever murders shall be liable to judgment.' But I say to you that if you are angry with a brother or sister, you will be liable to judgment; and if you insult a brother or sister, you will be liable to the council; and if you say, 'You fool,' you will be liable to the hell of fire. So when you are offering your gift at the altar, if you remember that your brother or sister has something against you,*

leave your gift there before the altar and go; first be reconciled to your brother or sister, and then come and offer your gift. Come to terms quickly with your accuser while you are on the way to court with him, or your accuser may hand you over to the judge, and the judge to the guard, and you will be thrown into prison."

Matthew 5:21–25

The demands that he makes go beyond the usual; people are to forgive without counting the cost, to lend without expecting repayment, to turn the other cheek, to "be perfected, even as your heavenly Father is perfect."

Self-satisfaction and self-congratulatory parties are not the new vision of life or the God that Jesus teaches. The Pharisees made God a taskmaster, measuring out rewards according to their obedience to his commands. By insistence on the security of a contract arrangement between God and themselves, they were blind to a fuller life he wanted to share with them as his beloved children (see Luke 17:5–10). God is like a recklessly generous landowner who gives rewards even to those who work a short time (see Matthew 20:1–16). God is also like the father embracing his youngest son who squandered half his possessions (see Luke 15:11–32). Open your heart, discover how great his love is for you, begin to live as his son or daughter; set out on the great adventure life is meant to be (see Matthew 6:30–33).

One problem in understanding what Jesus meant by the kingdom centers on apocalyptic speculation. Isn't it understandable that if you feel like an embattled minority in a corrupt world, desperate for relief, you would try to calculate the time when God's kingdom would arrive? Watching for signs in the stars or combing the Scriptures for clues, they ached for the day when their enemies would be destroyed by fire raining down from heaven; when the good, pious, Law-observant Jews would be vindicated, when all things would be as God intended them. The Zealots thought they could hurry things along by fighting the occupiers themselves.

The kingdom of God did not arrive that way. Jesus told them "you cannot calculate its arrival." If you focus your attention on the future you avoid present responsibilities. The future will dawn, but at a time you least expect it (see Matthew 24:22). Only the Father knows the day or the hour (see Mark 13:32).

The kingdom has also already begun. Even now its life is at our fingertips, if we will only open our hearts to it (see Luke 17:21). We look for signs in the sky, but we are blind to the signs before us (see Luke 7:22). We expect a kingdom we can enter without being transformed, a kingdom we earn, or we could bring about by force and making others conform to your rule. The reign of

God is something we have yet to imagine. We can taste it now, if we will open our hearts and listen. Begin to forgive as God forgives, live generously without counting the cost, and be willing even to surrender your life for love. If we believe, the new life we long for is possible now.

A TYPOLOGY OF RELIGIOUS AWARENESS

We have noticed the debt the Christian movement owes to the teachings of Jesus, and, in turn, his debt to the hopes, ideas, and concepts from Judaism. We have studied a central teaching of Jesus in his vision of the kingdom. The kingdom or reign of God would be a condition, a situation, not a piece of real estate. The kingdom is the answer to all human longings and hopes. But a process is best understood when we see its outcome. Let us summarize and clarify Jesus' notion of the kingdom with other answers people have believed across the ages. A template of religious awareness will help. It is not intended to exhaust every possible religious attitude, but to provide reference points for our study of New Testament perspectives. As we move away from a strict, literal reading of Scripture (literal fundamentalist) and away from extreme skepticism (secular postmodernism), we must read the Bible with respect to the culture(s) and philosophies that shaped its narrative.

According to Isaiah Berlin, a well-known twentieth-century philosopher, the history of ideas, as well as politics, literature, and aesthetics, is a history of particular patterns about life that dominates the epochs in which people lived who were responsible for writing, painting, or who produced particular pieces of music or art. In order to understand the world in which these people thought and lived, it is important to begin with a sensitivity to the fact that the earlier cultures, especially ancient ones, are stranger than we might imagine. The great transformations in the history of human awareness and understanding were more complex than an ordinary, for example, uncritical reading of the classics at first conveys.

The kinds of religious awareness outlined in the following text are not mutually exclusive. In fact, they may coexist in an individual's perception as well as compete for adherents in a culture. They continue to function, in one form or another, in the postmodern epoch.

Polytheism

The earliest model of religious awareness is based on the cycle of seasons and stages of life depicted in the ever-turning wheel of nature. There is a fascination with the cycle of life and the natural changes observed in the seasons. Things are born, develop, feed on each other, and die off, yet life continues on. Individual life emerges for the moment and then recedes again into the whole. Ultimate meaning is sought by these people in the endlessly recurring pattern, symbolized by a closed circle or mandala, the wheel of life, or the carousel. There is a materialistic focus and location for the activities of the deities in the world of nature and in the experience of people. The deities are powerful and reveal their influence in every manifestation of the life force.

Polytheism typifies the conception of the divine in this type of religious awareness. The gods work their powers through objects in the sensible world. In fact, the great systems of antiquity worshipped the power of bulls, the spell of sex, the sun and stars ruling earth's daily and yearly cycles of sleep and re-awakening. The less-formulated systems of our own time parallel these, for example, with adoration of money, youth, or military power. Some early religion systems in North America and Asia understood that life included revelations from divinities that were perceived in spatial terms. Their worship rituals emphasized nature as mediating the divine power and control over life. The divinities alternately permitted and ended chaos.

An example of the pattern is found in the story of the seventeenth-century French Jesuits who worked among the Huron people in upstate New York and Canada. At first, these Europeans were welcomed by the native people. It was only after sickness (smallpox) devastated them that anger against the Jesuits erupted. The priests were beaten, tortured, and shipped down the Hudson River to the Dutch Calvinist settlement at New Amsterdam. To the native people the Jesuits had interrupted the normal cycle of life. Their interruption introduced a strange sickness to the people. When the Jesuits returned a few years later, they were killed.

People who worship in this first pattern of religious awareness measure their own personhood with a closed horizon of understanding and find their definition as a piece of the world. They name good and evil in terms of life's established order; whatever promotes it is good, whatever has the power to disturb it—the alien, the chaotic, or even the simply different—is unclean or sinister. The word *sinister* originally meant left-handed and embodies the feeling of dread that the ancient people had at the sight of something out of order in a right-handed world.

Human destiny and salvation, in this view, is achieved by fitting into the system, by enjoying life's gifts for their season and then letting go with dignity. Five thousand years ago in the "Epic of Gilgamesh" is written a classic statement of this first attitude or type of religious awareness.

> *Gilgamesh, whither runnest thou?*
> *The life which thou seekest thou wilt not find;*
> *(For) when the gods created mankind,*

They allotted death to mankind,
(But) life they retained in their keeping.
Thou, O Gilgamesh, let thy belly be full,
Day and night be thou merry;
Make every day (a day of) rejoicing
Day and night do thou dance and play.
Let thy raiment be clean,
They head be washed, (and) thyself be bathed in water.
Cherish the little one holding they hand,
(And) let the wife rejoice in thy bosom.
This is the lot of (mankind....).

There are many comforts in this perspective—the sun rises again after the worst of nights. There also is an element of fatalism that follows from it. The pattern does not address the presence of the less gifted in our midst, those who never get their turn—do they matter? And what about the recurring restlessness, the sense of incompleteness that people feel as they ride the ups and downs of life? Is there no deeper meaning, nothing more to life than a ride on a great carousel that leads to nowhere? The first pattern of religious awareness has no answer for these questions.

Platonic Forms and the Ideal World

In response to these questions, a second viewpoint developed in which this world was perceived as not able to deliver ultimate meaning but only deception. The reason for human restlessness, they claimed, is that humans do not belong in this world of matter. Greek philosophy and literature in the classical age supported these views. If you read Plato, for example, you will notice that his thinking was dominated by mathematical models. His thinking operated with the idea that there are certain axiomatic truths, as in geometry, unbreakable laws from which it is possible by logic to deduce certain infallible conclusions. It is possible to gain this kind of wisdom by a special method that Plato (ca. 427–347 BCE) suggested, and thus the most perfect paradigm with which we can organize our lives is available in mathematics. If we can achieve it, then all forms of suffering, ignorance, stupidity, and vice will disappear.

The ordinary impulses we have that delight when we are healthy, and fight against illness and growing old, do not represent our true self. Instead, they deceive us into a denial that all will eventually come to an end. True reality is not the side of us that is finite, earthbound, or even the visible body in which we live. It is the invisible soul within that is alien and restless in the material world because it is made for another sphere.

The idea that there is perfection apart from our existence, or a perfect vision or state of being, and that it needs only a particular kind of discipline or method to attain, influenced many other thinkers after Plato, descending down the centuries in Western thought to this day. Invariably, subsequent patterns seem to liberate people from confusion and errors in an otherwise unintelligible world. The physical world is passing, temporal; our true home is eternal and immaterial. In the visible world we find darkness, illusion, and death. In the other world—Plato's world of ideal forms—is our true home of light, truth, and immortality. According to this ideology, the world as we ordinarily experience it is the enemy.

The divinities of this second pattern of religious awareness are the antitheses of the visible world. They are "totally other." Certain mystical traditions that are found in Buddhism and the antihistorical strains known in Judaism and Christianity, especially those with Hellenistic influences, embody this outlook. The world, as we experience it, is where perfection is mirrored incompletely. The spiritual realm is the realm of the infinite gods. It is eternal; only the gods are immortal. Brahmanism and other "sects" mentioned above in which asceticism and mortification of the senses are practiced are designed to assist the mortal soul in moving out toward an eternal realm and infinite truth.

According to them, to be limited by the horizons of the visible world, to be deceived by the impulses of our senses and flesh, is to be lost in unreality. But those who can untangle their soul from worldly desires are on the way to salvation. They are able finally to face even their own death untroubled. The disciplines of detachment, mortification, and asceticism or stoic indifference allow the informed to live in this world without being trapped by it. This type of religious awareness values separation, escape, and negation of the visible.

This second pattern probably finds its fullest realization in the principles and system formulated by the Buddha after his great insight under the Bo tree. They are not unfamiliar today in Western cultures. Dualistic strains have recurred in Western culture through the centuries. Profane existence is a trap. Humans try to escape the evil in this material realm through activities that concentrate on spiritual destinies.

For some people the only known answer to the enigma of life in this world is either a materialistic affirmation of meaning as offered by the experience of this world alone, or the condemnation of worldly existence in favor of some spiritual destiny and reality. Judaism and Christianity are not immune from these perspectives, but they offer a third and distinctive religious pattern of awareness.

JEWISH AND CHRISTIAN REALITY

Each of the previous points of view denies a portion of human reality for the sake of making sense of the rest. The first view rules out the impulse toward transcendence; it embraces the established order of life as if it is divine. It labels as demonic any challenge to the sovereignty of this order, even the challenge of a prophet who invites people to imagine something different. The second view refuses to admit the flawed but evident goodness found in the visible world.

The third view, however, holds out both at once. With the religions described in the first pattern of awareness it affirms the centrality of the earth. With the religions of negation and escape it recognizes the incompleteness of everything finite, yet it is not afraid to delight in summer mornings, giving and receiving selfless love, and other simple satisfactions.

How does it do both? The ideas from which both Judaism and Christianity spring include ideas about life, the relationship of tribe members to one another, and notions about realities, such as duty, forgiveness, and regulations given by authorities. So, too, the universe is explained. But these explanations are presented in ways that would have been totally unintelligible to the Greeks. Ideas such as those found in the Psalms, for instance, would be unimaginable to Plato or Aristotle (ca. 384–322 BCE). The idea that the entire world reacts personally to the command of the Lord, the idea that all relationships animate and inanimate must be interpreted in terms of the relationship of human beings or a divine personality is remote from the Greek conceptions. There is an absence among the Greeks of the idea of obligation and the absence of the notion of duty. This outlook is difficult for people to grasp who read the Greeks through imagery affected by the Jewish Bible; however, by translating the human restless quest for meaning into expectation, into trust that something more is under way and the present situation is only temporary, Judaism and later Christianity imagined a future in which all the promises of creation are fulfilled. In biblical language it is called the "kingdom of God."

The essential word is *future*. Biblical imagery, as we have noted, is predominantly of time, not place. The kingdom of God is not another place, another world, to which our souls will escape at death. Strictly speaking, for this third pattern of awareness there is no "other world." The kingdom is another time, the age to come in this dimension, the day of resurrection, when somehow our entire being will be reintegrated in a life beyond imagining. And not our personal being alone, but all of creation—transformed, aglow with the Creator's presence, making abundantly clear the reason he made it.

A truth found in the second pattern is acknowledged. Biblical religion knows that the present state of the world falls short of its destiny. The kingdom and renewal of the world begin with the proclamation of Jesus yet it remains unfinished. Mark emphasizes that the Lord's disciples fail to understand what is taking place in his ministry even though they have been given special information (see Mark 4:40; 6:52; 8:17–18). The tension is even greater when Jesus responds to Pilate, "My kingdom is not from this world. If my kingdom were from this world, my followers would be fighting to keep me from being handed over to the Jews" (John 18:36; see also John 1:10; 8:23, 47). And yet there is also the truth of the first model. While in the making, the world is God's handiwork, his self-expression, in which he reveals his invisible glory from time to time. The Creator transcends the world but is not its opposite. The Creator is the source and meaning of it all. In the midst of its dreariest and saddest days, those who share this pattern affirm a faith that God rules history, working everything somehow unto good.

In this pattern God does not work alone. The meaning of humanity is found in the fact that people are made in God's "image and likeness." We are the visible counterpart of the invisible Creator. Although we still belong to an unfinished world, we are also called to participate in co-creating it. The true meaning of human restlessness is the summons not to escape the visible world, but to love it with God's love—creative, critical, forgiving, and costly.

This is the boast of biblical religion; it is also its nemesis. The history of Israel recognizes that people forget that they are creatures, not the Creator. They grasp at some kind of lordship for themselves based on their own shortsighted ideas of what ought to be. This becomes especially tempting as they learn how fragile their achievements are before the earthly powers that conquer them. Is there really a loving purpose behind it all? Instead of joining in the struggle to bring forth the kingdom, commending the outcome to the Creator's hands, Israel and Christianity too often shrink back abetted by a religion that says, like the first pattern, "Why be a hero; accept what is." Or like the second pattern, "Forget it; the world has no future anyway." Either answer is too easy. The nobility and burden is to go on caring, hoping, and laboring at the crossroads of the present and the future. The kingdom has already begun, but it is not yet complete.

Below a certain level of awareness, some people tend to think that every detail of their favorite customs, rituals, traditions, or way of life is something fixed and sacred—even handed down by God. Israel had come a long way from that type of elementary formulation. Its sacred Torah explained God's will but made no effort to cover every possible detail or human situation. People were expected to understand certain general principles and thereafter apply them in the daily circumstances of their lives. The Jews believed that, if they honestly tried to serve God, the Lord would be with them and guide them. God would speak in their conscience. As the prophet Isaiah says, "On that day the dear shall hear / the words of a scroll, / and out of their gloom and darkness / the eyes of the blind shall see. / The meek shall obtain fresh joy in the LORD, / and the neediest people shall exult in the Holy One of Israel" (29:18–19). At least this was the mentality of the great formative figures of the Old Testament.

By the time of Jesus it seems there was a loss of nerve. People no longer dared to believe that God was still speaking. Religious Jews searched through what God had said in the past to find, for every possible question, the safety of an earlier answer. They compiled lists of opinions from every authority. They no longer trusted their own judgment, or trusted God was at their side. They wanted to be safe against God's watchful eye, and a web of traditions provided the shelter their anxieties demanded.

This shift placed a heavy responsibility on those in religious leadership— too much responsibility. Leaders began to be more certain about God's will than they had any right to be. They took their own opinions very seriously, and allowed the "traditions of the elders" to acquire a quasi-sacred status (see Mark 7:1–8, 14–15, 21–23). The life of the community began to sink into a mire of these sacred traditions and some among them cried out for something else.

The message of Jesus was one that cut right through the tangle. None of the Jewish traditions is condemned, but all are placed in a different perspective. These traditions exist only to encourage and heighten human sensitivities to God's presence, to guide and nurture the immature who have yet to see for themselves. Jesus recommends a life of love and forgiveness rather than malice, of sensitivity and generosity rather than selfish isolation. When traditions begin to stifle this growth, they usurp the place of God's will. "You abandon the commandment of God and hold to human tradition" (Mark 7:8). This is one reason why the New Testament is fond of short, pithy insights like "love the Lord with you whole heart and mind, and love your neighbor as yourself," which are offered in place of long, tedious lists of approved behavior. In the fifth century, Augustine states the idea more dramatically, but it is the correct idea, "Love, and then do what you will."

REVIEW QUESTIONS

1. Search the Web for the Greek word *agape*. Explain how agape, the root word for "Christian caring," implies something more than "philia" and "eros."
2. *Kingdom* is described in this section as a situation or condition that will occur here on earth. Name a few characteristics of "the kingdom."
3. Judaism at the time of Jesus was a diversified movement; that is, Jews held to a number of alternate beliefs. Name these groups and identify their special beliefs or preferences.

FOR FURTHER STUDY

1. Holloman, Henry W. *Kregel Dictionary of the Bible and Theology: Over 500 Key Theological Words and Concepts Defined and Cross-Referenced* (Grand Rapids, MI: Kregel, 2005). From an evangelical scholar whose sympathies are clearly delineated. A useful resource, especially compared with other dictionaries.

2. Klauck, Hans-Josef. *The Religious Context of Early Christianity: A Guide to Graeco-Roman Religions* (Minneapolis, MN: Augsburg Fortress, 2002). A careful discussion of cults and practices in popular Mediterranean deities at the time Christianity emerged.

3. *Theological Dictionary of the New Testament.* Edited by Gerhard Kittel and Gerhard Friedrich. Translated by Geoffrey W. Bromley (Grand Rapids, MI: Eerdmans, 1985). An exhaustive reference work originally in nine volumes. The rich etymology of each word in the Greek New Testament is searched for in its Hebrew original and usages in the later Septuagint.

4. Bauer, W. *A Greek-English Lexicon of the New Testament and Other Early Christian Literature,* 3rd ed. Edited by Frederick William Danker (Chicago: University of Chicago Press, 2001). Best used in a library due to the expense. If not for the beginner or general reader, it is a trove of important information of word choice, usage, and meanings in the language used by New Testament writers.

5. Brown, Raymond E. *The New Jerome Biblical Commentary* (Westwood, NJ: Prentice Hall, 1999). Written as an update to an earlier commentary edited by Joseph Fitzmyer, S.J. This volume includes leading biblical scholars in the Roman Catholic tradition. Many helpful essays regarding biblical formation, inspiration and inerrancy, and canonicity. Also by Brown, An Introduction to the New Testament (Anchor Bible Series), Vol. 1 (New York: Doubleday/Anchor Bible, 1997). A readable introduction that sidesteps the tangle of scholarly debates and concentrates on the final form of the New Testament list of canonical books.

6. *The Catholic Study Bible.* 2nd ed. Edited by Donald Senior and John J. Collins (Oxford: Oxford University Press USA, 2006). Uses the *New American Bible* translation of the Scriptures and is deferential to Catholic concerns and teachings yet is ecumenically sensitive. Excellent glossary of biblical terms and essays aimed at beginners.

7. Johnson, Luke T. *The Writings of the New Testament: An Interpretation* (Minneapolis, MN: Augsburg Fortress, 2003). This differs from a number of excellent introductory books in that he offers short commentaries on each text and tends to avoid the professional jargon found in scholarly books. Students find his writing clear and understandable. Johnson is a prolific writer and appeals to a general audience.

8. Carson, D. A., and Douglas J. Moo. *An Introduction to the New Testament.* 2nd ed. (Grand Rapids, MI: Zondervan, 2005). These evangelical scholars seek to reestablish the historical starting point in biblical interpretation; that is, they wish to move away from literary, sociological, and feminist additions to an interpretative method. The opening essay sets the focus of their perspective. It is a readable book, and read alongside works by Johnson or Brown will offer the student a glimpse of the multiple ways scholar "interpret" the biblical texts.

5

Paul and the
New "Way"

For some years after the death and resurrection of Jesus, the apostles and their followers were considered to be a religious movement within Judaism. They observed the Torah and the Jewish calendar of holy days; they offered sacrifice in the Jerusalem Temple; and they studied the Scriptures in local synagogues. Of course, the Scriptures they studied were what Christians today call the Old Testament. At the time, there was no New Testament.

JEWISH CHRISTIANS

Although Jewish by most standards, the first Christians had a noticeably different faith, outlook, and commitment to mission. They believed that God had called them to carry on Jesus' mission to announce the dawning of the kingdom of God. They came to understand that it would be through them that God was preparing the hearts of all people for a new age. Based on Old Testament prophecy and the workings of the first apostles, they established a core set of teachings. This first generation of Jesus' followers interpreted the Jewish holy books and culture to identify parallels, predictions, and justifications for their new "way." One of the first titles given to the movement was the "followers of the Way."

The first proclamations of Jewish Christians to fellow Jews resembled the teaching and style of Jesus. The reality of the crucifixion added weight to their challenge, and the resurrection was interpreted as divine testimony to the urgency of their focus on the kingdom. Not surprisingly, Jesus' warning that "the kingdom of God is at hand" became a dominant theme. In Luke's idealized description of Jesus' proclamation, some sold their property, gave the proceeds to a common fund, and started preparing themselves for the end of the world on earth. Others hurried to proclaim the word; they believed they would not finish proclaiming the new way to all the towns of Israel before the end finalized history. "When they persecute you in one town, flee to the next; for I tell you, you will not have gone through all the towns of Israel before the Son of Man comes" (Matthew 10:23).

These first Christians were considerably successful. Part of their success was due to the fact that they were not asking fellow Jews to give up being Jewish; they were not making converts to a new religion but to a renewal movement, of sorts, within Judaism (see Acts 9:2). The only major enemies of the early disciples were the Sadducee high priests whom they continued to condemn as having plotted against Jesus. "Meanwhile Saul, still breathing threats and murder against the disciples of the Lord, went to the high priest and asked him for letters to the synagogues at Damascus, so that if he found any who belonged to the Way, men or women, he might bring them bound to Jerusalem" (Acts 9:1–2; see also Acts 4:11 and 5:17). The attitude of the religious and pious Pharisees was much more accommodating: "So in the present case, I tell you, keep away from these men and let them alone; because if this plan or this undertaking is of human origin, it will fail; but if it is of God, you will not be able to overthrow them—in that case you may even be found fighting against God!" (Acts 5:38–39).

CONFLICT BETWEEN JEWS AND JEWISH CHRISTIANS

Tension mounted between traditional Jews and Christian Jews. Jesus was not only considered by Christians to be a "new Moses"—the bearer of a new law—he was above Moses, reinterpreting the Torah and claiming an unprecedented, even absolute, divine authority. So long as the disciples continued to observe the Torah (also called the Law) and precepts of temple worship, this would cause no great dissension. But what if they called the traditional Law into question?

Some followers of Jesus were faced early on with the specific challenge to ignore several key precepts of Judaism. The challenge occurred first among the converts from the more international, Greek-speaking group of Jews known as Hellenists. Perhaps it was their educational and cultural background that helped them to apply Jesus' teaching to the global community. When one of their leaders, Stephen, proclaimed eloquently that Jesus "will change the customs that Moses handed on to us" (Acts 6:14), even the Pharisees, who had up to this point remained somewhat neutral to the movement, became incensed. Persecutions broke out, and the Hellenists fled. One of the Pharisees, Saul, a zealous young student from Tarsus in Asia Minor, as we have noted, pursued them for prosecution.

Balancing the Law With the New Law of Jesus

It is important to remember that not all of Jesus' disciples were immediately persecuted—only those who were charged with "subverting the Law of Moses." In the heart of the Jewish capital, Jerusalem, the Palestinian apostles of Jesus remained untouched. "That day a severe persecution began against the church in Jerusalem, and all except the apostles were scattered throughout the countryside of Judea and Samaria" (Acts 8:1). They did not agree with Stephen; to them the Torah remained sacred. They quoted Jesus' saying that not an iota of the Law would pass away until the consummation of the world (see Matthew 5:18). Eventually it took a special act of God (the illumination or vision described in Acts 10) to convince Peter that his ancestral customs were not as inviolable as he had once presumed. "The circumcised believers who had come with Peter were astounded that the gift of the Holy Spirit had been poured out even on the Gentiles, for they heard them speaking in tongues and extolling God. Then Peter said, 'Can anyone withhold the water for baptizing these people who have received the Holy Spirit just as we have?' So he ordered them to be baptized in the name of Jesus Christ. Then they invited him to stay for several days" (Acts 10:45–49).

Meanwhile the Hellenist Christians, who were now scattered to international lands, began to baptize Greek Gentiles into their fellowship. "[A]mong them were some men of Cyprus and Cyrene who, on coming to Antioch, spoke to the Hellenists also, proclaiming the Lord Jesus" (Acts 11:20). In Antioch the followers of Jesus were the first to be called "Christians" (Acts 11:26b). The disciples back in Jerusalem were staggered. Converts, they claimed, must first be circumcised and observe the dietary laws of the Jews. Otherwise any Jew who associated with them or who ate with them would be rendered ritually unclean and not permitted to enter the temple.

Even when Peter was convinced by his vision that the Jewish Christians were no longer bound by the dietary and other Jewish laws, another dilemma remained. Other Jews would ostracize them if they had meals with gentiles. How could they carry on Jesus' mission in Palestine if they allowed the uncircumcised into their community as equal participants?

Peter's leadership began to develop in this difficult period. Somehow he managed to keep together the two opposing parties: one which insisted their mission was only to the "lost sheep of the house of Israel" (Matthew 15:24), and the other which insisted on baptism for the uncircumcised without concern for Jewish traditions. Peter fled Jerusalem around the year 43, leaving the community of Jesus' followers under the care of the more conservative, cautious, Torah-observant, apostle James. Peter would return to the capital in the year 49 for the first gathering of community leaders, known in Christian history as the Council of Jerusalem. Although Peter continued to be the mediator between James and Paul (see Acts 15), his primary ministry was elsewhere.

Paul's Mission for Jewish Christian Unity

The center of the distinctively Christian community was moving away from Jerusalem. Once known as Saul the Pharisee, Paul the apostle to the gentiles struggled with the consequences of the realization of an independent movement. He shared in Peter's effort to keep the Jewish and gentile converts from breaking connections, or fellowship, with each other. He sometimes disagreed with Peter's methods. "But when Cephas came to Antioch, I opposed him to his face, because he stood self-condemned" (Galatians 2:11).

It is important to remember that these disagreements are not easily assessed. One way to keep a balanced view is to recall that the connections were never broken completely between Paul and the Jerusalem Christians. A clear example is found in Paul's Second Letter to the Corinthians. Paul urges that a collection be taken up, of all things, and sent to the mother community in Jerusalem.

> *And in this matter I am giving my advice: it is appropriate for you who began last year not only to do something but even to desire to do something—now finish doing it, so that your eagerness may be matched by completing it according to your means. For if the eagerness is there, the gift is acceptable according to what one has—not according to what one does not have. I do not mean that there should be relief for others and pressure on you, but it is a question of a fair balance between your present abundance and their need, so that their abundance may be for your need, in order that there may be a fair balance. As it is written, "The one who had much did not have too much, and the one who had little did not have too little."*
>
> 2 Corinthians 8:10–15

In every community Paul visited on his missions to convert the Gentiles to Christ he took up a collection, and these are mentioned in 1 Corinthians 16:1–4; 2 Corinthians 8 and 9; and Romans 15:25–27. The collection was meant to relieve hardships in the communities of Palestine, but readers were never given a complete description of how the funds were used or collected. There was a famine a decade earlier; Paul had some involvement in a smaller collection then, and this earlier situation is alluded to in Acts 11:30. The continuing need in Jerusalem is never explained. Some commentators suggest that the Jerusalem community was so convinced that the world was about to end that they sold everything, shared everything, and now possessed no more resources.

Paul is silent on the topic. He does offer a rationale for the gift giving. If the Corinthian community is not wealthy, should they impoverish themselves to help? Paul says no, but if they have extra resources and someone else is in need, they have no choice but to respond. The last line of the passage above gives a reference to the manna in the desert as found in Exodus 16:18. In that case, excess needs became rotten and useless. Just as useless in the long run, according to Paul, are the things we keep for ourselves while others remain in need. Paul's motives are not easy to assess. He was concerned with ethics, but he also wanted converts to give witness to the love of God. He wanted them to demonstrate to the world the new condition or kingdom that God revealed in the risen Christ.

Paul became consumed with building up the morale of the Palestinian Christians. They faced economic troubles, and their way of thinking was a minority opinion in the growing Christian community. They continued to preserve the many Jewish customs among Jesus' followers, as Jesus did, but the leaders of the church progressed to a new incorporation of the old Law (Torah) and the new Law (Jesus). Paul had been the chief mediator of this new adjustment. In the end, the new religious climate eased the strained but unbroken relationship between the Hellenist Christians and Palestinian Jewish Christians. Above all, insisted Paul, "Because there is one bread, we who are many are one body, for we all partake of the one bread" (1 Corinthians 10:17). And he reminds the Galatians "you were called to freedom, brothers and sisters; only do not use your freedom as an opportunity for self-indulgence, but through love become slaves to one another" (Galatians 5:13). See also Romans 12:5 where he states, "so we, who are many, are one body in Christ, and individually we are members one of another."

Finally, Paul's method of proceeding seems to be a combination of flattery and gentle insistence. He reminded his audience how good the Macedonians were to donate to the collection, even though they were poorer than the Corinthians. In fact, says Paul, they gave more than Paul asked. Then he pointed out that he knew the Corinthians would be generous in helping a church community in need (see 1 Corinthians 16:1–4). Paul continues this theme in 2 Corinthians where he adds a theological challenge to the call for giving aid: "but it is a question of a fair balance between your present abundance and their need, so that their abundance may be for your need, in order that there may be a fair balance. As it is written, 'The one who had much did not have too much, and the one who had little did not have too little.'" Paul's challenge alluded to his desire for the unity of Christian factions. Those on the losing side of disputes that would inevitably arise must not become embittered against others. Likely the most challenging lesson from Paul was his interpretation of possessions and property. When we have more than we need, and others are in want, we owe the surplus to them. I wonder how far we are supposed to go today with Paul on this; it may be farther than many prefer.

The End of the Jewish Christian

Paul understood the new Christian community, a collection of Jews and Greeks, to be the new Chosen People of God. He continued to go into the Jewish synagogues in each city he visited. He preached his "good news" or Gospel message to them. According to Paul, those who refused have lost membership as the people of God. Slowly the number of international, non-Jewish converts grew until they outnumbered those of Jewish origin.

A small community of Christian Jews in Palestine continued to carefully observe Jewish laws with the stubborn hope to convert their fellow traditional countrymen to the new way of Jesus. In the years 60–65, as Zealot opinion prevailed and Palestine organized for a war of independence against Rome, Palestinian Jewish Christians did not cooperate with war plans. They thought that God's kingdom was not to be achieved by warfare. When the armies gather, "Then those in Judea must flee to the mountains, and those inside the city must leave it, and those out in the country must not enter it" says Luke 21:21, and they did. Jerusalem was demolished by the Roman army in the year 70, and Jewish Christianity slowly disappeared from history.

THE GLOBALIZATION OF CHRISTIANITY

A remarkable spread of Christianity unfolded in the wider Mediterranean world around the time of the fall of Jerusalem. The profound and challenging proclamation of Jesus that brought hope to the people of Palestine began to take hold throughout the empire. Because it was possible to present Jesus' message in a few short parables, as he often did, his teaching spread quickly. In fact, by the turn of the first century a growing number of Hellenist Christians began to regulate their new Christian doctrines and rituals.

Before the crucifixion, Jesus addressed his people (Jews) who had a clear religious identity. There was a context for his words, a vocabulary he could use, a religious tradition he shared with his listeners. Many years later, when his disciples went out to spread his message to the world, they had no such context. Not even the word "God" had the same meaning. In short, the message of Jesus had to be translated into an entirely new way of living.

Along with this transition came the realization that their mission was much more global than they first had anticipated. The apostolic generation (those who knew Jesus firsthand) believed that history was coming to an end. Jesus was expected to come back, triumphantly, very soon "to judge the living and the dead" (1 Peter 4:5). People in such a frame of mind do not write volumes for posterity or establish codes of community laws for future generations. They gradually realized that there might be an indefinite period yet to come before all things were accomplished as they first had thought.

These two factors combined challenged the community to organize itself. They claimed that they were guided by the Spirit of God and Jesus himself in their midst and were able, even as first-century Christians, to accomplish the organization of a new religious movement to include all who lived in the empire.

Review of Key Events Leading to Separation of Judaism and Christianity

1. Judaism at the time of Jesus was a diversified religion. There were several types of Jews: Pharisees, Zealots, Hellenist Jews, Essenes, Emigrants. Each of these groups supported distinct teachings.

2. Jesus died sometime between AD 30 and 33.

3. The first disciples of Jesus were Palestinian Jews, yet Hellenist Jews were part of the new community within a few years of Jesus' death. Stephen was identified as a Greek Jewish convert to Jesus.

4. Stephen dies about the year AD 36. Luke, in his Acts of the Apostles, identifies Stephen's verbal attacks against the authority of Temple leaders as the cause of his demise.

5. After Stephen's death, persecution broke out against Greek followers of Jesus. There was no indication in the New Testament that James and the Palestinian Jews in the Jerusalem Jesus movement were disturbed or attacked.

6. Paul converted from Hellenist Judaism to the "Way" sometime around the year AD 36.

7. Paul's innovations to traditional Jewish teachings caused difficulties for leaders of the Jerusalem followers of Jesus. Jewish leaders gathered in the year AD 49 to clarify core doctrinal matters.

8. Paul was able to continue his innovations beyond Jerusalem across the empire.

9. A war broke out in Palestine during the year AD 66. The Romans destroyed the Jerusalem Temple in the year AD 70.

10. A more stringent form of Judaism developed after AD 70.

11. A final separation rested on several factors: increasing numbers of Hellenists to the Jesus movement, the development of a more specified Judaism in the years after the loss of the Temple, and distinctive developments within each group of mutual exclusion.

13. Many converts to the new movement come from gentile communities, not from Palestinian Jewish communities.

PAUL AND THE FIRST ORGANIZED CHRISTIANS

Paul, a Roman citizen as well as a former member of the Pharisee movement, wrote several letters that are the earliest Christian writings in existence. Written throughout the 50s and early 60s, these "epistles" provide a special vantage point from which to view critical elements of the first communities. Except for Paul's Letter to the Romans, which Paul wrote to introduce his thinking to a community that never heard of him, the letters are unsystematic, specific, and totally engaged in the particular needs and concrete issues of his readers. His letters include questions of discipline, encouragement, and clarification, even to the practical details of collecting money for the poor.

The personality that emerges from these writings is passionate, strong, and intelligent. His presence may have been so powerful, in fact, that some scholars have suggested that he, instead of Jesus, ought to be counted as the true founder and architect of the Christian faith and church.

In their favor, it must be granted that Christianity did not emerge as a religion in its own right, distinct from Judaism, for some years after Jesus' resurrection. As noted earlier, the disciples at first confined their ministry to the "lost sheep of the house of Israel," the way Jesus had done (see Matthew 15:24).

The missionary insight did not begin with Paul; its origins go back to the Jewish Hellenists whom Paul had persecuted before his conversion to the "Way." These were the first people to understand that Jesus' Gospel had broken the confines of the Torah and Palestinian Judaism, and this was precisely the provocation that may have outraged the Pharisees like Saul of Tarsus.

This new insight and commitment entailed a simultaneous struggle on two fronts: not only was there the missionary task itself with its multiple demands (which Paul comments on, for example, in 2 Corinthians 11:26–30), but there also was opposition from the Jewish Christian groups.

> ...[F]or a night and a day I was adrift at sea; on frequent journeys, in danger from rivers, danger from bandits, danger from my own people, danger from Gentiles, danger in the city, danger in the wilderness, danger at sea, danger from false brothers and sisters; in toil and hardship, through many a sleepless night, hungry and thirsty, often without food, cold and naked. And, besides other things, I am under daily pressure because of my anxiety for all the churches. Who is weak, and I am not weak? Who is made to stumble, and I am not indignant?
>
> 2 Corinthians 11:25–29

The followers as a whole were still far from a final break with Judaism, especially in Palestine, where many continued carefully to observe the Torah. They demanded that any Greek converts do the same. But Paul had other ideas.

> *"All things are lawful," but not all things are beneficial. "All things are lawful," but not all things build up. Do not seek your own advantage, but that of the other. Eat whatever is sold in the meat market without raising any question on the ground of conscience, for "the earth and its fullness are the Lord's." If an unbeliever invites you to a meal and you are disposed to go, eat whatever is set before you without raising any question on the ground of conscience. But if someone says to you, "This has been offered in sacrifice," then do not eat it, out of consideration for the one who informed you, and for the sake of conscience—I mean the other's conscience, not your own. For why should my liberty be subject to the judgment of someone else's conscience? If I partake with thankfulness, why should I be denounced because of that for which I give thanks?*

1 Corinthians 10:23–30

From the distance of two millennia, it is understandably difficult to imagine that the first communities would ever have had much of a problem distinguishing themselves from Palestinian Judaism. In fact, the separation was the greatest single crisis these fledging churches faced. The question was supposedly resolved in the Jerusalem Council in the year 49, but five years later Paul's converts in Galatia, for example, were continuously harassed by "Judaisers" who told them they would not enter the kingdom of God unless they were circumcised.

Besides a natural loyalty to their Jewish traditions and the early teachings of the disciples, the pro-circumcision "Judaisers" appealed to a theological principle to defend their positions. The Law of Moses was given by God himself and was intended to stand until the end of time. Even Jesus had said that "not one letter, not one stroke of a letter, will pass from the law" until all things are fulfilled (Matthew 5:18).

The missionary response, as it came to be articulated by Paul, contained a radical and astonishing counterprinciple. Granted that the Torah was intended to continue until the new kingdom or age of God broke into history, nonetheless its role is now ended because the kingdom is already under way. All things have been accomplished; the kingdom is at hand, but it is not yet complete. Left unqualified, such a claim would easily be refuted by experience. For example, some might claim that this world of confusion and suffering surely cannot be the new creation planned by God for those who love him. It is important to recall that the "kingdom of God" referred not only to a private, spiritual salvation for the soul but also the resurrection of the body and life everlasting in a transformed creation where God's will is done on earth as it is in heaven.

One passage from Paul's writings is frequently quoted: "[Y]ou are all children of God through faith. As many of you as were baptized into Christ have clothed yourselves with Christ. There is no longer Jew or Greek, there is no longer slave or free, there is no longer male and female; for all of you are one in Christ Jesus" (Galatians 3:26–29). The contemporary world has seen these words used to argue for full equality of women in the church and in society generally and other minorities. None of these important causes was in Paul's mind when he wrote. When we quote him, we should begin with what he intended to say. We analyze his intentions below.

THE LIFE OF PAUL THE APOSTLE

It is necessary to reconstruct Paul's life. Modern scholarship has identified two sources for information. The first concerns biographical details found in The Acts of the Apostles, written in the 70s. The second source is material found in letters that bear his name in the New Testament—most were written during the 50s, but some were not collated into books until the turn of the first century. Scholars offer several approaches to evaluate these sources.

First, some have complete trust in the details found in The Acts of the Apostles, placing events and theology from Paul's letters into the spectrum provided in Acts. A second scholarly group understands the material in Acts to be under the editorial hand of its author, Luke. As a result, they warn that caution is needed when relying on those items. A third group of scholars indicate that Paul's letters are the primary source of biographical data, but supplemental data can be found in Acts.

A Brief Reconstruction of Paul's Life

1. Paul was born sometime between 5 and 10 (see Acts 7:58, where he talks about "a young man named Saul"; also Philippians 3:4-6).
2. He was born in Tarsus in southeast Asia Minor (see Acts 22:3ff).
3. Many Graeco-Roman Jews of the time period had double names: Saul (his Jewish name), Paul (a Hellenistic name). Scripture records that he descended from the tribe of Benjamin (see Philippians 3:5 and 2 Corinthians 11:22).
4. The Letter to the Philippians reveals that he was a Pharisee (see Philippians 3:5).
5. He seems to be well educated, familiar with the Greek Jewish Bible (Septuagint, LXX), and Hellenistic rhetorical skills.

6. Paul claimed to have had a dramatic revelation of seeing and hearing the risen Christ on the road to Damascus. He claimed this experience as justification and authority for his mission as an apostle.

7. Paul converted to the "Way" of Christ about AD 36. He saw a light, heard a voice, was blinded and helped to a house, and scales fell off his eyes after a few days.

8. Paul returned to Jerusalem about AD 40 after a sojourn in Damascus, Syria. The followers of Jesus in Jerusalem continued to observe Jewish customs.

9. Paul lived among Hellenized Jews in Cilicia (capital of the area where Tarsus is located) around AD 40-44.

10. Paul returned to Antioch (the city where the term *Christian* is used for the first time) around AD 44-45. Some scholars speculate Peter (Cephas) was the leader of the community there.

11. During AD 46-49 he went on his first "mission" journey from Antioch to Cyprus. This journey occurred ten years after his "conversion." He visited communities of Hellenized Jews and returned to Antioch.

12. The leaders of the new community gathered in Jerusalem in AD 49 (this meeting is known as "the council of Jerusalem"). Major doctrinal questions included the following: Do Christians have to be Jewish before becoming Christian? Do Christians have to observe the Law of Moses, including dietary regulations, avoiding games and pagan ceremonies, and other aspects of the Law?

13. Paul went on a second mission from AD 50-52, setting out again from Antioch to northern Galatia, Macedonia, and Corinth. Scholars indicate that 1 Thessalonians is written during this mission. Paul returns to Jerusalem and then back to Antioch.

14. From AD 54-58, Paul's third mission began from Antioch through northern Galatia to Ephesus. He remained three years in Ephesus and may have been imprisoned there. Scholars believe he wrote letters to the Galatians, Philippians, Philemon, and 1 Corinthians during this time.

15. In AD 57 Paul goes through Macedonia toward Corinth (this is when he wrote 2 Corinthians).

16. During the winter of AD 57 at Corinth he wrote his Letter to the Romans.

17. Paul returned to Jerusalem in AD 57-58.

18. Sometime during AD 58-60 Paul was arrested in Jerusalem and imprisoned for two years at Caesarea.

19. Around AD 60-61 Paul was sent to Rome as a prisoner.

20. Paul remained a prisoner in Rome from AD 61-63.

21. Sometime after the summer of 64, Paul was put to death by Nero in Rome.

RESURRECTION ACCORDING TO PAUL

As Paul explains it, Christians shared a special experience. For although the rest of the world is still "groaning [as if] in labor" (Romans 8:22) for a day of salvation yet to come, according to Paul, that day has begun through Jesus. In Jesus, the will of God is perfectly fulfilled, even in death, and the life of the world to come has already begun. Rising from the dead, Jesus has entered upon the dazzling fullness of life that we can scarcely imagine, but which we too were made to share.

Those who join themselves to Jesus can already experience the kingdom yet to come. If they are willing to "die" with him, trusting the Father enough to give away what they have in love, then they will also "rise" with him and begin to live out today the God-like life of glory that lies ahead. They share now in his spirit, which becomes the principle of their lives as it is of his, and in a genuine sense they share his very self, his risen existence. They are to become his risen body on earth.

This may suggest a different view of the risen Christ than today's fundamentalists, postmodern, or even many mainstream Christians imagine. We are mistaken to make the Christian teaching of the resurrection as ordinary as Jesus simply getting back on his feet on Easter morning and soaring off to heaven forty days later. According to Paul, risen life is a dimension of existence beyond anything we can yet comprehend—one which is described sometimes as "enthroned at God's right hand" and sometimes as in the midst of believers "wherever two or three are gathered together in my name." To be a Christian, by Paul's descriptions and definitions, is to begin by faith to experience this new existence. As he says, "For to me, living is Christ" (Philippians 1:21); "[I]t is no longer I who live, but it is Christ who lives in me" (Galatians 2:20); and "[I]f anyone is in Christ, there is a new creation" (2 Corinthians 5:17).

When against all expectations people encountered Jesus raised from the dead, they recognized him as the same person they had known before, but he was living in an entirely new mode of existence. He entered locked rooms and disappeared without notice; he transcended the limits and frustrations of everyday life.

This is not to say, as some people imagine, that Jesus "went back to being God." He was and remains truly human, but in the resurrection his humanity is brought to a new condition that transcends everything we know of being human. Paul describes it as something like the difference between a seed that is buried in the earth and the plant that eventually grows up from it. It is the same substance, but in a totally new condition. "So it is with the resurrection of the dead. What is sown is perishable, what is raised is imperishable. It is sown in dishonor, it is raised in glory. It is sown in weakness, it is raised in power. It is sown a physical body, it is raised a spiritual body. If there is a physical body, there is also a spiritual body" (1 Corinthians 15:42–44).

When Paul wrote those words he was thinking not only of Jesus but also of himself and everyone who formed the community of believers at Corinth. For—and this is likely the most important insight to overcome the distance between our contemporary way of thinking and that of the New Testament—although the resurrection of Jesus is totally unlike anything else that happened in the past, it is not so unique in view of what one day will happen to everyone. We too will rise from death; we too will enter a transformed condition. Jesus is only "the firstborn within a large family" (Romans 8:29), "the first fruits of those who have died" (1 Corinthians 15:20). The resurrection of Jesus on the first Easter morning anticipated what will take place in every human life.

The Physical Reality of the Resurrection

The physical dimensions of the resurrection event remain the most difficult to define. Although Jesus was truly risen from the dead, his glorified condition makes it doubtful that "seeing" or "hearing" Jesus was like seeing or hearing anything else in the world. When Paul encountered the risen Christ on the road to Damascus, the company with whom he traveled saw nothing (see Acts 9:7). The Gospel narratives disagree on details, suggesting that they are dealing with a reality beyond the reach of ordinary language. If resurrection means entering into the fullness of life for which God created people, then when they met the risen Christ, they met their destiny.

Faith and the Resurrection

The Gospel narratives reveal what these experiences meant for the first followers and the adjustments they made in how they lived their lives: it is precisely the uncertainty about the outcome of life that makes some people so faint-hearted when they think about it. We tend to grasp at the objects we can reach because we doubt the harder but better things God has in store for us. Meeting the risen Christ, Peter and the others stood before the outcome of history, the next dimension of existence. The experience of Easter transformed them from frightened and disillusioned individuals into courageous pillars of faith. Imagine the slow and painful processes to learn to hope in God; imagine the years of living, the experiences that test, break, heal, and stretch the human heart. Now imagine a single event that compresses all that inner growth and more into one moment of agony and joy; of losing familiar certitudes and discovering new ones; of walking on water; of seeing the past, the present, and the future in God's embrace. This is some of what the first believers underwent.

Witnesses of the Resurrection

As we will see, several early or fundamental elements in the Christian tradition concern the resurrection. First, all the Gospel accounts report the events associated with the resurrection to have been set in motion by women. Mary Magdalene went to the tomb to mourn. She found the tomb empty and went to tell the disciples. This is known as the "empty tomb" narrative. Second, Luke 24:12 offers an early tradition that Peter visited the tomb alone, found it empty, and walked away without any certain idea as to what had happened. Third, there are several appearance stories that are centered in two locations: Jerusalem and Galilee (see Matthew 28; Luke 24; John 20, 21; and Mark 16). Fourth, in 1 Corinthians 15, Paul does not mention the women or indicate where the appearances of the Risen One took place. He seems to imply that the appearances were widespread yet not uniform in content. Fifth, there is mention of angels at the tomb. Matthew 28:2 states that an angel opens the tomb. Luke 24:4 has two men in dazzling garments appearing to the women at the tomb. It seems the women are commissioned to go and proclaim the news. Sixth, in Paul's listing of those who experienced appearances, Peter and James are not the subjects of narrative traditions. In Mark 16:7 it is the women, not Peter, who are commissioned to tell the others. Seventh, there are few citations from the Jewish Bible in connection with the resurrection, even though expressions indicating connection with the Scriptures are found in 1 Corinthians 15; Acts 2:23; and Luke 24:27, 44ff. More surprising is the frequent use of the phrase "according to the Scriptures" in the accounts of the passion and death of Jesus. Finally, the resurrection is unlike Elijah's assumption into heaven or even the cultural myths of heroes and leaders taken up into heaven in full view of everyone on earth. The resurrection of Jesus is not witnessed. In short, it seems the New Testament proclaims the resurrection is mysterious—in the beginning some followers met the risen Christ, and others did not. The faith of the community rests on those who claim to have met him—and that they were transformed from unbelievers to believers. And the believers live to imitate his teachings and message.

Passion Narratives

It is important to keep in mind that each of the canonical Gospels includes what are termed *passion narratives*. Individual authors gather themes that they have woven throughout their Gospels. In short episodes each author reports on the final hours of Jesus' life: a last meal with his friends; the arrest; interrogation by religious leaders; a trial before the Roman Pilate; and the horrific scene of the crucifixion, death, and burial. We must recall that the Gospels were written for those inside the Christian movement. They include interpretations of history, theology for members, and are not meant to be explanations for outsiders.

Personal Reflection on the Resurrection

As ongoing students of the Bible, sometimes it is helpful to integrate interpretation and study with real-life experience. Are there moments in our own lives that remind us of our mortality—or of the possibility of resurrection? Paul worked hard to teach people about the life-changing resurrection of Jesus. What does it mean to us?

Last Wednesday was a brilliant, warm spring day. After some errands, I decided to visit my parents' grave. Because of my work as a clergyman, I have been to that cemetery many times for other people, but I resist going there for myself. I am not a cemetery person. Fortunately, some members of my family visit the grave regularly and bring decorations and flowers and even the little people (great-grandchildren).

When I arrived at the grave, I broke up. No, not weeping. I started to laugh out loud. Loud laughter in a cemetery gets people to look at you the way they do in a movie theatre when your cell phone goes off. "Who's that inconsiderate loon?" Neatly placed on the headstone were several small stones. That's a Jewish custom. Observant Jews place a stone on the headstone each time they visit. I said in my heart to my parents, "What's this? Did you convert and not tell me? Did someone down here switch? Wait 'til next year, they'll have Buddhist prayer wheels flapping all over you." And then more solemnly, "See, we haven't forgotten you. We will never forget you. I'm missing you today. Someday, I'll see you again. Amen."

When I looked up, the beauty of the place was overwhelming. It was luminous with bright flowers and palm crosses and birds chirping. Yet isn't the expression "a beautiful cemetery" an oxymoron? I turned to head back to my car and stopped. I thought of Mary Magdalene. She's in the press these days with claims of her social relevance, reappearing in a number of forms as someone to be revered or mourned for popular amusement.

A long time ago, she visited a grave. She had nothing else to lose. Other friends were busy trying to save themselves. She felt she had lost everything. All she had now was his grave. Because Magdalene went to a grave she became the first Christian preacher. Yet at first she could see nothing. Why? Because she kept looking farther away than he was. She kept looking for a dead body, an object; he was alive in another way. He was beside her.

Today we are most at home with objects; things we know that are within an arm's reach. If we see something, we believe we have verifiable, concrete, or objective truth. Hope is never necessary if you have all the answers. And Easter is about hope.

Let the little ones have their chocolate bunnies and colorful baskets. They are in the springtime of life when everything seems green and new. For the rest of us, we decide at different times whether to live by faith and hope, or that it is best and more reasonable to have all the answers. If we live with Easter hope, we are not immune to sadness and loss. We live with a promise that beyond this dimension of existence there will be a reunion. We will be transformed beyond our wildest imaginings. It is said that everyone is offered the possibility of this type of faith.

But we live in the here and now. There is so much contradictory information around. Is it wise to trust in Easter hope? What if it is all mistaken? What if we are misled or duped? The skeptic's cry is understandable.

We, who try to make the act of faith, which grows in Easter hope, agree it is a risky decision. It would be easier to believe that the spark of life that is within each of us is destined to rise up for only several decades and then to recede into nothingness. There are other gods to believe in, gods who offer other comforts and pleasures. But God in Jesus the Christ says we have been made in an everlasting way.

When we stand by the grave of a loved one and wonder if all is ended, Christ says you are human when you feel and think as much. Your intuition that your loved ones are alive is not an illusion or sentimentality caused by grief. Think of your scientific definition for energy. Does energy ever end? Potential energy becomes kinetic and vice versa, a cycle that seems to propel us on and on. Why, then, is it so difficult to imagine the energy of a loved one is now transformed in another dimension of life? This is no proof. It is a perspective we use to interpret life, loving, and dying. To grow into this perspective takes a lifetime of faith and love. If we come to believe him, the way we live in this unfinished world will be different. We will live with his perspective, even when our hearts break.

I looked up again, turned and walked back to their grave. I placed a rock on their headstone, a big fat one.

PAUL AND THE LAW OF CHRIST

Paul was a born leader, a relentless advocate, someone on the move, whose practical contributions to the formation of Christianity cannot be underestimated. Before he began to teach about Jesus, Paul admits that he had a profound personal experience that changed his outlook and life. He claims that he met the risen Christ. Even so, Paul is not exempt from criticism by other Christians. For instance, he reports in his Letter to the Galatians that some defenders of the Jewish faith had visited his converts and told them they could be saved only if they would be circumcised and begin to observe Jewish laws. There were strong arguments, as we have seen, on their side—Jesus had insisted that the Torah should be observed, but these visitors accused Paul of watering down divine requirements in order to make his own name more popular in the Hellenist world.

Paul's response is understandably harsh. He understood their feelings; he had once been a student of the Pharisees, outstanding in his zeal for that movement, and he was pained by the rift that his conversion and preaching had caused, but he was convinced that the Law of Moses had now been superseded: Christ Jesus was enough.

The pro-circumcision people should have known better. Five years earlier the council had agreed that Paul was correct. The Torah was not to be imposed on non-Jewish converts (see Acts 15). Paul offers one argument after another to demonstrate that Christians stand before God no longer on the basis of how well they have observed a code of rules but how willing they have been to accept God's love as an unmerited gift.

Paul does not teach that a person should act in any way that he or she pleases. He knew that shallow people might take his words as an invitation to abandon not only the Torah but other moral guidelines. The person with a heart open to God in faith will live or view life characterized by "love, joy, peace, patience, kindness, generosity, faithfulness, gentleness, and self-control" (Galatians 5:22). The person who is closed to God, on the other hand, will tend toward fornication, impurity, licentiousness, idolatry, sorcery, enmities, strife, jealousy, anger, quarrels, dissensions, factions, envy, drunkenness, carousing, and things like these" (Galatians 5:19–21). This is not an exhaustive list; they are Paul's examples to illustrate interior attitudes or personal postures. Two of them are essential: living "by the Spirit" and yielding to the "desires of the flesh" (see Galatians 5:16–18).

Flesh and Spirit

"Flesh" and "spirit" are often misunderstood. Paul's statement that "what the flesh desires is opposed to the Spirit, and what the Spirit desires is opposed to the flesh" (Galatians 5:17) has been explained by some Christian teachers, for example, as referring to the tension between the human body and soul—as if every bodily desire is evil and only the soul's impulses are good. Other times it has been presented as the love of God in opposition to the love for the world. These simple comparisons lead people to forget that in order to love God correctly we must love his world too, as God does. "Love of self versus love of neighbor" is also an inadequate formulation.

According to Paul, *flesh* is the limited, finite, and fragile human situation. Humans scratch and scramble and deny the inevitable end of death as long as possible. We attach ourselves to the tangible and passing securities that we find in life. *Spirit,* on the other hand, is the sense of God's life within us, giving us confidence that we actually have a future; that we do not have to cling to the tangibles we have at this moment (as mortal beings) because God created us in an everlasting way.

The interplay between flesh and Spirit is the last perspective that Paul offers the Galatians regarding his teaching on Christ. It has nothing to do with lawlessness. It implies a thorough obedience, a wholehearted devotion to God's will, but it breaks the limits of the Torah and of every other written law. It provides people with an extraordinary freedom, the freedom of no constraints. According to Paul, this freedom allows the believer to do exactly what he chooses, because he acts out of love of God.

Paul's Response to Judaisers

Paul's Letter to the Galatians had a specific purpose: to refute the argument of the Judaisers. As noted previously, they were converts to the teachings and way of Jesus, but they believed that anyone who wanted to be saved was obligated first to follow Jewish customs and laws. They continued to think of themselves as Jewish even after their baptism, and they maintained Jewish dietary regulations, worshiped at the Jerusalem Temple. According to them, Jesus had done the same, and thus his mission was not to abolish Judaism but to present it in a new way.

Christianity gradually began to separate itself from Judaism. Acts 6:14 records the first stirrings of the schism. The notion was initially regarded with suspicion even by the apostles. Peter slowly accepted it, as we noticed, after a supernatural encounter narrated in Acts 10, but not everyone agreed with his view. The first gathering of community leaders in council at Jerusalem in 49 tried to settle the issue. Paul fiercely repeated his arguments to the Galatians, the same ones he had used five years earlier during the Council of Jerusalem. According to Paul, salvation is the fulfillment of Scripture (Old Testament). And he argued for the superiority of living life in Christ rather than under the demands of Torah.

Paul and Social Standing

Under Jewish law many people were considered inferiors. Gentiles (non-Jews) were considered by Jews to be beneath everyone else. Slaves were held as property, and some were able to participate in the local household and its religious life in very restricted ways. The status of women was not much better. The attitude toward these people is summed up in words from a prayer intended for daily recitation by first-century pious Jewish men:

Blessed art thou O Lord our God, King of the Universe,
that thou hast not made me a foreigner.
Blessed art thou O Lord our God, King of the Universe,
that thou hast not made me a slave.
Blessed art thou O Lord our God, King of the Universe,
that thou hast not made me a woman.

Paul rejects these social distinctions, but not according to modern standards. Paul was a person of his own times. The fact that society defined higher and lower positions for its members was something he simply took for granted (see also 1 Corinthians 14:34 or Colossians 3:18–22). He advised women and slaves to accept their roles graciously. Today, we understand social roles as human or cultural creations that need to be changed when necessary. In Paul's time it was thought that things were what they were, beyond anyone's power to adjust them. Besides, Paul thought the world as we know it was fast approaching its last days, and soon there would have been no need to make any permanent changes.

Paul does not fault the Torah because it describes inferior roles for certain groups. What bothers him is that, in his eyes, the Torah was elevating certain social categories to the level of God's will. It told people that they had superior or inferior status even in God's eyes, simply because of sexual, social, or racial identity. Paul discovered in Christ something that went beyond any such exclusivist or superficial understandings. The human status before God, according to him, depends only on the free interior opening of the human heart to divine love.

This breakthrough in religious understanding had consequences for human society, but Paul never envisioned them. Unfortunately, we are still discovering and enacting them today—as explored above, the unfolding of Scripture is an eternal genesis of insights and delayed applications. With respect to human status, Paul articulates one basic insight: before God all human beings, in God's sight, are radically equal and precious.

PAUL'S CREED

Paul includes specific doctrinal instructions in his letters. Later Christians would refer to these teachings as *creeds,* or statements of belief. An interesting list of beliefs is found in Paul's First Letter to the Corinthians. Some critics refer to it as an early "creed." Following his conversion or *metanoia* to Christ, Paul learned these core messages and beliefs of the new movement of followers of the "Way." First, the central elements of the Way concern the death, burial, resurrection, and appearances of the risen Jesus to the community. There is no narrative of Jesus' life and words. It is more a proclamation of faith, the bedrock teachings for the new movement. Second, Paul does not invent them. Rather, he received them as part of his instruction in the new movement. This seems to indicate that early on the new movement clarified for itself its special beliefs and teachings. Scholars have puzzled over the date of the formulation. Suffice it to say, the formulation predates Paul's conversion and is the starting point for his special interpretations.

> *Now I would remind you, brothers and sisters, of the good news that I proclaimed to you, which you in turn received, in which also you stand, through which also you are being saved, if you hold firmly to the message that I proclaimed to you—unless you have come to believe in vain.*
>
> *For I handed on to you as of first importance what I in turn had received: that Christ died for our sins in accordance with the scriptures, and that he was buried, and that he was raised on the third day in accordance with the scriptures, and that he appeared to Cephas, then to the twelve. Then he appeared to more than five hundred brothers and sisters at one time, most of whom are still alive, though some have died. Then he appeared to James, then to all the apostles. Last of all, as to one untimely born, he appeared also to me. For I am the least of the apostles, unfit to be called an apostle, because I persecuted the church of God.*
>
> 1 Corinthians 15:1–9

THE MEANING OF THE WORD *GOSPEL*

It is important to notice that Paul's use of the term *gospel* does not refer to what we might imagine to be a document. Instead, it refers to preaching about core beliefs. He offers a clue to the development the New Testament: preaching came first, letters and narratives later. The word *gospel* as it appears in the New Testament never refers to a written document. The expression "in the gospel" is found in early writings, but it is not included in the New Testament. The *Didache* 15.3, and the *Second Letter of Clement* 8.5, written early in the second century, use the expression "in the gospel." The first clear reference to "gospel" as a written document is found in the writings of Justin Martyr during the second century (see *Apologies* I 66.3). In the writings of Irenaeus ("Against Heresies," 1:1; 3:1; 6:3; 8:1; 9:1; also 10:3–6) we first find names of the evangelists attached to the four Gospels.

In the Greek translation of the New Testament, the term *gospel* refers to "the message of salvation." The word *gospel* is derived from the Old English word "godspel," which is a translation of the Greek term that meant "good announcement" or "good news." The word was often associated with the good news of a military victory. At times, it was associated with the birth or presence of the emperor, which constituted good news for Romans. In the Greek translation of Jewish Scriptures (Septuagint or LXX), the term had similar meanings—translating the Hebrew word *bsr*, a term for Israel's victory and God's victory over enemies.

The New Testament usage of the word *gospel* is derived from a translation of the Old Testament Hebrew term "to bring joyful (or good) news." Two passages, in particular, are significant. Isaiah 52 states, "How beautiful upon the mountains / are the feet of the messenger who announces peace, / who brings good news, / who announces salvation, / who says to Zion, 'Your God reigns'" (v. 7). Please notice the parallelism: peace = good news = salvation = God reigns.

The second passage is Isaiah 61:1–2: "The Spirit of the Lord GOD is upon me, / because the LORD has anointed me, / he has sent me to bring good news to the oppressed, / to bind up the brokenhearted, / to proclaim liberty to the captives, / and release to prisoners, / to proclaim the year of the LORD's favor." Please notice the elements included: healing from captivity or slavery and oppression.

In the New Testament, the term *gospel* first appears in the letters of Paul where the heart of his message concerns the suffering, death, and resurrection of Christ and its power for justification and salvation (see Romans 1:16). Paul did not coin the term or apply it to his own writings. He does refer to the "gospel" of his Galatian opponents ("As we have said before, so now I repeat, if anyone proclaims to you a gospel contrary to what you received, let that one be accursed!" [Galatians 1:9]). Whether Jesus used the term continues to be debated.

FORMATION OF THE GOSPEL

For our study it is important to keep in mind that a period of approximately thirty years had elapsed between the death and resurrection of Jesus and the composition of the earliest New Testament Gospel. Scholars speak of three stages in the history of Gospel formation: first, the actual ministry and preaching of Jesus; second, a period in which his associates preached about his teachings and their faith in his resurrection was celebrated in communities of fellow believers; and third, a later period in which the Gospel texts were composed in different communities. The stages are not neatly divisible. They help us to chart a development that ended with the written narratives and Gospels.

Jesus' Ministry and Preaching

It is important to keep in mind that no one followed Jesus around Galilee, taking down every word he spoke or detailing every encounter or activity. After the resurrection, Jesus' companions recalled what he had said and done—not every action or word, but those which pertained most to his message about the kingdom of God. There was, in other words, a selective memory at work from the beginning. The recollections of witnesses formed what scholars today refer to as "Jesus material." But these materials were memories by the members of the new movement of Jesus followers. Some were eyewitnesses to the events, particularly the companions or apostles of Jesus.

Preaching of Disciples

The second stage in the development of the New Testament is a period inexactly placed under the simple heading of "preaching." It is important to recognize that the postresurrection faith of believers impacted or shaped their memories of Jesus. Their recollections were meant to bring people to faith or to confirm the faith that the message was preached. Additionally, as the message spread into the Hellenist world of Greek Jews, and gentiles, the earliest materials were necessarily translated from Aramaic into Greek. They would rephrase vocabulary, geographic details, and speech patterns to make their translations intelligible. For example, if we compare the two versions of the Lord's Prayer (Matthew 6:9–13; Luke 11:2–4), scholars alert us to a transformation that took place in usage. The text in Matthew reveals a change in wording that reveals use of the prayer in the liturgy. The prayer shows other changes that reflect the shift from a predominantly Jewish to a non-Jewish or gentile community. There are changes not only in language but perspectives regarding apocalyptic themes.

Community Witness

Lastly, scholars tell us that the set forms of narratives that recount the final days of Jesus, known as the *passion narratives,* were established very early as the community tried to decipher the impact of the incarnation, life, death, and resurrection of Jesus. Paul's creed in his First Letter to the Corinthians could have developed during the same period. As the stories were told and retold, translated, and directed to different communities, new issues would spark adjustments and reorganization of the Jesus material, and new teachings were offered to the next generations of believers. These teachings became solidified in the Gospels.

REVIEW QUESTIONS

1. It is important to understand that Paul's preaching and letters include a special emphasis on the Lord's death and resurrection. What does *resurrection* mean? What does it *not* imply?
2. Identify some of the ingredients that contributed to a final separation between Judaism and Christianity.
3. Explain Paul's understanding of *flesh* and *spirit*.

FOR FURTHER STUDY

1. Refer to your favorite commentary and read an article on Paul's theology. For example, see the *Anchor Bible Dictionary* entry for "justification."
2. Murphy-O'Connor, Jerome. *Paul: A Critical Life* (Oxford, UK: Clarendon, 1996). An evaluation of Paul's persecution of the early Christian community.
3. Bassler, Jouette M. *Navigating Paul: An Introduction to Key Theological Concepts* (Louisville, KY: Westminster John Knox Press, 2007). The author refers to modern scholarship underestimating Paul's creative pastoral sense. Paul practices a theology not as a systematic thinker but an innovator. She explains her positions with scholarly documentation and a lively text.
4. Fee, Gordon D. *Pauline Christology: An Exegetical-Theological Study* (Peabody, MA: Hendrickson, 2007). Fee has written on the Holy Spirit. Here he offers a clear exposition of Paul's use of the Septuagint. This book is for those familiar with Paul's basic terminology and concepts.
5. Schutz, Howard, J. *Paul and the Anatomy of Apostolic Succession* (New Testament Library Series; Louisville, KY: Westminster John Knox Press, 2007). A careful analysis of the rise of Paul's leadership in the New Testament period.
6. Meeks, Wayne. *The First Urban Christians: The Social World of the Apostle Paul*. 2nd ed. (New Haven, CT: Yale University Press, 2003). Meeks analyzes the letters of Paul. In a revised introduction he explains developments in New Testament scholarship over the past two decades.
7. Byrne, Brendan. *Romans* (Sacra Pagina Series). Edited by Daniel J. Harrintgon (Collegeville, MN: Liturgical Press, 1996). This series of individual volumes by Roman Catholic scholars offers a variety of biblical methods in use by scholars. Byrne uses a literary-historical approach in his analysis of Paul's letter.

8. Polaski, Sandra H. *A Feminist Introduction to Paul* (St. Louis, MO: Chalice Press, 2005). This volume includes a carefully written summary of the many issues recent scholarship has identified. She offers a lively discussion, without polemics, as to where Paul's ideas leave off and faithful extensions may be developed.

6

The Gospel According to Mark

DATE

The Gospel According to Mark is the oldest Gospel. Most date it to sometime between the years AD 65 and 75. Its chronological position is somewhat different from the order of the Gospels in most Bible translations. Most often these other materials list Matthew first. A number of reasons have been advanced as to the priority given to Matthew. First, Matthew's version was thought to be the most complete picture of Jesus' ministry that was available. Second, it is the longest version and took more time to hand copy. Third, Matthew's community was considered ancient and deeply respected for its life and practice. For instance, it is Matthew's version of the Lord's Prayer that Christians pray. In fact, Matthew seemed to give evidence of early liturgical practices in the way he formulated some passages. There is a consensus today that Mark is the first narrative or extended story of the words and deeds of Jesus.

AUTHORSHIP

The debate in scholarship about the date of origin centers on Mark 13 and the question of whether Mark knew or anticipated the destruction of the Jerusalem Temple in 70. From the second-century tradition of Papias, who is cited by the church historian, Eusebius, in the fourth century, Mark is called the "interpreter/translator" of Peter, who "wrote down accurately, however, not in order, all that he recalled of what was either said or done by the Lord. For he had neither heard nor followed the Lord, but later followed Peter who used to adapt his instructions to the needs of the moment (or audience) but not with a view to making an orderly account of the Lord's sayings." This Mark is usually identified as the John Mark mentioned in The Acts of the Apostles, whose mother owned a home in Jerusalem. He had accompanied Paul and Barnabas on the "first missionary journey" and may have helped Peter and Paul in Rome during the early 60s.

Other commentators, drawing from Mark's text, posit a Greek speaker, who was not an eyewitness to the ministry of Jesus. The evangelist makes a number of inexact references to the geography of Palestine, and these cast doubt that he had lived there. The author seems to have drawn on an oral and written reshaping of the Jesus tradition as he composed his Gospel narrative. The author of Mark's Gospel seems to write for a Christian community that has experienced persecution and failure.

SYNOPTIC PROBLEM

The traditions that Mark drew on to form his narrative would have been selective, focusing on the message shaped by the preaching and memories of fellow believers who were eyewitnesses to the life of Jesus. His account was written for the purpose of strengthening personal faith by situating the word and deeds of Jesus in a new and powerful frame.

It is important to know the goals and expectations as we read particular genres (poetry, history, science, and so forth). Scholars have grappled with this question for some time and have centered their attention on Mark's approach. It is assumed that Mark's narrative is eventually copied by the authors of Matthew, Luke, and to a lesser extent, John. Scholarship presents a number of pathways they use to research Mark's influence. It is a complicated story, but for our purposes as an introduction, it is important to keep in mind that the New Testament Gospels do not fit neatly into any other category of ancient literary genres.

In the late eighteenth century a scholar arranged the four New Testament Gospels in parallel columns for comparison and study. This parallel column arrangement is called a *synopsis,* with a single view or seen together. What became clear is that The Gospel According to John seems to include a different sequence and interpretation of the message of Jesus. Mark, Matthew, and Luke present equivalent narratives, miracle stories, and parables. These three Gospels are called the *synoptic Gospels.* Even with great similarities, certain differences baffled scholars. The question of how to explain the complex of similarities and differences is called the *synoptic problem.*

The Complexity of the Synoptic Problem

1. Length—Mark 661 verses, Matthew 1,068 verses, and Luke 1,149 verses
2. Triple tradition—370 verses appearing in all three Gospels
3. Double tradition—220 verses common to Matthew and Luke in different contexts in each and not found in Mark
4. Special sources known only to individual Gospels—30 verses in Mark, 330 verses in Matthew, and 520 verses in Luke
5. Infancy narratives in Matthew and Luke—these cannot be reconciled with one another
6. There are significant differences in material contained in resurrection stories of all three Gospels

Griesbach-Farmer Hypothesis

Scholars have proposed several solutions, including the suggestion of complete independence of the Gospels from one another. The Griesbach-Farmer hypothesis proposes that Matthew was used by Luke, and that Mark draws from both Matthew and Luke. Another solution is called the *two source theory*.

Two Source Theory

The two source theory proposes that Matthew and Luke drew on Mark's material and several other outside sources. The latter sources are known as *Q sources*, or simply Q, taken from the first letter of the German word *Quelle*, meaning "source." Although the two source theory does not solve every problem, it solves more than it creates and, since the mid-nineteenth century, it has held the field among the majority of New Testament scholars.

Before we proceed, the content of Q needs further explanation. First, it is important to recognize that Q is a scholarly theory, a hypothesis, concerning approximately two hundred thirty verses of shared passages in Matthew and Luke. Scholars consider that Luke is less likely than Matthew to have adjusted the original language and often cite his verses as closest to the original content of Q, and, therefore, closest to the way Jesus would have spoken. Even without a written copy of Q, scholars find hypothetical Q an acceptable reconciliation of the shared verses.

Contents of Q

Synoptic comparisons allow scholars to speculate about the type of early Christian community that formulated and preached these sayings of Jesus. Some scholars claim that it was written in Greek by preachers who lived perhaps in western Syria. They were itinerant preachers, like Jesus. There is no narrative or story line included in the source. Instead, Jesus is presented as the last of God's prophets who is rejected by God's people. Some scholars see Jesus as a teacher of wisdom. Other scholars emphasize that there is no theology or interpretation of the death of Jesus in Q and thereby posit a very early date for its composition. The verses form a litany of the parables, sayings, and maxims Jesus used. Included in Q are some of Jesus' most memorable teachings, such as, the Sermon on the Mount (Matthew 5—7 and the equivalent Sermon on the Plain in Luke 6, praise for John the Baptist, and two versions of the Lord's Prayer).

There are additional theories concerning other verses not shared but found separately in Matthew and Luke. For our purposes, it is important to recognize the debt owed to scholarship and its in-depth analysis of sources. Now let us turn to the text considered by scholars to be the first and oldest Gospel.

Twelve Elements of Mark's Gospel

1. It is the shortest of the Gospels and full of continuous activity.
2. There is no infancy story, and Jesus never teaches the Lord's Prayer. Jesus teaches only twelve parables in Mark.
3. His closest companions have the greatest difficulty understanding Jesus' identity, and his family members come to take Jesus home. They feel he's mad (see Mark 3:21), while the demons seem to understand Jesus' identity (see Mark 1:23-26, 34; and 3:11).
4. Jesus' miracles do not seem to give people the correct interpretation of his identity. They misunderstand him as a miracle worker. In one miracle it takes Jesus two times to cure a blind man (see Mark 8:22). In another place, Jesus uses spit and his fingers to perform a cure (see Mark 7:33-34).
5. Few individuals really know Jesus' identity: early in the Gospel a demon screams out his identity and is silenced by Jesus; immediately following his death the Roman centurion at the foot of the cross blurts out, "This indeed was God's Son." He is not criticized.
6. Mark's Gospel seems to be arranged in such a way that Jesus' activities point to Jerusalem and the cross on Calvary. Mark's audience needs to learn that if you want to follow Jesus, you must integrate following him even to the cross. In other words, discipleship will entail unjust suffering.
7. Mark's Gospel is written in Greek. It was either a hasty Greek translation, or the author did not know Greek thoroughly.
8. Mark includes Aramaic phrases in three places: Mark 5:41; 7:11; and 14:36.
9. The "Son of Man" is Mark's favorite title for Jesus.
10. Mark is the only Gospel in which Jesus refers to himself as a carpenter (see Mark 6:3).

11. Mark is the one Gospel where Jesus lacks knowledge concerning the end of the age (see Mark 13:32).
12. During the passion narrative, the witnesses against Jesus do not agree on the charges against him (see Mark 14:56) and Jesus cries out in agony on the cross. Matthew and Luke tone down the horrific details of the crucifixion.

JOHN THE BAPTIST

I live in the shadows of New York City. To rise above the sense of your own self-importance is no small achievement. Where I live, some would wonder whether the idea of self-forgetfulness is a sound idea in the first place. A New York street scene is never dull. People of various shapes and sizes, gender and nationality, status and education seem to scurry around seeking to maintain a slender hold on their personal dignity. This one sneaks a glance at a department store window to check his reflection, not the displays. That one bristles as she is cut off by a cyclist at an intersection. Some wear uniforms, but not lightly. Others read amid the chaos of a subway ride. A few yell into cell phones, the newest human appendage: "Can you hear me?" With a fleeting glance, a passerby with an iPod stares back a challenge, "I can do whatever you can do." Urbanites are poignantly serious—about their hair style, their car, their dog, their space, their anonymity. Arrest them, but "don't push." Hire them for peanuts, but "don't look down" on them. Heal them, to be sure, but treat them the same as the rich patients in the private rooms upstairs. People take pride in the way they fold a napkin or roll up their sleeves, the way they lean on a building or sit in a chair. Greatness is tied to knowledge of this "deal" and that technique or shortcut. Like a surging tide, the voice of the people, its gestures and style, asserts a fundamental claim to self-importance.

To say the least, the story of personal uniqueness is a complicated one. No one cares to be compared to someone else, except favorably. But society is built on such mutual assessments. Grades are given at school. Some make the team; others are cut. Jobs are awarded, promotions given. Despite all the complaints about nepotism and who-you-know, expertise often becomes the criterion for advancement. Opportunity is never really equal, and not everyone succeeds. How, in the face of this obvious pressure to compare, can we take personal uniqueness as an absolute or an unarguable point of reference? Is valuing our individuality simply a defense mechanism we use against the harsher demands of reality? As we say in New York, "Are you kidding me?"

The New Testament pictures John the Baptist as different. "The one who is more powerful than I is coming after me; I am not worthy to stoop down and untie the thong of his sandals" (Mark 1:7). This hero of Christianity is mentioned by each of the four canonical Gospels and in The Acts of the Apostles, but he was long gone before Jesus died. This rugged and blunt symbol of the urgency of God's kingdom was a crowd pleaser, even if he preached near the wilderness and not in the city center. Some critics understand he was a dissident priest. At the time there was a deep struggle between Jewish priests of various stripes. Yet John defers to another in Mark's story. He reportedly sees in Jesus something different, something better. His special talent or uniqueness in that circumstance became a non-issue, and that is equally difficult for an urbanite to fathom.

Scholars tell us Jesus may have been one of John's disciples. In fact, historians argue that it was possibly through his association with John that Jesus came more and more to discover his own role in the kingdom's arrival. More certain is the assessment that the apocalyptic language of John's teachings seems dual. He warned and denounced the Jerusalem leadership, and he exhorted people who came out to the river to live uprightly and to act justly toward others. He urged them all to prepare for a coming doomsday or time of judgment by God.

How, then, do we explain John's self-forgetfulness? John gives us the answer, "I have baptized you with water;, but he will baptize you with the Holy Spirit" (Mark 1:8). To get to the point of his remark, we must understand the significance of baptism in the Holy Spirit for New Testament writers. Commentators point out that the Spirit was perceived by them as someone full of surprises. Like the wind and the gale, the Spirit kept people off balance. The Spirit of the new creation is remembered to brood over the baptism waters as it did at the beginning of creation. Out of the sameness of things, the spirit again is creating diversity. To the community that was Mark's spiritual home, Jews found themselves in the same place with gentiles, free people with slaves. Contours once thought to clash now meshed. The spirit seemed to give the Christians a community with a diversity of talent, background, temperament, and appeal. The community came to see this diversity as a sign of the spirit. Comparisons became not only inevitable but nonthreatening, A positive purpose could be served by them: to explore the diversity of the one Spirit of God.

John the Baptist, according to Mark, caught something of this spirit from Jesus, but Mark does not set out to tell John's story. John's baptism was a public ritual designed to recognize the need to repent and live a holy life. Mark has his focus on Jesus, but John was able to see his own mission and talent as different from that of Jesus. He could say the truth about Jesus and his own truth in the same breath. He could postpone commentary on his own uniqueness, because he found himself in the company of someone like Jesus, who set store not on uniqueness but on diversity of talent.

Not all of John's disciples became followers of Jesus. There is a tradition maintained by the Mandean people. Today they continue to recognize the

Baptist but not Jesus. Could the presence of John in each of the Gospels signal an ongoing attempt to convert John's followers to the Way? Scholars study this possibility too.

The habit of expecting great things from others and understanding our own anxieties about uniqueness is difficult to form, but it is the opening of Mark's Gospel. Mark seems to suggest that it helped someone like John recognize someone like Jesus when he arrived.

John's popularity is also mentioned by the first-century Jewish historian, Josephus, in his twenty-volume work, *Jewish Antiquities.* We learn from him of still other early first-century apocalyptic preachers, such as Jesus son of Ananias, who terrified Jerusalem citizens and annoyed magistrates with his wailing forecasts of approaching doom. Josephus explains King Herod Antipas' reaction to John the Baptist in a similar vein: Rather than waiting for trouble to develop, Herod struck at John early on and eliminated him.

> *When others too joined the crowds about him [John the Baptist], because they were aroused to the highest degree by his sermons, Herod became alarmed. Eloquence that had so great an effect on mankind might lead to some form of sedition, for it looked as if they would be guided by John in everything that they did. Herod decided therefore that it would be much better to strike first and be rid of him before his work led to an uprising, than to wait for an upheaval, get involved in a difficult situation and see his mistake. Though John, because of Herod's suspicions, was brought in chains to Machaerus, the stronghold that we have previously mentioned, and there put to death, yet the verdict of the Jews was that the destruction visited upon Herod's army was a vindication of John, since God saw fit to inflict such a blow on Herod.*
>
> Josephus, *Antiquities* 18.116–119

COMPARING MARK WITH THE OTHER GOSPELS

Mark has a number of concerns that differ from those of Josephus, and some of these clearly distinguish him from the other Gospel writers. Each of the four evangelists brings a personal and particular slant to the writing—a different religious background and experiences, his culture, his concerns.

Primary Objectives

Scholars indicate that Matthew writes from the perspective of a typical first-century rabbi: his major interest is the Torah; God's law is to be obeyed. For him Jesus is the greatest of rabbis, who saves his people by "teaching them to obey everything that I have commanded you" (Matthew 28:20). Luke is a Hellenist, whose highest concern is universal love; his Jesus is the gentle friend of the needy, the merciful and patient forgiver of sins. "Oh, how foolish you are, and how slow of heart to believe all that the prophets have declared! Was it not necessary that the Messiah should suffer these things and then enter into his glory?" (Luke 24:25–26). John's Gospel comes from the background of a proto-Gnostic Jewish sect, or a Hellenized Jewish group in which salvation is identified with knowing the truth. John's Gospel presents Jesus as "Truth" incarnate, the true Light; a perfect revelation of the Father. "The true light, which enlightens everyone, was coming into the world. He was in the world, and the world came into being through him; yet the world did not know him (John 1:9–10). We will continue the discussion of these themes later.

Miracles

This type of analysis is an oversimplification; besides their differences the evangelists have a great deal in common. They clearly portray the same Jesus of Nazareth, but the events of his life take on slightly different significance depending on who tells the story. Jesus' miracles, for instance, to John are best termed *signs,* symbolic revelations of the truth that makes us free. To Luke they are merciful actions, great kindnesses toward one's neighbor. To Matthew they are tokens of authority, authenticating Jesus' teaching of the new Law.

Judgment

Mark 1:21–28, more than the other three Gospels, seems to expect this "present age" to end very soon. In this Mark is typical of the first generation of Christians; the other Gospels, at least in the final forms handed down to us, represent a slightly later perspective.

> *They went to Capernaum; and when the sabbath came, he entered the synagogue and taught. They were astounded at his teaching, for he taught them as one having authority, and not as the scribes. Just then there was in their synagogue a man with an unclean spirit, and he cried out, "What have you to do with us, Jesus of Nazareth? Have you come to destroy us? I know who you are, the Holy One of God." But Jesus rebuked him, saying, "Be silent, and come out of him!" And the unclean spirit, convulsing him and crying with a loud voice, came out of him. They were all amazed, and they kept on asking one another, "What is this? A new teaching—with authority! He commands even the unclean spirits, and they obey him." At once his fame began to spread throughout the surrounding region of Galilee.*

This expectation of an approaching end, for Mark, is one facet of an apocalyptic outlook. Typical on the popular level of Palestinian religion at the time was a notion that saw the world locked in a terrible conflict between supernatural powers, some for good and some for evil. Although created by God, the world was now under the control of alien forces—disease, death, occupation by foreigners—any threatening reality people could not understand. Because of these forces, human life was diminished, jeopardized to the point that many people were selfish, petty, and quarreling over what small securities they could find. What was needed, in this apocalyptic view, was a new power, a mighty divine agent or champion more powerful than human enemies—someone who would defeat every evil power and restore the world for God.

This is the way Mark presents Jesus: a conqueror, full of "mighty works." Little space in his Gospel is given to narrating scenes or even Jesus' teachings, for example, in comparison with the other evangelists. Jesus' mission is to cast out the unclean powers and announce the imminent judgment and victory of God.

The Cross

If we read the passages as an isolated unit, with no reference to the rest of Mark's Gospel, this would be the image of Jesus you would be given: Jesus is God's agent or champion. But Mark has something more central to add to this, so important that it is actually the major theme of his narrative. Jesus' identity is not completely understood by those who look at his power as something that eliminates trouble. The victory by Jesus is paradoxically found in the acceptance of the cross on Calvary. The power of disease, strife, and death is broken, not by a simplistic wiping them from the face of the earth, but by personal choices and refusals to fear them. The power of Jesus—the power that can save the world—is the power of faith, the confidence to trust, despite everything, in God's love. The Jesus of easy victory by "mighty works" had no trouble finding an enthusiastic reception by the downtrodden Palestinian Jews. On the other hand, when Jesus tried to speak about the cross, even his chosen disciples became discouraged and confused. It is perhaps this fact, as much as the cultural difference, that makes Mark's picture or icon of Jesus the least remembered of the Gospels.

Outline of Mark's Gospel

At some point it is essential for a serious student to read Mark's text in one sitting. The Gospel was first *heard* by people. In any case, Mark's is a short read of only 661 verses. Chapter titles, numbers, and verses were added by copyists to the biblical manuscripts at various times in Christian history. In addition to chapters and verses, scholars often chart the movement of Mark's narrative through outlines.

Section 1: Jesus the Healer and Preacher in Galilee (Mark 1:1–8:26)

a. John the Baptist; one day of work; hometown troubles (1:1–3:6)
b. Selection and instruction of inner circle; miracles and parables lead to misunderstand by Jesus friends, relatives, and the crowds (3:7–6:6)
c. Disciples are sent out to preach; feeding the multitudes; walking on water; misunderstanding; another feeding of the multitudes; and further misunderstanding (6:7–8:26)

Section 2: Jesus the Suffering Messiah (Mark 8:27–16:8)

a. Three predictions of suffering and death; Peter's mistaken understanding; the Transfiguration; Jesus' teachings (8:27–10:52)
b. Last days in Jerusalem: triumphant entrance; trouble in the Temple; speeches and teachings about the end (11:1–13:37)
c. The Last Supper; passion narrative; death; burial; empty tomb (14:1–16:8)
d. Appendix: a later addition (16:9-20)

HISTORICAL CONTEXT

By the end of the second century, Clement of Alexandria mentioned Rome as the location of Mark's composition. Roman Christians by the year 68 had undergone Nero's fiery persecution. The emphasis in Mark's narrative on the failure of the disciples to understand Jesus, as we will see below, and their flight from him suggests a persecuted community (see Mark 13:9 and 12–13). Mark's audience spoke Greek and did not know Aramaic; thus Mark finds it necessary to translate Aramaic terms. In the area where this community lived many Latin words were used in the Greek language, and Mark's readers are acquainted with this custom. But Mark's readers seem unfamiliar with some of the more basic Jewish customs and practices, especially Palestinian ones. Nonetheless, the author assumes they know some religious terms from Judaism, such as *rabbi* and *Satan*. For the most part, scholars conclude that the community addressed seems to be composed of gentiles. As suggested from the content of Mark 13, readers might have had an overly eager expectation that Christ would soon return. The author of Mark's Gospel seems to urge them to remain watchful and not be misled.

EMPHASIS ON THE CROSS

The author sets the message of salvation, or "Gospel," in narrative form. The climax of the story is found in the cross of Christ. Indeed, virtually from the beginning of Jesus' ministry, one detects the shadow of the cross. Some time ago, scholar Martin Kaehler called Mark's Gospel "a passion narrative with an extended introduction." Mark's story moves quickly, creating a sense of urgency that matches the proclamation that the kingdom of God has drawn near. The plot of the story moves along unflinchingly from conflict and misunderstanding to the cross.

The Messianic Secret

A special feature of Mark's narrative is what has been called the "secrecy" surrounding the true identity of Jesus. Demons recognize Jesus and are silenced. Those whom Jesus cures are forbidden to make his identity known. This feature is termed the *messianic secret*. Jesus is explained only in light of his death on the cross. The messianic secret is a literary device Mark uses to structure his narrative and to deliver his interpretation of Jesus. *Christology* is a field of study that interprets the meaning of Jesus' life, death, and resurrection. Mark Christology begins by proclaiming that Jesus is "the Christ, the Son of God." A correct understanding of these titles is possible only if one accepts the cross. A Christology based on power and glory, such as Jesus-the-wonder-worker, is a false understanding of Mark's Jesus. Only when Jesus dies on the cross does a Roman centurion correctly state the truth of his identity.

For Mark the title of "messiah" or "Christ" cannot be accepted for Jesus if it is associated with earthly power. For example, when Peter boldly proclaims that Jesus is the Messiah, he is stiffly rebuked. To deny that the Messiah must suffer is not only wrong; it is demonic (see Mark 8:33).

The Son of Man

Jesus refers to himself as "the son of man." This is a mysterious self-designation more than a title, that is used with present, future, and suffering/rejection emphases. For Mark, the true identity of Jesus is hidden to all who do not see with the eyes of faith based in a true understanding of the centrality of the cross. So, too, discipleship, like Christology, must not deny the cross. If anyone wishes to follow Jesus, they must share in Jesus' cross. Mark models discipleship as this kind of Christology or faith interpretation of the meaning of Jesus Christ. Mark also includes three predictions of the passion, as mentioned in the outline of his Gospel, and he follows them with a prophecy that envisions persecution of his followers. As the Son of Man came to serve, disciples should serve the needs of everyone. The repeated failure of the disciples to understand this particular interpretation of Jesus is a challenge not only for the first community of believers but for all Christians. The failure of the disciples was followed by a promise from Jesus to see them in Galilee. This is meant to help a community of disciples who have undergone persecution and perhaps failure not to lose faith in the presence of threats.

Kingdom and Cross

Before Mark wrote, the term *gospel* meant a short announcement of salvation. His announcement, or gospel, was that Jesus' teaching that "the Kingdom of God is near (or at hand)." Paul's "gospel," as we have seen, centered on the resurrection of Jesus. According to Paul, the kingdom actually began when Jesus rose from the dead. Mark recognizes that the entire life story of Jesus is the "good news." The teachings Jesus offered, the things Jesus did, and particularly the manner in which he faced death led Mark to arrange and assemble what he found recounted by others into a simplified narrative of Jesus' public life and ministry. Some scholars have argued that Mark offers a synthesis of Paul's theological interpretation of Jesus with the sayings and stories about Jesus' life that characterized the teaching of Peter.

Historical Context and the Cross

Mark's Gospel is not a biography. The author collected some of what was circulating in the early churches as oral stories. These were not materials in the care of scholars or librarians. Mark makes no effort at chronological order; he does not offer a cause and effect presentation. Instead he diagrams the meaning of the Jesus' life and ministry in sixteen chapters. Eight are devoted to Jesus' preaching and healing ministry in Galilee and eight to the fateful last journey to Jerusalem and death. Incidents are inserted into this diagram whenever they serve Mark's message.

The finished Gospel reflects the time in which Mark wrote. He lived when war was about to consume the Palestinian Jews; Peter and Paul had died at the hands of the Emperor Nero; discouragement and loss abounded. Mark's answer to the people of his community was the cross. Jesus is a different kind of messiah, proclaimed Mark, and he will soon return and be vindicated, but he is only understood correctly in light of the cross. Everyone has failed repeatedly to understand this revelation, and Mark seems to think his audience needs to face it too. Only by following the Master on the way to his cross will they enter into his glory.

THE CENTRALITY OF FAITH

Faith can be defined in many ways. For example, one might say, "I trust you, but I am not certain of the things you do." Or "Is it you that I trust or only some version of you that I project on you?" One might even say things such as, "I trust you implicitly," when the more proper language is, "I trust you explicitly." A similar pattern often occurs when we talk about faith in God. For some people the certainty is there, but so is the obscurity. Mark's portrayal of the misunderstanding of Jesus' identity is no exception. A key theme in

Mark's narrative is that faith has many meanings and just as many mistaken conclusions.

Like Mark, Paul tried to have the Corinthians look at these matters with the "eyes of faith." "[F]rom now on, let even those who have wives be as though they had none, and those who mourn as though they were not mourning" (1 Corinthians 7:29–30). The tangible things he mentions have a certain solidity and depth to them. By comparison, faith seems vague and unsubstantiated. He says that if faith invariably seems intangible by comparison with other things, then treat those other things with reserve. Playing them down, so to speak, is not a pretense to give faith a chance to compete, but the muting of these realities in favor of the other is risky. One could end up with too much pretense and then make use of faith to escape the realities of the world. This need not happen. Paul's "as though" is *not* ideology; it is a technique, a way of holding oneself back so that faith has a chance to grow. Anyone who has tried to trust knows that we sometimes distract ourselves from dealing with things in another person so as to concentrate on the good reasons we have for trusting. When Paul suggests that we do this with marriage, business, and other matters, it is his way of expressing the reality of our personal faith.

Faith and Everyday Experience

Faith is not always contrasted to normal experience. Sometimes it is presented in continuation with them. Mark recounts how Jesus called his first disciples together (1:16–20):

> *As Jesus passed along the Sea of Galilee, he saw Simon and his brother Andrew casting a net into the sea—for they were fishermen. And Jesus said to them, "Follow me and I will make you fish for people." And immediately they left their nets and followed him. As he went a little farther, he saw James son of Zebedee and his brother John, who were in their boat mending the nets. Immediately he called them; and they left their father Zebedee in the boat with the hired men, and followed him.*
>
> Mark 1:16–20

Jesus does not ridicule their profession before inviting them to join him. To the contrary, common fishermen are invited to be fishermen of another type. Their knowledge of the lure, weight, winds, and nets will be taken up into more exciting work, "I will make you fishers of men." Faith, as Mark seems to report the incident, will be more of the same thing, and many things yet to be known. What the followers will need to practice, so to speak, is something they know a lot about. And while they mended nets in the past, their trust in Jesus is in continuity with what they have come to know in their lives.

It remains a delicate matter whether we are to look on faith as something close to our native abilities and instincts, or as something foreign, and an entirely new gift. An English theologian, John Cardinal Henry Newman, once said, "Belief engenders belief," by which he meant that people have a far greater experience of faith in their lives, even before it develops into religious faith, than they might suspect. Even so, faith does remain murky to some people.

Losing Faith

Some people lose faith. Judas Iscariot is one of the Gospel characters who lost faith in Jesus. His story is popular in the media. The absence of sufficient details in the New Testament about him may foster the cottage industry that now surrounds his contemporary popularity. Even those who are unfamiliar with the New Testament stories are able to identify the character known simply as "the betrayer."

Mark says very little about Judas Iscariot, at least compared with the other Gospel writers. Mark preserves a picture of Judas who was a member of the inner circle of Jesus' followers, the "Twelve," a group that Mark refers to eleven times in his Gospel. Judas is with Jesus throughout his ministry and participates in the Last Supper. Mark simply says that Judas is the one who handed Jesus over (Mark 3:19; 14:10, 44). The original band could not protect itself from his departure, and some scholars indicate that in Mark's estimate the figure of Judas is a stark reminder that the community must continue to ask the Judas question, "Surely, not I?" (Mark 14:19). In other words, according to Mark, present-day followers of Jesus are not exempt from losing faith, even in the risen Christ. Judas observed the miracles performed by Jesus and heard his preaching and parables, and none of it became bedrock for him to gain lasting faith. Other Gospel writers and church theologians offered different reflections concerning Judas. Mark seems to be satisfied to invoke Judas as yet another person who misunderstands the Nazarene.

Faith and Miracles

What people most readily turn to God for seems to be miracles. Someone is in a tough spot, aching and hurt, and they call on someone who can make all troubles go away. God promises, according to the Bible, that in the end all our tears will be wiped away. He will even wipe our tears today. He seems to be able to come to our assistance through miracles, but miracles are not what God is about. Easy escapes from limitations, sufferings, or death are not the answer.

Mark juxtaposes two subjects in his Gospel: miraculous cures and forgiveness. The first chapter of his narrative draws attention to Jesus' reluctance to become known only as a miracle worker. People flock to him, according to Mark, with their frustrations and pains while Jesus struggles to avoid that particular kind of popularity (compare John 2:23–25; Matthew 4:1–10; and Mark 2:1–12).

FORGIVENESS OF SINS

According to Mark, Jesus did not come to save people from every cross or difficulty; he came to save people from sin, through acceptance of the cross. The second chapter of Mark begins to introduce this theme. In this miracle scene, Jesus does not actually "heal" the man. Instead, he says "your sins are forgiven" (v. 5).

Which is more difficult: to heal a person's illness or their sins? Anyone can know the correct answer, but which would we rather have seen if we had been on the scene in Capernaum? Certainly the bystanders were disappointed, so Mark focuses on the scribes, who were hostile. "Who is this guy to start forgiving sins? No one forgives sins but God." Certainly at the time there were a number of Jewish rituals that allowed forgiveness of sins in the name of God. These scribes were not objecting to the fact that God's forgiveness was pronounced but that is was pronounced outside the official Temple and Torah channels. Miracles do happen, they would say, but forgiveness? According to the scribes, forgiveness was not available to Jesus to wield.

Mark assembles the scene with a great sense of drama. His narrative is the shortest of the four Gospels: 661 verses. Please notice that the first time Jesus mentions forgiveness of sins is the first time Jesus' enemies are singled out in the crowd. The charge against him that they use is the same one that will condemn him to death. "It is blasphemy!" (Mark 2:7) is the same charge made at the end of his life (14:64). Then in case the reader has any doubt about the source of hostility, Mark presents yet another scene of forgiveness at a banquet celebrated in God's kingdom; again the scribes are outraged (vv. 13–17).

Jewish leaders were not upset that someone was pronouncing sins as forgiven. Jesus' words "Your sins are forgiven" were heard in Judaism before. It is perhaps the freewheeling way that Jesus offers this divine forgiveness. He does not measure it out in careful doses, as the authorized channels do. He does not demand the official sacrifices, burnt temple offerings, atonement rituals. He forgives as if God would be as generous to one who worked only an hour as he would to someone who worked all day, or as if he would welcome back a son who squandered half of the family fortune. Jesus makes it sound as if it is God's joy to forgive.

Before we condemn the scribes, we might ask ourselves, following Mark, whether we are ready for Jesus' idea of forgiveness. According to Mark, Jesus wants to tell people that there are no obstacles to forgiveness on God's side, but obstacles remain in people. If we are not ready to love God as he loves us, then we impede divine forgiveness. If we would rather not take responsibility for changing our lives, and ask only that God not hold us accountable, we prevent divine forgiveness from touching us. If we are not ready to forgive others who trespass against us, then we have walled out the forgiveness God longs to share. Mark seems to indicate that few are ready, at first, for the emphasis on forgiveness. In fact, a number of people continue to find this version of forgiveness not believable. In a strange way, Mark's Gospel contains more miracle stories than the others, but miracles do not lead people to have faith in Jesus. They contribute to his rejection and demise.

THE SHEPHERD

After the cross, the image of the shepherd is the most familiar depiction of Jesus. What an actual shepherd does for the sheep is clear enough: he gathers and watches over them, and guides them "along right paths." But when Jesus is described as the "shepherd" and people as "sheep," and the shepherding is only a metaphor, there are more ways than one to imagine what it entails.

The Shepherd King

The concept of kingship is found in the Book of the Prophet Jeremiah, a writing that was very popular during the lifetime of Jesus among Palestinian Jews. Jeremiah imagines that God will send a true shepherd like King David to govern the people. Pious Jews were suffering under foreign overlords. Some longed for a powerful messiah-king who would overthrow the Romans just as David had overthrown the Philistines and allowed God's law to guide the people.

Mark tells us that Jesus is the long-awaited shepherd, but his shepherding is very different from what was promised in the writings by Jeremiah. He can be called a king—but only after the word has been disconnected from its usual meanings. In this regard, the Gospel of Mark shares theology with the Gospel of John. The differences between the Gospels of Mark and John are multiple, yet the opening verses of Mark have been favorably compared to a prologue. Mark relies on a number of titles for Jesus; he is "my [God's] Son, the Beloved" (Mark 1:11 and 9:7), "the Son of the Blessed One" (14:61), "God's Son" (15:39), and Jesus is the Christ ("Messiah") (see 2:35; 14:61; 15:32). Mark clearly portrays Jesus as one who teaches with authority (Mark 1:21–22, 27) even as he is misunderstood by his closest disciples who are instructed in his true identity.

Mark's story alludes to other images that are well known to an audience that is familiar with images from the Old Testament. Jesus is God's anointed

Son, as were the Israelite kings of old. As a result, Jesus is God's royal Messiah. Mark makes certain—as does the Gospel of John—that Jesus does not fulfill ordinary expectations of a kingly Messiah. Jesus is God's servant, his Beloved one (Mark 1:11), much as Isaac, the only son of Abraham, was so loved. God is pleased with his anointed son, Jesus. Jesus has the Spirit of God and is now more powerful than John the Baptist. Jesus is a teacher more than a kingly ruler.

This theme is verified in the Gospel of John. When the Roman procurator, Pontius Pilate, pressed him with the question "So are you a king?", Jesus answered "You say that I am a king" (see John 18:37). His kingship is not the same as Pilate and others imagine. Kings usually lord it over their subjects and rule by coercive power (see Mark 10:42). He does not want subjects but friends (see John 15:15) who will share his mission.

The Shepherd-Teacher

The title that Jesus accepts from his followers and the role in which he presents himself to the people of Palestine is not king but teacher. It is by teaching that he is a shepherd. "As he went ashore, he saw a great crowd; and he had compassion for them, because they were like sheep without a shepherd; and he began to teach them many things" (Mark 6:34). A shepherd-king is different from a shepherd-teacher.

Both kinds of "shepherd" offer security, but they offer it in contrasting ways. A king tells others what they must do. If he is powerful enough to make everyone conform to his plans, things run smoothly and safely. A teacher lacks this kind of power. A teacher offers knowledge, insight, the security of understanding, and the means to interpret what people experience in their lives.

Unity is another objective of the shepherd-teacher, but like the term *king*, unity has various meanings. The king sees to it that everyone works together according to his prearranged plans. Unity is like bees in a hive or gears in a machine. The teacher looks for the unity of a common language and conversation, with the possibility of shared commitment and vision. The teacher ultimately asks and offers something greater than any king would offer. No king would ever wish to make his subjects into other kings. He is the only and permanent authority, the final decision-maker. But the teacher wants to hand over all knowledge, to enable a student to carry on where the teacher leaves off, to help someone else fall in love with wisdom. If this is a king, it is a very peculiar one. According to Mark, Jesus was much more of a "shepherd-teacher" than Jeramiah's "shepherd king."

As a teacher Jesus used hyperbole, aphorisms, and a variety of wisdom sayings.

If your hand causes you to stumble, cut it off...And if your eye causes you to stumble, tear it out; it is better for you to enter the kingdom of God with one eye than to have two eyes and to be thrown into hell, where their worm never dies, and the fire is never quenched.

Mark 9:43, 47–48

Palestinian rabbis (that is, "teachers") used these types of exaggerated remarks to make their points. Like the other rabbis, Jesus presumably wore a cloak with tassels on it. Mark 6:56 indicates a number of sick people who begged Jesus to let them touch the tassels of his cloak. The tassels were a special reminder for pious Jews that they should moderate their earthly desires. It would have been understood that hand and eye for Jesus must be subordinate to the concerns of God's will.

The exaggerations in the passage are not completely unknown in our own colloquial speech: "It cost me an arm and a leg" or "I'd give my right arm for one of those." Jesus' teachings about "chopping off" or "plucking out" are extreme in their expression and it does not mean we must take them literally, nor does it mean we should take them less than seriously, as if Jesus "didn't really mean it." He meant it, but what did he mean? Jesus' lesson concerns the type of personal determination, the choices people make, rather than dismemberment. It is the same sort of lesson he taught in the parables about the kingdom: the kingdom is a hidden treasure for which everything else must be sacrificed.

The seriousness of moral and religious choices is taught by Jesus when he says that it is better to enter life with one hand than with two hands be thrown into Gehenna. What was Gehenna? J. R. R. Tolkien, in his trilogy, *The Lord of the Rings*, suggests this sort of place in his "land of Mordor," which sends up vapors and noxious fumes. Gehenna is as hideous as the land of Mordor. History identifies it as a valley on the southern edge of Jerusalem. Jews believed that long ago it was the site of a shrine to the god Moloch, who demanded the ritual sacrifice of children in a fire. By the time of Jesus, it was Jerusalem's fiery dump, where flames consumed the city's refuse. The point of the imagery, allowing for Semitic rhetoric, is a warning, explained in the previous few verses: every good gift of God can also be a danger to salvation. The spiritual gifts received by Jesus' closest friends could be their undoing, if they lead to selfish and exclusivist attitudes. What God has given they must share. His followers are not to work in their own name. They are servants, not masters; they are to seek the interests of others; they are to be "of use" rather than "to use." They are not to pretend that God's gifts are under their personal control.

So Jesus called them and said to them, "You know that among the Gentiles those whom they recognize as their rulers lord it over them, and their great ones are tyrants over them. But it is not so among you; but whoever wishes to become great among you must be your servant, and whoever wishes to be first among you must be slave of all. For the Son of Man came not to be served but to serve, and to give his life a ransom for many."

Mark 10:42–45

HOW MUCH DID JESUS KNOW ABOUT HIMSELF?

The second section of Mark's Gospel, as mentioned before, includes passion predictions and the final days of Jesus' life in Jerusalem. It contains theological (understanding of God) and Christological (understanding of Jesus) formulations that have challenged scholars to interpret Jesus' understanding of himself—an exercise that is meant to help us understand what Jesus had in store for all of us.

Jesus' Understanding of His Divinity

One of the more interesting clues about Jesus comes from the account of the transfiguration:

Six days later, Jesus took with him Peter and James and John, and led them up a high mountain apart, by themselves. And he was transfigured before them, and his clothes became dazzling white, such as no one on earth could bleach them.

Mark 9:2–13

Six days earlier Jesus had predicted his passion and explained to his inner circle of friends the necessity of his death on a cross. It is thought that Mark balances the passion prediction with this episode.

The term *theophany* is often used to describe the experience. It means that God reveals something in a spectacular occurrence. The transfiguration episode has been used to answer a contemporary question concerning Jesus' awareness of his divinity. It is a gigantic question in biblical research and theology. Even so, it is difficult to speak of the transfiguration without saying something about Jesus' self-awareness.

For some Christians the transfiguration is interpreted as a deliberate pulling back of the human side that covered Jesus' divinity. Jesus' inner circle of friends were aware of his divine origins. For others, the spectacular episode is a retrospective; that is, in light of their later belief in the resurrection, Mark pushes the revelation of Jesus' identity back to the transfiguration. The disciples came down the mountain and did not behave as true believers, especially when Jesus' passion begins to unfold. The special event of witnessing the transfiguration did not give them absolute or unwavering faith in Jesus.

Another group of Christians, literal fundamentalists, insist that it is critical to imagine Jesus as somehow immune from the maze and ordinariness of human life. They conclude that Jesus had foreknowledge and perfect self-understanding of his divinity. Jesus is divine, they say, and he was vividly conscious of it throughout his earthly ministry. It seems they are unfamiliar with a basic principle of reading the New Testament. That is, most of what is said about the historical Jesus by the Gospel writers is first offered long after the resurrection. It is in light of the resurrection that they come to new understandings of Jesus, which, while factually accurate, may not have been certain to those who experienced them at the time the events occurred. The Gospel writers reinterpret the life and career of Jesus based on the witness of faith that emerged in the wake of the resurrection. Thus while Jesus indeed may have been aware of his divinity, the Gospels do not express it literally.

The transfiguration has been called a number of things by scholars: a misplaced resurrection story, a second version of Jesus' baptism, a pious fable that expresses that believers gradually came to see Jesus fulfilling Jewish prophecies, or a strong affirmation of the kingship of Jesus throughout his earthly life.

JESUS' UNDERSTANDING OF HIS KINGSHIP

Another issue emerges after the resurrection and may be summarized with a question: Did Jesus emphasize his kingship during his earthly life? In Mark 6:14–16, King Herod hears about Jesus and the stunning miracles he performs and how the crowds are stirred up with speculations about his identity. The corrupt king agrees with the first and possibly most popular view that Jesus is John the Baptist raised from death. Others speculate Jesus is Elijah, or a prophet unlike any other in history. King Herod says, "John [the Baptist], whom I beheaded, has been raised" (v. 16).

When Jesus asks his closest disciples at Caesarea Philippi, "Who do people say that I am?" Peter is the last to respond and says, "You are the Messiah" (Mark 8:29), and Jesus does not deny it. Yet Jesus sternly orders them all "not to tell anyone about him" (Mark 8:30). This restriction may be Mark's way of continuing one of his favorite themes: the closest disciples fail to understand who Jesus is until after his death and resurrection, and a reluctant Peter and the others continue to have only a partial understanding of his identity and significance. The episode may be linked to Mark 6:14–16 in which the same list of popular titles for Jesus is mentioned. Jesus has more to reveal about his identity, and these will shatter common understandings of messiah and other titles.

Two further incidents in Mark's Gospel offer a partial answer to our question. At his trial Jesus stands before the Sanhedrin and is asked by the high priest, "Are you the Messiah, the Son of the Blessed One?" (Mark 14:61). He replies, "I am; and 'you will see the Son of Man / seated at the right hand of the Power' / and 'coming with the clouds of heaven.'" At first this seems to indicate clearly that Jesus accepts, at least, the elusive title Son of Man. We need to be cautious in coming to a judgment. We have noticed that a spectrum of expectations circulated in Jesus' day around the idea of the Son of Man. Here Jesus adds a reference from Daniel 7:13, "As I watched in the night visions, I saw one like a human being / coming with the clouds of heaven. And he came to the Ancient One / and was presented before him." Near the end of his life, Jesus accepts not a kingly designation but the "Son of Man" title, a title also rich with variant meanings for his contemporaries. Jesus is an agent or prophet of God who inaugurates during his ministry the beginnings of a new age on earth for God's people. Jesus has more to reveal, especially in his passion, death, and resurrection. For any kingly glory that might lie ahead, there are constant reminders of the sacrifices to come.

Finally, it is Pontius Pilate who orders a sign hung on the cross that reads, "The King of the Jews" (Mark 15:26). The inscription appears in each of the four canonical Gospels in various forms and summarizes the criminal judgment against Jesus made by Pilate. Mark has the chief priests and scribes standing at the foot of the cross repeat the same words, "'Let the Messiah, the King of Israel, come down from the cross now, so that we may see and believe.' Those who were crucified with him also taunted him" (Mark 15:32).

Our survey suggests that Jesus is personally more inclined to accept identification as the one who announces the in-breaking of a new age of God than to apply to himself the usual terms for an expected priest, prophet, anointed king, or any combination of them. Mark repeatedly emphasizes that Jesus' contemporaries, disciples, and enemies misunderstand him. The more decadent or hostile leaders (the high priest, scribes, and Pilate) use truthful titles for Jesus in mocking tones.

When Jesus screams out and dies, according to Mark, it is a gentile centurion who exclaims, "Truly this man was God's Son!" (Mark 15:39b). No one contradicts the Roman. The centurion's admission returns Mark's narrative to the opening lines, "The beginning of the good news of Jesus Christ, the Son of God" (Mark 1:1). The soldier's words of faith are the first positive effect of Jesus' voluntary passion and death. In Mark's point of view, the royal throne of Christ is his cross, although Jesus steadfastly avoided the term *king*.

UNDERSTANDING THE PASSION NARRATIVES

Mark's outline of the last days of Jesus is later used and edited in distinct ways by Matthew, Luke, and John. In the following chapters we will study their adjustments to Mark's outline and the additional information they incorporate from other sources. Each writer develops a passion narrative, a series of episodes and interpretations of the last hours of Jesus, to suit his own theology as a climax to that particular Gospel. These stories are rooted in the memories of the earliest followers and eyewitnesses to the events of Jesus' life and the ongoing faith of later communities of believers.

Keep in mind several lessons presented in this book in trying to understand these developments. First, the historical trajectory of Gospel formation—preaching, teaching, and worship—precedes the written documents. Special challenges confront church communities, such as the death of eyewitnesses, separation from Judaism following the destruction in 70 CE by the Romans, and the influx of gentile and Hellenist converts.

Each Gospel writer offers a narrative to strengthen readers' faith and preserve the central teachings given in the earthly ministry of Jesus to interpret the meaning of the risen Christ. Within the passion narratives certain details of the final hours of Jesus' life include episodes with embarrassing behavior by Jesus' friends. These are never glossed over. They are instructive to Christian readers who observe equivalent behavior by other members or themselves.

Gathered together the Gospel passion narratives offer specific details of the Palestinian world Jesus knew. Later Christians, especially preachers, harmonize these into one continuous story. On the popular level, the passion of Jesus becomes a story filled with double-dealing, intrigue, jealousy, fear, and even greed with nearly everyone alive at the time accused of deicide. Yet a close reading and critical analysis of the passion and death of Jesus reveals that the Gospel writers understand the death of Jesus in less dramatic ways.

As we have seen, Mark teaches that the death of Jesus was the price he voluntarily paid for the message he preached. Jesus' teachings disturbed the sensibilities of religious and political leaders. He was misunderstood by pious people and his closest associates. It was not a matter of politics or bad marketing of the message that led to Jesus' demise. Mark's story suggests that Jesus in his teaching and ministry often alluded to the cross of Calvary, and these suggestions also were misunderstood. No eyewitness to the ministry had a clear vision of Jesus' identity until after his death on a cross.

The arrangement of Mark's narrative is no accident; it is his perspective on how to understand Jesus' identity. Jesus ministers under the shadow of death, and the agony in Gethsemane nearly overwhelms him (see Mark 14:34). Mark presents Jesus as knowing human emotions. He is moved by pity, anger, frustration, compassion, and sorrow (see Mark 1:41; 3:5; 8:17; 14:6; and 14:33). Mark's picture of Jesus is organized to evoke a special type of faith in Jesus and to help readers understand their discipleship. As we have seen, God's voice announces it from heaven at Jesus' baptism (Mark 1:10–11), evil spirits and demons scream about his divine connection (Mark 1:24, 32–34; 3:11), and Peter blurts out a naïve understanding of Jesus' identity (Mark 8:29–30). According to Mark, only the Roman centurion acknowledges correctly Jesus' identity (Mark 15:39). The death of Jesus gives courage to one member of the Jewish establishment, Joseph of Aramethea, who asks Pilate, the Roman establishment representative, for the body of Jesus to bury (Mark 15:43–46). Pilate agrees. Joseph buries Jesus as Mary Magdalene and his mother, Mary, watch (Mark 15:47).

The original ending of Mark's narrative (Mark 16:8) is not the form we find in the Bibles we read today; at least, that is the opinion of biblical scholars based on their studies of manuscripts. They advance the view that later copyists added several short episodes (Mark 16:9–20), perhaps to soften Mark's original blunt ending in 16:8.

The shorter ending includes a brief story in which Magdalene and another woman walk to Jesus' tomb on Sunday following Friday's crucifixion in order to anoint Jesus' body. They are troubled only by the prospect of rolling away the stone at the entrance to the tomb. When they arrive, they find the tomb open. They enter and meet a "young man" (v. 5) who announces "he has been raised" (v. 6). He gives them orders to return to Peter and the others and tell them to go to Galilee for a reunion with the risen Jesus. The women disobey and "they went out and fled from the tomb, for terror and amazement had seized them; and they said nothing to anyone, for they were afraid" (Mark 16:8).

This shorter ending continues Mark's theme of misunderstanding Jesus' identity even when news of his risen life is first revealed. It is difficult to understand Jesus. He does not fit the ordinary expectations of people.

The Factual Events

Several factors impact the development of the passion narratives. The first is the factual events themselves. The Gospel writers knew these and provide an outline that included the Last Supper, arrest by Temple police, trial, and conviction to death by the Roman prefect Pontius Pilate. According to the Gospels, Jewish Temple leaders plotted against Jesus. He had spoken against their authority and even disturbed the money exchangers who worked for them. The Gospel writers included the embarrassing detail of Jesus' betrayal by one of his inner circle. The passion narratives also include Peter's denial of Jesus and the disappearance of Jesus' closest friends during his trial and crucifixion.

The Increasing Size of the Passion Narratives

The second element is an expansion of the narratives as history moved along. If Mark was the earliest formulation and John's the latest, we notice that the role of Pilate is diminished in a way that follows the historical trajectory of the writings. Pilate's role is reduced, while hostility and blame toward the Temple leaders increases. The Gospels of John and Matthew, both written more than a decade after Mark, assigned major roles to Jewish leaders in the plot to kill Jesus. The sad history of developing hostilities between Christian and Palestinian that actually occurred many years after the passion are carefully braided into the narrative.

The Fulfillment of the Old Testament

The final element is the Gospel writers' use of the Jewish Scriptures. The death of Jesus was interpreted in the context of key passages from the Septuagint Bible. The prophetic insights of Zechariah, especially chapters 9–12, help to color the narratives of Jesus' passion and death. So, too, certain ancient psalms, especially Psalms 22 and 69, as well as the so-called suffering servant chapters of the prophet Isaiah (52:13—53:12), were useful references. The death of a "righteous one" in the Book of Wisdom (chapters 2, 4, and 5) was also useful to illustrate God's purpose. In short, the death of Jesus is a fulfillment of the divine plan revealed throughout the holy writings of the Jewish Scriptures.

One way to conclude our study of Mark is to take the ideas presented in this chapter and to offer a contemporary application—a meditation of sorts. As we begin, bring to mind Mark's shorter ending for his story, the scene of the women fleeing the empty tomb and telling no one. Imagine a private meditation in which you try to think through your own fears and unmet expectations about Jesus.

Matthew adjusts Mark's passion narrative to suit his own theology, and he inserts additional details. Certain themes developed in his passion account are ones familiar to his readers. They were introduced from the beginning in his infancy narrative. For example, Matthew calls Jesus *Emmanuel*, God-with-us. (Matthew 1:23; 18:20; 28:20). It is possible that this title is easily understood for Matthew's audience of gentiles and Jews. In the aftermath of the destruction of the Temple in Jerusalem, many Jews wondered where God would now present himself. Matthew responds: God reveals in Jesus of Nazareth.

Some interpreters claim that if we had only the infancy narratives of Matthew and Luke, we would have each theme that is developed in the respective Gospel narratives. In other words, the infancy narratives are Gospels in miniature. So, too, the passion narratives may be understood as miniatures. Themes identified and developed throughout the body of the Gospel are summarized in the passion narrative. For example, Matthew emphasizes, more than the other Gospel writers, how the death of Jesus fulfills Jewish prophecies. The passion is not only a politically unjust decision; it is also the completion of Jesus' divinely appointed role as minister of salvation. If you take the time to line up the following passages, you will see confirmed the connection of themes in Matthew's infancy with his passion narrative: Matthew 1:22–23; 2:5; 17:23; along with 26:31 and 27:9.

Matthew uses apocalyptic imagery in his story of the infancy and in the passion account. A guiding star announces the birth (Matthew 2:2) and guides gentile astrologers to find the child Jesus. Graves open and people rise from the dead simultaneously to Jesus' death on the cross (Matthew 27:51–53). He also expands Mark's account of Judas' betrayal with details of thirty pieces of silver, and Judas' guilt feelings after deal making with the Temple authorities. It is Matthew who introduces the theme of Judas' suicide and the warnings by Pilate's wife (Matthew 27:19). No one is an innocent bystander to the death of Jesus.

Luke seems to follow Mark's outline and emphasizes Jesus at prayer during the final hours of his life. Angels are present in Luke's infancy narrative. They announce to lowly shepherds the birth of the savior. In Gethsemane, angels arrive to minister to Jesus in what only Luke describes as the "agonia" or agony in the Garden of Gethsemane. Luke also adds details, such as Jesus staring at Peter's after his third denial of ever having known Jesus. Only after the stare does Peter weep with deep regret (Luke 22:60–61). Only Luke reports that Pilate and Herod became friends after condemning the innocent Jesus (Luke 23:12).

The innocent Jesus demonstrates enormous understanding and compassion even on the road to Calvary. Only Luke mentions Jesus greeting the weeping women of Jerusalem (Luke 23:27–20), and Jesus' promise to the repentant thief who hung on a cross next to him: "This day you shall be with me in paradise" (Luke 23:43).

Finally, John's Gospel begins with a hymn proclamation of the eternal origins of Christ. There is a cosmic drama in John's portrayal and narrative: life and death, truth and falsehoods, light and darkness. We will discuss these themes in depth later. For John, Jesus is never a martyr or a victim. Instead, he willingly lays down his life to bring light into a darkened world. Jesus is aware of all that takes place. Jesus is not surprised by his impending demise. He gives Judas permission to leave the Last Supper to betray him (John 13:27–30). John emphasizes that Judas leaves under the cover of darkness to complete the plot: "and it was night."

The Passion and Faith

When you love someone and they die, all kinds of emotions and feelings well up in the human heart. The death of a loved one seems wrong and unfair. It is not logical. It is in no way deserved for someone who had so much and so many to live for.

In raising these questions we raise basic issues of what belief in Jesus entails. Doubt is part of believing. Faith does not mean the absence of doubt. Some people claim their doubts as the only final explanations. Then they live believing doubts are the only truths. Others, perhaps an increasing few, claim their doubts as their own and move into something we call faith.

If life on this planet were all that any of us were ever to know, then death would be the end of everything. And we might wish it to be the same for us rather than to live without a loved one. All we would have would be our tears.

If it could only be proved that Jesus rose from the dead, every doubt would be answered and satisfied. If we could prove that life and those of our deceased loved ones continues in some way beyond the edge of death, then every uncertainty would be erased. Is there a proof for faith? There is no combination of words that can explain all doubt away.

It is not difficult to prove that Jesus lived and died, but his resurrection goes beyond the ordinary, common experience we share. The resurrection was a breakthrough that opened humanity to something that eyes have not seen nor our ears heard.

When Jesus was arrested, his friends ran away in fear. His death crushed them. They hid. Then something happened. Something changed them from disillusioned and beaten people. They claimed that they met Jesus risen from the dead. His new life made them realize that every other instance of life cannot compare to the love of God. They said that their outlook on life, their understanding of what the meaning of life entails, was a gift that Jesus gave to them. He promised that they too would have unending life; that everyone will share it. Yet their testimony of faith really is no proof, is it?

There are some who think the risen Jesus was some kind of hallucination—that Peter, Thomas, and the others were so guilt ridden and grieving that they imagined the stories. The decision about Jesus and the possibility of life beyond death remains a personal one.

To the unbeliever the world is nothing but an energy field. Life is nothing but a complicated mechanism; awareness and love are nothing more than illusions. Believers, they say, are escapists, unable to face the harsh truth of mortality, clinging to childish, magical dreams about how everything will turn out happily in the end.

We who believe agree in part. Yes, instinct and physical forces provide a type of explanation for our conscious lives. But there is an unexplained remainder not reducible to those levels. There is a further question that some of us ask: the question of ultimate meaning, the question of *God*. In the end, questions about the death and resurrection of Christ are questions about belief in God.

Do we concede to being alone, a mere accident, a meaningless spark tossed up to flash for a few decades of life and then fall back into nothingness? Or do we dare hope that we exist in one who knows and holds; who created us, with whom something more is always possible. That we make a difference; that our loving and hoping are important; that even death is not the final moment in the journey of life.

There are easier gods to believe in, gods who make fewer demands and offer other comforts, gods who offer a compromise for those who are afraid. But the God of Jesus says we will live on beyond death. God raises the dead. God always offers a new beginning.

REVIEW QUESTIONS

1. Read Mark's Gospel in one sitting. What qualities or characteristics in his story do you notice? What aspects of a "life of Jesus" does Mark ignore?
2. How does Mark interpret the suffering and death of Jesus?
3. When it is said that the Gospels include a number of theologies. What is a theology? How is it that there seems to be a variety of theologies in the New Testament?

FOR FURTHER STUDY

1. Donahue, John R., and Daniel J. Harrington. *The Gospel of Mark* (Sacra Pagina Series; Collegeville, MN: Liturgical Press, 2005). The authors concentrate on the settings of the communities in which Mark was formulated and their use of the Old Testament; the nature of the finished literary character of the Gospel is analyzed.
2. Maloney, Francis J. *The Gospel of Mark: A Commentary* (Peabody, MA: Hendrickson, 2002). Very much for the beginner. This book is a literary analysis of the text; if read along with Donahue and Harrington, it will demonstrate the difference between a scholarly and nonscholarly treatment. Maloney is worthwhile and accomplishes what he intends to offer.
3. Errico, Rocco A., and George M. Lemsa. *Aramaic Light on the Gospels of Mark and Luke* (Smyrna, GA: Noohra Foundation, 2001). Part of a series originated by Lemsa to introduce the Aramaic substructure of the canonical Gospels as well as the ancient history of the region to contemporary Westerners. For those with a special interest in learning the Aramaic underpinnings for certain key concepts in the New Testatment.

4. Juel, Donald H. *The Gospel of Mark* (Interpreting Biblical Texts Series; Nashville, TN: Abingdon, 1999). A short summary of issues included in Mark's Gospel. Juel's focus, as other volumes in the series, is not on the world created by texts as much as the world created in the reader by the Scripture texts. A book a beginner will enjoy.

5. Hahn, Scott, and Curtis Mitch. *The Gospel of Mark.* 2nd ed. (Ft. Collins, CO: Ignatius Press, 2001). The text uses the *Catechism of the Catholic Church* and the writings of the Fathers of the Church as bedrock for the study. Enthusiastic and clearly written.

6. LaVerdierre, Eugene. *The Beginning of the Gospel: Introducing the Gospel According to Mark* (Collegeville, MN: Liturgical Press, 1999). A rhetorical and literary analysis of Mark in which Father LaVerdierre offers and explains his thesis: Mark's community understood that the return of Christ *(parousia)* was imminent.

7. Collins, Adela Yarbro. *The Beginning of the Gospel: Probings of Mark in Context* (Minneapolis, MN: Augsburg Fortress, 1992; 2nd rev. ed.: Eugene, OR: Wipf & Stock, 2001).

8. Collins, Adela Yarbro, and Harold W. Attridge. *Mark: A Commentary* (Hermeneia: A Critical and Historical Commentary on the Bible Series; Minneapolis, MN: Fortress, 2007). Collins identifies perspectives advanced by major scholars of Mark during the past few decades. The primacy she gives to the apocalyptic literature now understood as "not of one piece" is joined to her exposition of the popularized biographies of the first century as opening up a pathway to understand Mark's content choices and his literary composition. This is a serious work by a premier biblical scholar.

9. Fitzmyer, Joseph A. *The One Who Is to Come* (Grand Rapid, MI: Eerdmans, 2007). Especially see pages 134–145 for more information on the expectations circulating in Jesus' day about the "Son of Man."

10. Foster, Paul (ed.). *The Writings of the Apostolic Fathers* (New York, T&T Clark, 2007). Helmut Koester offers a thoughtful introduction, and each document is introduced with a summary of manuscripts and approximate dates of origin as well as a summary of contentious issues among scholars. Useful is the inclusion of the *Didache.*

11. Matera, Frank. *New Testament Christology* (Louisville, KY: Westminster John Knox Press, 1999). See pages 7 and 260 for his comparison of Mark's opening verses with a monologue.

7

The Gospel According to Matthew

Special Elements in Matthew's Account

1. Scholars observe a "rabbinical" style in Matthew's style and theology. He portrays Jesus as the fulfillment of Jewish expectations "that the Scripture might be fulfilled."
2. Isaiah 7:14 predicts a virgin conceiving; Micah 5:2 predicts the birth in Bethlehem; Jeremiah 31:15 predicts the slaughter of the innocents by Herod; Joseph and family flee to Egypt as predicted by Hosea 11:1.
3. Old Testament parallels are found in Jesus coming out of Egypt like Moses (Exodus 1:11) The death of Herod and the death of the Pharaoh are equated (Matthew 2:19ff and Exodus 2:23; 4:19).
4. Like Moses, Jesus on a mountain delivers a new law from God. (Compare Exodus 19 and 20 to Matthew 5:1.) Matthew presents Christianity as Judaism in fullest form.
5. Matthew tends to substitute the word *heaven* for *God.* He prefers the expression *kingdom of heaven* rather than *kingdom of God.*
6. He seems to soften Mark's texts where Jesus corrects the disciples even as he follows Mark's outline. Peter receives special prominence (Matthew 16:17ff) rather than rebuke as in Mark's version.
7. There is a universal theme in Matthew's interpretation of Jesus' teachings on the kingdom. Matthew is the only Gospel writer who uses the world *ecclesia* (Matthew 16:18 and 18:15-22).
8. Dreams and prophecies are important to Matthew (Matthew 1:20ff; 2:12ff; 27:19).
9. He includes apocalyptic parables by Jesus (Matthew 13:47-49; 25:42-44; 25:1-38).

10. Luke and John record resurrection appearances of Jesus in Jerusalem. Matthew follows Mark's tradition of Jesus appearing in Galilee and commanding disciples to convert the world (Matthew 28:19ff).

11. Matthew was thought by many early Christians to be the earliest Gospel written. This is mentioned by Irenaeus about the year 190. Ignatius of Antioch about the year 110 makes use of Matthew's infancy story. So, too, the *Didache* refers only to Matthew's Gospel.

12. The liturgical form of the Lord's Prayer (Matthew 6:9ff) continues to be used by Christians even as scholars suggest Luke's version (11:2ff) follows more closely the Aramaic usage by Jesus and Matthew's version resembles the prayer forms used in synagogues.

A PROPHECY FULFILLED

Matthew is the first Gospel listed in many Bibles. Does your Bible follow this tradition? The historical formation of the New Testament as presented in this book follows an opinion held by many contemporary biblical scholars. They consider Mark to be the oldest or first written gospel. Today we understand that the texts of the New Testament developed out of the life and practice of the church. Preaching, teaching, and worshipping preceded the written documents that eventually came to be known as the New Testament in the form used today. Matthew follows the order of events in Jesus' ministry as Mark narrates them. Matthew and Mark are interrelated in some way, and, as we studied earlier, there are a number of scholarly solutions or hypotheses to explain the connections. Even if these are not fully satisfying, the special features of Matthew's narrative offer other clues as to why his Gospel is listed first in the canonical New Testament.

There is an ancient opinion from church leaders and theologians who recognize Matthew as the first to write a Gospel. Saint Augustine in the fifth century agrees with the earlier Clement of Alexandria (ca. 150–215/216) and his student, Origen (ca. 185–254), regarding the priority of Matthew. Origen writes:

> *Concerning the four Gospels which alone are uncontroverted in the Church of God under heaven, I have learned by tradition that the Gospel according to Matthew, who was at one time a publican and afterwards an Apostle of Jesus Christ, was written first; and that he composed it in the Hebrew tongue and published it for converts from Judaism. The second written was that according to Mark, who wrote it according to the instruction of Peter, who, in his General Epistle, acknowledged him as a son, saying, "The church that is in Babylon, elect together with you, saluteth you;*

and so doth Mark my son." And third, was that according to Luke, the Gospel commended by Paul, which he composed for the converts from the Gentiles. Last of all, that according to John."
Origen, from the *First Book on The Commentary on Matthew,*
translated by Roberts-Donaldson

The accuracy of this ancient position is questioned, yet no one doubts the frequency with which Matthew's account is quoted by other early church leaders and theologians. Matthew's account is thought by some to have been part of the instructional format used with aspiring church members. The length of Matthew's narrative offered a more thorough interpretation of Jesus and was often quoted.

Matthew's robust account of the meaning of Jesus' life is clearly evident in the multiple verses he offers to illustrate how Jesus fulfills Old Testament prophecies. He uses the prophet Isaiah many times. In Matthew 1:25 he quotes from Isaiah 7:14 to explain how Jesus' miraculous conception fulfills Isaiah's prediction. The prophet Micah identifies where the Messiah is to be born and is a useful reference for Matthew 2:15. The violence of King Herod and the murder of innocent children finds Matthew 2:18 repeating Jeremiah's lament (Jeremiah 31:15). Hosea 11:1 helps Matthew justify the flight into Egypt (Matthew 2:15) in fulfillment of Hosea's predictions. Thereafter Matthew has quotations from Jewish Scripture to verify why Jesus enters Galilee (Matthew 4:15–16), the meaning of Jesus' miracles (Matthew 8:17), his inner spirit (Matthew 12:8–21, the purpose of his teaching in parables (Matthew 13:35), his triumphal entry into Jerusalem (Matthew 21:5), why he is taken and killed (Matthew 26:56), and how Jewish prophecy is fulfilled in the betrayal by Judas (Matthew 27:9–10).

Matthew focuses on Jewish prophecies and concerns to his community of Christians who are understood variously as a mixed community of Jewish and gentile Greek speakers who seem less interested or familiar with the apocalyptic "Son of Man" than Mark's community. Matthew has a distinctive interpretation for Jesus, his role and for his community, and God's plan for human salvation. He had the need to retell the story of Jesus in order to address a new community with special needs and issues. Writing in the aftermath of a total destruction of the Jerusalem Temple a decade or more earlier, Matthew defines who the "new Israel" is and how Jesus is the "new Moses." For Matthew the Messiah is God's final and special agent, who is eternally present with God's people and who, on a mountaintop, initiated a new age with Jesus as master and teacher (Matthew 28:16–20). It is the risen Christ who speaks God's message and interprets God's Law for Jews and gentiles and commissions Jewish and gentile

Christians alike to a worldwide mission to convert all nations. Jesus tried to teach to his Jewish contemporaries during his lifetime (Matthew 10:5–6) and following the resurrection to world (Matthew 28:19). Matthew provides justification for a Christian community to understand how it derives from Judaism but now must see itself as established by One who fulfilled ancient prophecies and promises of God's final revelation.

Nervousness about what is historical or real in the Jesus story for believers is confirmed when they face the extreme assertion that Jesus never lived. The truth is that we have only a few, short historical references to Jesus in ancient non-Christian writings. As a response, one type of sensitivity that has developed among some fundamentalist Christians is a view that no single detail of Jesus' actual life is more significant than any other. What is essential for faith is that the Son of God became human to save humankind. He lived a life of holiness. He died to atone for our sins. He rose from the dead and is now an effective force in those who seek to live holy lives. Advocates of this perspective never mention a virgin birth, the nightmares and dreams of Joseph, the plot against the child by a dishonest king, or the visit of the Magi. The reason they do not emphasize these stories is to honor more the activity of God sending a savior than the significance of human participation in the story of God's salvation.

Other Christians are more selective than fundamentalists in their use of details and themes in the story of Jesus' earthly life. For example, television evangelists often offer a special selectivity and emphasis. Although they may invoke the name of Jesus in their preaching, they read and interpret the biblical narratives with a firm conviction that Jesus was always the Christ. Christ is the divine savior. Christ knew all things throughout his earthly visitation. As a result, they find certain biblical passages more significant than others, such as Romans 1:3–4, where Paul writes, "[C]oncerning his Son, [he] was descended from David according to the flesh and was declared to be Son of God with power according to the spirit of holiness by resurrection from the dead, Jesus Christ our Lord." In other words, they focus on a limited number of details about Jesus' earthly life. They prefer to emphasize his later impact on others, beginning with the resurrection.

There is a third group of Christians who are found in every denomination. These people sidestep historical questions completely. They have a vague outline of the details of Jesus' life and teachings and that is sufficient. They are indifferent to questions about the nature of Jesus' divine origins, the content of his earthly teachings, resurrection, or present whereabouts. If curiosity prompts them to ask what the original biblical storytellers literally understood about the details in the infancy narratives, they understand "faith" not to rest on details or complete information. Faith is a feeling or a sentiment they experience. They have no interest to elaborate on historical facts.

The context of Matthew's infancy narrative does not center on the relationship of Mary to Jesus. Still less does he want to emphasize the merits of virginity. Instead, he attempts to interpret Jesus' special relationship to God, and to underscore the special authority Jesus embodies. The reference to Isaiah bears this out: Jesus is God with us. Yet Matthew also gives some deliberation to the virgin who conceives the Messiah. For this reason, Christians have interpreted his faith as extending to the fact of Jesus' virginal birth and its significance. They understand that Matthew teaches a theological or faith interpretation of the facts of Jesus' life.

Official and unofficial versions of the Christian faith do not always coincide. People do not always follow official teachings for the best of reasons. Even those who do follow them may not catch the intended significance of a teaching. Believers may have some experience in sensing certain items in a personal history that are important and those that are not. They may also know, with Cardinal Newman, that we believe because we love. They understand that love can be blind, that it may exaggerate, but they also know that love may be unerring in its intuitions.

DATE

One fact that has been widely debated is the date of Matthew's composition. The parable in Matthew chapter 22 indicates the author knew of the destruction of Jerusalem by the Romans in the year 70: "The king was enraged and sent his troops, destroyed those murderers, and burned their city." A banquet invitation was refused by certain guests, and the destruction of their city corresponds to the time period when Roman armies demolished the city and Temple. Other commentators notice the triadic formula in Matthew 28 as the most advanced formula in the New Testament that moves in the direction of later Trinitarian theology. "Go, therefore, make disciples of all nations, baptizing them in the name of the Father, and of the Son and of the Holy Spirit" (Matthew 28:19).

The passage suggests a time for the composition of the Gospel in the late first century. On the other hand, scholars know there is a tradition from Papias, written as early as the year 115, in which a claim is made that Matthew's Gospel was copied first, and Ignatius of Antioch, about the year 110, remarks on the place of honor Matthew's version held in the ancient churches.

No other Gospel version is cited more frequently than Matthew in noncanonical Christian writings. For instance, in the *Didache*, written sometime between the years 80 and 120, Matthew is the one Gospel that is mentioned. Taking all this information into consideration, a number of scholars conclude that a date of composition for the Gospel of Matthew is best understood as having taken place sometime between the years 80 and 90. The high regard for Matthew in the ancient churches is not disputed.

AUTHOR

It is unknown what connection, if any, the Gospel has with the Matthew who was Jesus' disciple, or why it includes the apostle's name. The author may have had access to records that Matthew made, or the author's community may have claimed Matthew as its founding preacher. In any case, the present form of the Gospel was written in Greek. It was not a translation from Aramaic and was written after the lifetime of the apostle Matthew. Most of the narrative depends on Mark's outline, and the author fills this out with teachings of Jesus from other sources. Other reasons for the high estimation given to Matthew by the ancients may be found in the way in which he tells the story of Jesus itself, the demands of discipleship, and Matthew's distinctive claim that in Jesus there is a final revelation in human history. The resurrection of Christ fulfills all Jewish hopes, and a new Israel has been formed in his name.

Scholars suggest that the author was a teacher with a rabbinic style and was likely from a community that had maintained ties with Jewish religious life for as long as possible. A few clues are offered in the text to verify this assumption. The community has strong roots in Judaism as witnessed by the concern for the Law of Moses. Jesus has come "to fulfill the Law and the Prophets" (Matthew 5:17–18). There are several of these "formula quotations" that function as special notations for the reader, interpreting a particular event in the life of Jesus as a fulfillment of the Jewish Scriptures. So, too, there is a respectful concern for Jewish questions and practices as well as bitter criticisms of the Pharisees and scribes. These elements seem to suggest a split had developed between Matthew's community and the synagogues. The evangelist speaks emphatically of "your" and "their" synagogues (Matthew 4:23; 9:35; 10:17; 12:9; 13:54). It remains debatable whether the break with the synagogues had taken place or if the Pharisees and followers of Jesus continued to find themselves competing voices within Judaism before or following the devastating war with the Romans that began in the year 66.

With all his Jewish sensitivities, it seems odd that the author of Matthew is the most bitter against the pious Pharisees. One explanation lies in the context of his writing. In their preparations for the disastrous war with the Romans, the Jews had found proof that the gentile followers of Jesus, as well as the Jewish Christians, could not be trusted to put Judaism first in their lives. The Jews were fighting for God's kingdom, but the Christians did not believe it would be obtained from warfare. When the remnants of the Jewish nation regrouped after their loss of the Temple, they came under the leadership of the Pharisees. The Zealots had failed in the fighting, and the Sadducee Temple priesthood and aristocracy was ended. At this time, Christians were no longer welcome in the synagogues. Despite this hostility, Matthew continues to preserve an instruction from Jesus to "do whatever they teach you and follow it" (Matthew 23:3).

AUDIENCE

One of the sensitivities in Matthew's Gospel is a preference for the use of the expression *kingdom of heaven* in place of *kingdom of God*. This is a pious Jewish way to avoid a casual use of God's name. Jesus is compared with Moses as the revealer of a new Torah that fulfills all the promises of the original covenant with Israel. Jesus teaches a more perfect way of life. At the same time, Matthew's Gospel is very open to the gentiles. The arrival of the Magi (2:1ff) anticipates the coming of gentiles to faith in Jesus, and the closing scene of the Gospel presents the risen Lord sending his disciples out to make disciples of all nations.

The community Matthew addressed was thoroughly familiar with Judaism and may have included a considerable gentile presence. The personality of the author that emerges from the Gospel is that of a careful teacher, willing to repeat and amplify his examples for the sake of clarity. He is less interested in the urgency of actions by Jesus that we saw in Mark. He shortens some of Mark's narratives and extends the length of many of Jesus' sayings. The result is a more solemn, less dramatic, portrayal of Jesus' life than the other evangelists present. For example, Mark seems to ask for followers to be willing to face the cross, whereas Matthew asks for obedience to all the commandments Jesus has given.

THE MESSIAH

Jesus and Abraham

Matthew's prologue (1:1—2:23) presents a genealogy for Jesus that begins with Abraham, the father of Israel (Matthew 1:1–17). Matthew designates Jesus as "the son of David, the son of Abraham" (v. 1). As noted earlier, David lived a thousand years after Abraham, but he is mentioned first. One possible explanation is that the kingly ancestor of Jesus the Messiah is the royal anointed one (see Matthew 1:16).

The character of Abraham is central to the Jewish understanding. Jesus is called by many names in the New Testament: the new Adam, the new Elijah, the new Moses, the new David, but he is never called the new Abraham. Abraham set the model for the Jewish monotheistic faith tradition. Jesus' faith, like Abraham's, would take him through the same kind of adventurous clinging to God throughout life. Abraham's faith is a way of seeing more possibilities for life where others see only death. Such faith involves submission to the demanding claims that are sometimes made on us. Faith means recognizing that you are not God.

The Infancy Narrative

In the first episodes of Matthew's infancy narrative, the mystery of Jesus is proclaimed in his miraculous birth by the power of God's Spirit (Matthew 1:18–25). The birth is also part of the revelation. The Messiah is not identical to anyone else in human history. The birth fulfills the prophecies known to Israel regarding a final leader from God. Notice the name Matthew gives to Jesus: *Emmanuel*, which means "God is with us."

From his baptism by John in the Jordan River, throughout his ministry of healing and preaching the arrival of God's kingdom, Mark's interpretation demands that disciples integrate into their own lives an understanding of the centrality of Jesus' cross and death. With Matthew we see the many themes woven into a narrative that centers on the birth of Jesus. Luke offers his special interpretation of the birth. Later, John interprets Jesus as the Word of God who from eternity incarnates himself into human reality.

COMPARING MATTHEW AND PAUL

One way to notice development in ideas presented in the New Testament is to apply some of the knowledge we now have in a comparison of the ways in which two biblical writers express themselves: Paul and Matthew. Two passages suggest themselves as a good place to emphasize the similarities.

Matthew 4:12–33

This passage provides an example of how Matthew offers an extraordinary scene of God's might or power breaking into human history, finally setting it right. A world that has lived in darkness suddenly sees a great light; for people who have lived in the shadow of death a new day begins to dawn. Jesus, according to Matthew, goes through all of Galilee, teaching and preaching the news of God's kingdom come. One of the signs of the kingdom is his curing people of all sorts of diseases. When he approaches Peter and Andrew, then James and John, he tells them: "Follow me" (v. 19). Immediately they drop their nets, jump out of the boats, turn away from their families, and walk with Jesus.

1 Corinthians 1:10–17

Paul, on the other hand, is not so quick to emphasize the joys of Christ's coming. Insofar as we can reconstruct the epistle, the Corinthians had regular contact with Paul. In a recent letter to him, they may have congratulated themselves for the ways they tried to solve their local difficulties. Paul had other sources of information about them and was not satisfied with their reports: "[I]t has been reported to me by Chloe's people…" (v. 11). Paul criticized them throughout the letter for a lack of concern for each other, particularly the weakest members of the community. He noticed their vanity, their lack of reverence at worship, and a few poor attitudes regarding marriage.

The first issue Paul attacks, though, is what he considered their greatest failing: a spirit of division and rivalry. "What I mean is that each of you says, "I belong to Paul," or "I belong to Apollos," or "I belong to Cephas," [in Aramaic rock or *kefa* is equivalent to the Greek word *petros*)] " (v. 12). In short, Paul understands the Corinthians are making religion into a contest in which they look down on one another. Near the end of his letter, Paul chides them for vying for the most spectacular charismatic gifts.

Divergent Views?

These passages present two divergent pictures of early church life. One gives the picture of everything moving along as God intended. The other picture reflects the struggles of human conversion. Despite their failings Paul felt affection for them. A few years later he commented, "I wrote you out of much distress and anguish of heart and with many tears, not to cause you pain, but to let you know the abundant love that I have for you" (2 Corinthians 2:4). Even as he attacks their arrogance, he calls them, "God's temple" and tells them "that God's Spirit dwells in you" (1 Corinthians 3:16), and later he calls them "the body of Christ" (1 Corinthians 12:27). Paul recognizes human weakness but continues to believe that God has called them to be holy (1 Corinthians 10:31; see also 1 Thessalonians 4:1–12) and God's power is still at work among them. It is on the strength of this belief that Paul challenges the Corinthian community of believers to regain their perspective. The center of their lives must not be themselves, not even a holy preacher. The center must be Jesus: "In whose name were you baptized?" "Who was crucified for you?"

In some ways, Paul's teaching is no different from the passage we read in Matthew. Matthew knew as he wrote it that he was simplifying: Peter did not in fact meet Jesus for the first time and suddenly turn into a perfect follower. For one thing, Peter had spent time with Jesus earlier. "One of the two who heard John speak and followed him was Andrew, Simon Peter's brother" (John 1:40), and Peter managed to continue to make mistakes for a long time afterward. "Then he began to curse, and he swore an oath, 'I do not know the man!'" (Matthew 26:74). Even so, Matthew does not describe the daily reality of discipleship but its inner essence. Paul understands discipleship as God's call. They each understand that most people will remain sinners and will need to be challenged many times to let go of their preoccupations, to count everything in life as secondary to imitating Jesus. According to Paul and Matthew, God's power to convert and transform people is available in the life of the community of Jesus' followers. It is a religious community with few rewards and punishments.

MATTHEW'S ETHICS

The morality in the Bible has been described as infantile because it appeals to ideas of rewards and punishments. A morally adult person chooses to do the good not because he or she will win a prize or avoid paying a terrible penalty. Such motives are for children. Children are unable to grasp important issues and consequences of their actions and need the authority of others who have the competence to offer them guidance. Only with maturity comes an ability to see for oneself what is right and what is wrong.

This is not only the position of some contemporary moral thinkers; it was the teaching of the ancient Greek philosophers. Socrates and Plato, for example, insisted that virtuous living is its own reward. As a result, when we pick up the Bible we find what might seem an immature morality based on rewards and punishments. For instance, the apostles in Matthew's Gospel ask Jesus about what rewards they will receive for following him (see Matthew 10:37–42). Jesus replies that those who parade their virtue before other people already have received their rewards. It is the one who endures hardships for the sake of justice who will be blessed, "for your reward is great in heaven" (Matthew 5:12).

The Scriptures have two points of view on this issue. One is the evolution within the Bible itself away from the early idea of external rules and the resulting rewards and punishments. In Israel's earliest days the typical thinking was basic: if someone sins, they could expect misery and even an untimely death. If someone was virtuous, they could expect a long, prosperous life, with talented children, and a peaceful old age. Yet these early ideas do not endure. More experience proves them too simple. The Book of Job stands as a classic statement of disillusion with the early formulations of rewards and punishments. By the end of the Old Testament period we begin to read ideas of rewards and punishments taking place after this lifetime; rewards in a life beyond death.

The teaching of Jesus seems to complete the development. He demands a moral responsibility that is beyond the obligations of any external law or regulation. No law is specific enough or goes far enough. What rule can demand you to marry one person and not someone else, or what rule can tell you to support a specific political strategy? Instead of obedience to a long list of rules and regulations, Jesus asks for obedience to God's Spirit poured out in everyone's heart. Even when he speaks with the traditional language of "rewards," he speaks of it in a new and unprecedented way. The just ones will receive a payment beyond expectation or calculation. It will be a gift that comes with an awareness of a personal relationship with God.

It is even more than an evolution toward moral autonomy. Those who seek something like the Greek idea of doing the right thing simply for its own sake are likely to be disappointed by Jesus' innovation. The Scriptures do not have the idea. The writers do not believe in it. The teachings of moral philosophy may be valid and good as far as they go, but they remain too abstract. In the world of real living the drama of good and evil is not resolved simply. Goodness is not always its own reward.

Moral thinking always presupposes a prior question or two. Given the facts of self-centeredness, insensitivity, indifference, and a measure of ruthlessness alive in human society, and the fact that our best efforts often turn out, in retrospect, to have been misguided, how can anyone expect to sustain a commitment to goodness? After all is said and done, does it make any difference if we try to do the good?

The answer does not lie in the realm of morality. It lies in the realm of religious faith. The ultimate ground of moral behavior is belief in the Creator's Spirit that lives with us. Jesus' use of the language of rewards and punishments offends those who suppose they are too mature to tolerate any "primitive" motivations, but it serves as an effective illustration of a fact that they may resist. Our moral decisions have a deeper significance—far greater than we ordinarily imagine. Wittingly or unwittingly, we live and act in dialogue with God. This is the New Testament's view of the foundation of morality. It is a bit deeper than a foundation for ethical behavior that says: "It's nice to be nice."

Typically those who try to define the distinctiveness of Christianity begin by discussing how it differs from Judaism. Jesus' words, especially in Matthew's writings, set up a deliberate contrast between the Law of Moses ("you have heard it said…") and Jesus' new law ("but what I say to you…"). A standard interpretation is that Judaism teaches an ethic of love and forgiveness within an immediate circle of family, friends, or the tribe. Judaism recommends also a strict eye-for-an-eye vengeance, especially with outsiders. These interpreters understand Christianity as teaching a superior ethic of love and forgiveness for all.

A number of problems result from oversimplifications. First, there is the issue of how Christians actually behave. Although Christians stake a claim on the insight to love one's enemies, do they actually live it out? When a person strikes them on one cheek, do they turn and offer the other? How many people live this way? The Christian world, it seems, has never been ready and is not ready today to live strictly according to this ethic.

Furthermore, if we think of Israelite religion as a static system instead of a living, developing movement, Christians may not have been the only ones who tried to improve on the original ethical theory. Granted, the regulations established by Moses thirteen centuries before Jesus were severe by contemporary standards, yet Jesus' words are not meant to be overlooked. Some commentators misunderstand that the Ten Commandments still remain as God's most complete revelation of rules and regulations for Christian people to follow. When asked to explain how their Christian religion differs from Judaism, they tend to mention something about believing that Jesus is the Son of God. When it comes to the conduct of their own lives, they make no mention of this passage from the New Testament.

Moving Beyond the Ten Commandments

Jesus was more than an apocalyptic prophet. He teaches very clearly that living by the Ten Commandments is not sufficient. What he asks his followers to practice moves radically beyond the teachings of the Ten Commandments. How so? The answer transcends the ethical level and touches the arena of his understanding of the human relationship to God. Jesus, according to Matthew, invites those who would follow him to make a daring leap, to believe in an unusual possibility. The possibility is described in the Sermon on the Mount (Matthew 5:1–12). As if heaven will come about on earth, as if people will actually begin to live in a way he teaches God intends for them: forgiving one's enemies as God forgives us; sacrificing personal interests for the sake of someone else; only returning good for evil; living as if the Spirit of God is alive in the heart of every creature making us all God's family not just in name but in fact; sharing now God's life and divinity. Christianity is not only an intellectual assent to the idea that Jesus is the Son of God; it is the practical assent to God that makes us a family, related to one another.

Overcoming Death

If we reduce the original mission and teaching of Jesus only to an apocalyptic proclamation of a messianic kingdom breaking into human history that is not yet complete, we might end up with only a partial interpretation of Jesus—He proclaims an urgent message with no real content. In other words, Jesus the apocalyptic prophet proclaims the end of history as we know it, but he has nothing to say about what happens afterward. Matthew 16:13–19 is an intriguing extension of Mark's affirmation that Jesus is the Messiah (see Mark 8:27–29; see also Luke 9:18–20). These include the content of Jesus' teaching. Translations of the passages offer several expressions: jaws of death, gates of hell, or the netherworld. Even so, they each indicate the power that rules this kingdom is the Hebrew Sheol or death. A "kingdom of death" in this case would be the best way to convey the original meaning intended by Matthew.

No one can offer a definitive reason for the existence of evil. On one level, the choice to do evil is precisely the choice to do something *un*reasonable, something stupid, and unexplainable, but when the Scriptures wrestle with this question, they do offer what might be termed a motive for evil. And the motive is death. The prospect of dying reduces everything that we have and know in this world. It tells us that nothing matters, that we are alone, that we ought to grab what we can while we are able.

The Scriptures proclaim that we do indeed matter, that God holds us in his infinite care, but when we fall short in our trust of God, we worship and give power to the idea of death. When we sacrifice the truth, personal integrity, our knowledge of right and wrong for the sake of personal advantage over others, we serve the kingdom of death. When we try to hide from the natural movement and passing of life itself with distractions, possessions, and frenzied activity, we are death's captives. With the image of a city or the kingdom of death, Jesus tries to describe the condition of people without faith.

In Matthew's narrative, Jesus explains this kingdom not only as the separate effect of death to our personal existence, but how our personal lack of faith interacts with everyone who is around us. If we try to live in faith, we are likely to be mocked and challenged not only by personal anxiety but also by the entire fabric of the games and avoidances established by society. "Who are you trying to fake with?" "Come on, everybody does it." The real monster is not a frightening sea beast but the ordinary messes caused by bad example, cowardice, apathy, self-absorption, and compromise that pull down even the best among us.

The Kingdom of Heaven

According to Matthew's report, the kingdom of death will not prevail. In the midst of life, Jesus has set up a rock, and on this rock he will build his own kingdom: a kingdom of faith in God, a faith that promises an eternal genesis for us.

We do not escape the ordeal of physical death, but we no longer need to live under its fear or gloomy shadow. We are able to discover that we are not alone in the universe. Our life is guaranteed. Instead of jealously guarding crumbs of merchandise that come into our possession, we can give thanks, break bread, and share what we have. We are reborn into God's family and are meant to be a source of hope in the world. The type of community that Jesus describes in this section of Matthew's Gospel will never be undone: it is God's work, and by his power and influential spirit it will endure always.

THE SERMON ON THE MOUNT (MATTHEW 5:1–7:28)

Matthew's version of the Sermon on the Mount is the central point of Jesus' teaching. It brings readers into contact with a Jesus who could be, depending on how we interpret the sermon, consoling or frightening. Several major interpretations have traditionally been offered about the sermon.

1. The first interpretation presents a severe Jesus. Every sentence of the sermon, for example, reads as a stern law. You *must* be poor in spirit, you *must* make peace, you *must*....

2. The second viewpoint presents a less demanding Jesus, but a didactic one all the same. Knowing full well that no one can live up to the ideals he presents, Jesus offers them to demonstrate how hopeless we are without God's favor, life, and grace. It seems in this interpretation that God wants to tone down all human boasting. In other words, you have to depend on God to avoid punishment for your sins.

3. Some claim that Matthew's frequent use of apocalyptic imagery coincides with the sermon's role as an interim ethical policy established by Jesus in anticipation of the immediate end of the world. Thus Matthew was calling for drastic measures to prepare people for the upcoming trial and judgment.

4. Another interpretation identifies the incompleteness of the Sermon on the Mount. Although it is filled with incredible directives, it is not a complete list of regulations for his disciples. What Jesus offers are symptoms, signs, and examples of what it means when the kingdom of heaven finally breaks into human history. The sermon thus describes the things people do as they gradually live as members of the kingdom. The person is changed. A simple way to see the point is to divide the sermon into two columns. The concluding phrases in one column describe the kingdom in traditional Jewish terms taken from the Hebrew prophets and faith. When God is in charge, there is care for people; there is consolation; there is a sense in people that they have ownership as God's heirs; there is mercy and sufficient food; there is recognition by God, and recognition or comprehension of God by people. In the other column are the opening phrases of the sermon. They describe those whose lives are drawn to serve God. A variety of conditions are listed: the lowly, the poor in spirit, the sorrowing, those who are trying and those who are single-minded, the persecuted, and those who work with the persecutors to make peace. In short, these types of people are often considered "losers." Change is perceived as difficult or impossible. They are never expected to be successful.

5. According to others, Jesus turns the two columns into one. He takes the people listed on one side (the opening phrases) and has them experiencing in themselves the signs of the kingdom of heaven. The lowly feel blessed. The poor in spirit actually feel as if they have ownership. Jesus demonstrates the power of God to transform the world into God's place. Down through the centuries, Christians sign themselves up in the first column and hope to further the signs of the kingdom that are in the second column. It is a strategy that makes sense. It is a hope based on Jesus' own example. But hope can be betrayed. If the Christian community is never seen to be lowly and poor and to be at work among the poor and lowly, hope will be betrayed. Matthew seems to have Jesus remind his church that a cozy, complacent community of believers will not convince others that God wants to transform them regardless of their status in life.

Several passages in Matthew encompass attitudes Jesus exhorts his followers to apply to their lives. Each is based on the Sermon on the Mount. In Matthew 18:3, Jesus says, "unless you change and become like children, you will never enter the kingdom of heaven." In verse 10, he says, "Take care that you do not despise one of these little ones…." And in Matthew 25:40, Jesus reminds his listeners, "[J]ust as you did it to one of the least of these who are members of my family, you did it to me."

Jesus' teaching is full of references to "little ones." He speaks figuratively. He does not mean children, but believers. Sometimes this is evident, such as in Matthew 10:42, where Jesus comments, "[W]hoever gives even a cup of cold water to one of these little ones in the name of a disciple." Other sayings are less obvious: "If any of you put a stumbling block before one of these little ones who believe in me, it would be better for you if a great millstone were hung around your neck and you were thrown into the sea" (Mark 9:42).

What qualities of childhood might Jesus have had in mind? In first-century Palestine the term *child* did not connote simplicity but insignificance. Historians point out that the idea of childhood as an ideal time of life is a modern fascination. The ancients understood childhood as fragile and incomplete.

THE BANQUET OF GOD

Despite the wishes of his disciples, Jesus directly contradicts the prevailing attitude of his time regarding status in society. Several instances in the Gospels show the disciples arguing over who was the greatest among them (see Mark 9:34) and who would have the most preferred seats at a banquet table (see Luke 14:10). Even when they prayed, disciples raised questions of who was the greatest among them (see Mark 12:39). In each case, Jesus sets himself against those mentalities. He never praises immaturity or weakness. He was not opposed to the development of personal gifts and talents, but he wanted his closest friends to be sober about their limits. Human strength is inadequate for the goals that really matter. No amount of shrewdness or power ensures our lives. Those who know that their lives are incomplete, who acknowledge that they rely on God alone, who agree to his rule over their lives, and seek to trust in God alone, will experience the banquet of life that God promises.

The association of the kingdom as a "banquet" is not only a symbol of unity and good times, but also a symbol of God himself. The banquet was a favorite image in the writings of Isaiah and was familiar to the Jewish people at the time of Jesus. "On this mountain the LORD of hosts will make for all peoples / a feast of rich food, a feast of well-aged wines" (Isaiah 25:6–9). In Isaiah's view, attention is focused on the host. A festive relationship with God need not wait until some distant point in time. If God is basically a generous host, people need to relate to God now in the same way. In Matthew 22:2ff, Jesus incorporates his appreciation of the banquet image in his practice of fellowship meals with his friends. The New Testament tells us that he ate with various types of Jews who normally would be excluded from table fellowship due to some type of ritual impurity: prostitutes, tax collectors, sinners. Under Jesus' inspiration, without his personal example, his later followers would extend such table fellowship to the gentiles.

In the wedding banquet parable, Jesus adds another insight: some people try to ruin banquets. They find excuses not to attend. They are too timid to celebrate with others. They think the host has something else on his agenda with his invitations. They have resentments. "But they [the invited guests] made light of it and went away, one to his farm, another to his business, while the rest seized his slaves, mistreated them, and killed them" (Matthew 22:5–6).

As if to destroy the image of the banquet he has built up, Matthew adds four verses (11–14) in which the king suddenly becomes ungracious. After inviting everyone in from the byroads, the king begins to worry about how people are dressed. Some commentators see this as a reference to early Christian ceremonies. Matthew's "many are called, but few are chosen" seems to be part of his anti-temple polemic. In this view, the invited guests would be those Jews who will not accept Jesus; the chosen represent the Christian community. The king in these verses points out that the Jews have missed the spirit of the messianic banquet.

THE VINEYARD

Another image associated with the banquet is wine. The wine harvest was probably the most joyous of Israel's agricultural feasts. The fullness of life is often associated in biblical references to a time when vats are overflowing, singing as the grapes are pressed. A vineyard was a special place. Other property might provide grazing for animals or grain for bread, but the extra effort devoted to caring for the vines would end in toasts at a wedding and celebrating God's goodness with family and friends.

The heady joy of the grapes was a frequent metaphor for a woman's love (read the Song of Solomon 8:11ff). Isaiah 5:1–7 would gain the immediate attention of listeners when he mentions a friend's efforts when the grapes produce nothing. The man undoes his vineyard and returns the land to raising grain. "What more was there to do for my vineyard / that I had not done?" (v. 4).

The disappointed friend in Isaiah's story is God, and the vineyard is Israel. Where are the grapes God desired? Isaiah seems to say that God has done all he can do for Israel. Now it is up to Israel to change its ways. By New Testament times the idea of Israel as God's vine had become well understood. When Jesus invoked the metaphor, it was an association he audience would not miss.

Yet Matthew's parable of the vineyard not only uses Isaiah's imagery, it revives it. Jesus fills it with fresh prophetic fire and a renewed challenge. God's choice of Israel demands a response. God's people are expected to be fruitful. The responsibility now falls on the Jewish people. They are the "vineyard" and their failure to yield grapes is what Jesus questions. Later, in John 15:1–8 we will see that Christ alone is the true vine, and the lives of his community are fruitful only to the extent that people live in full dependence on him. The ancient words of Psalm 80:14 are reversed, "Turn again, O God of hosts; / look down from heaven, and see; / have regard for this vine." God is no longer asked to change, but the followers of the risen Christ must live as if they are God's chosen vineyard, set aside, carefully planted, joining together in a banquet of love and forgiveness.

THE LORD'S PRAYER

Today Christians continue to pray Matthew's version of the Our Father in liturgy and private devotions. It is a memorized prayer. Scholars long ago identified Luke's version as closer to the Aramaic language Jesus spoke, but the preference for Matthew's form endures and has ancient testimonies to its use in the liturgy. For example, the *Didache* presents Matthew's version to converts shortly before their baptism and includes the famous doxology, "For Thine is the kingdom, the power, and the glory. Amen."

As we will see in the next chapter, Luke seems to avoid editing what he receives as the words of Jesus. His version preserves a personal more than a communal or liturgical style that Matthew seems to add to the prayer. A well-known guide used by some biblical analysts indicates that shorter versions include fewer editorial embellishments.

Even so, Matthew and Luke report that Jesus and his disciples prayed, but they never mention that Jesus asked his closest friends to memorize a specific prayer. In Matthew's case the Lord's Prayer, as it has been known in English since the Protestant Reformation, is included as part of the Sermon on the Mount and Jesus' warning not to call attention to themselves when they pray.

Scholars puzzle over the popularity of Matthew's version in Christian devotion and in the liturgy. It is a rich discussion. For our purposes, it is sufficient to be aware that the Gospel texts do not identify the words Jesus and his disciples used during the many occasions where they are found at prayer. Notes at the end of the chapter offer references for further study of the Lord's Prayer. Some elements of the prayer are worth noting as they demonstrate familiar themes developed by Matthew throughout his Gospel.

- Matthew begins his prayer with the expression *"Our Father, who art in heaven."* Luke simply states: *"Father."* Some scholars see Matthew's usage indicating a community prayer rather than a private or personal prayer. It resembles the prayer forms used in synagogues. The oldest English translation of the Lord's Prayer dates to the seventh century. Earlier Jerome translated the prayer into Latin. Tyndale offered a translation in the 1540s, during the reign of Henry VIII. The *King James* translation from the early 1600s retains several close translations from the Latin text.
- The next petition is *"hallowed be Thy name."* To *hallow* or to bless is familiar in Jewish prayer, where to honor God's name is well known in the Kaddish.
- *"Thy kingdom come."* The petition is a familiar apocalyptic hope for the completion of God's new age on earth.
- *"Thy will be done, on earth as it is in heaven."* This phrase is not included by Luke but is a request of God to bring about his much-expected kingdom on earth.
- *"Give us this day our daily bread."* The "daily bread" may refer to Exodus 16:15ff when God provided the manna for the starving Israelites wandering in the desert. It was thought by some contemporaries of Jesus that the "age to come" would include bread and no starvation, an endless banquet. This is a request to share in that kingdom's bread. The age of the kingdom would be a renewed time on earth free of dread and famine.

- *"And forgive us our trespasses as we forgive those who trespass against us."* The *King James* translation follows Jerome's text closely as uses the words "debts and debtors." Curiously Roman Catholics follow Origen's use of the Greek word *paraptomata,* which translates into English as "trespass" or "faults." The role of forgiveness is given added importance as a condition or sign that his followers will be forgiven by God based on the way we forgive those who have wronged us.
- *"And lead us not into temptation; but deliver us from evil."* It was thought when the kingdom dawned and the "servant of God" arrived, there would be a time of trial and testing of God's people. The prayer concludes with a somber expectation of a time to come that will be noteworthy for its difficulties and burdens as the kingdom break into human history.

REVIEW QUESTIONS

1. List several characteristics of Matthew's Gospel narrative.
2. How does Matthew demonstrate that Jesus is the fulfillment of Old Testament prophecies?
3. Explain Matthew's parables of the kingdom as a banquet and a vineyard.
4. Explain Matthew's version of the Lord's Prayer.

FOR FURTHER STUDY

1. Brown, Raymond. *An Introduction to the New Testament* (New York: Doubleday, 1996), especially chapter 8, "The Gospel According to Matthew," pp. 171–223.
2. Olmstead, Wesley G. *Matthew's Trilogy of Parables: The Nation, the Nations and the Reader in Matthew 21:28—22:14* (Society for New Testament Studies Monograph Series, No. 127; New York: Cambridge University Press, 2004). Olmstead uses redaction criticism to examine three parables in Matthew. This is a short and excellent summary of the parable form and its use by Matthew the redactor.
3. Origen, "Commentary on Matthew," trans. Roberts-Donaldson. Available at http://www.earlychristianwritings.com/text/origen-matthew.html
4. Wainwright, E. M. *Toward a Feminist Reading of the Gospel According to Matthew* (Berlin: de Gruyter, 1991).
5. The Lord's Prayer is analyzed thoroughly by Joachim Jeremias in *The Prayers of Jesus* (London: SCM, 1967). See also Brown, pp. 180ff.
6. Senior, Donald. *The Gospel of Matthew* (Interpreting Biblical Texts Series; Nashville, TN: Abingdon Press, 1997). Senior offers seven chapters in which he summarizes contemporary biblical scholarship on Matthean themes. He is ecumenical and readable.

7. Clarke, Howard W. *The Gospel of Matthew and Its Readers: A Historical Introduction to the First Gospel* (Bloomington, IN: University of Indiana Press, 2003). Clarke reviews contemporary scholarship views of Matthew and then traces the use of Matthew's Gospel across the centuries by believers and those who use Matthew to leave the church. This book will tease anyone interested in history.

8. Aune, David E., ed. *The Gospel of Matthew in Current Study* (Grand Rapids, MI: Eerdmans, 2001). Several scholars tackle thorny contemporary questions using Matthew to light a pathway to resolve them.

9. Luz, Ultrich. *Studies in Matthew.* Translated by Rosemary Selle. (Grand Rapids, MI: Eerdmans, 2005). More than a dozen essays in which Luz sees Matthew's original community familiar with the teachings of Mark and special sayings of Jesus from what is termed the Q source of sayings. To Luz, the Matthean community must reorient itself because of new crises. Luz includes essays on Matthew's ecclesiology.

8

The Gospel According to Luke

Special Elements in Luke's Account

1. Unlike Matthew's infancy narrative in which Joseph's perspective is emphasized, Luke relates material in which Mary is the "favored one" and full of grace ("The Lord is with you" (Luke 1:28). Mary and Elizabeth rejoice in God's mysterious ways (see Luke 1:39-49). Luke presents Mary as a spokesperson for the poor of Israel (Luke 1:46ff). Mary grows in faith and guides readers to the birth of John the Baptist (see Luke 2:50).

2. Luke places the birth of the church community at Pentecost. John's Gospel places it at Calvary. For Luke, Mary is in the Jerusalem community as a true believer and first disciple (see Luke 1:12ff).

3. Luke reports his narrative is an orderly account completed after reviewing available sources (see Luke 1:1-4). He addresses his work to Theophilus, whose identity is unknown. The name is translated "friend of God" and may symbolize the Christian reader, an influential gentile convert, or refer to those who show interest in the teachings of Christ. The name is never repeated by Luke.

4. Luke reports events in the childhood of John the Baptist and Jesus. He continues stories about children in the body of the narrative (see Luke 7:12; 8:42; 9:38).

5. Jesus is at prayer throughout the narrative (see Luke 3:21; 5:15-16; 6:12-13; 9:18, 9:29; 10:21-22; 11:1-13; 22:39-46ff).

6. Unlike Matthew, Luke avoids citing Hebrew prophecies as fulfilled in Jesus. Jesus is the prophet of God and the power of the Holy Spirit is in Jesus throughout his ministry (see Luke 9:30ff).

7. Jesus speaks in Nazareth but includes Gentiles in his message (see Luke 4:14ff). Jesus speaks kindly of Samaritans (see Luke 10:29-37; 17:11-19).

8. The role of women as disciples and believers throughout Jesus' life is emphasized by Luke (see Luke 8:1ff; 10:38ff; 18:1ff; 21:1ff; 23:27ff; 24:1ff).

9. Money and wealth occupy special parables and sayings from Jesus; God forgives and is merciful (see Luke 3:12-13; 4:17-19; 6:20, 24; 9:25; 10:35; 17:19-31).
10. The city of Jerusalem is the special focus of preparations for the death narrative of Jesus.
11. The resurrection appearances occur in or near Jerusalem, not Galilee.
12. Luke presents Jesus as concerned with misfits and outcasts (see Luke 7:1-10, 13-17, 22-23, 36-50). The special Spirit of Jesus is available now in all who form a prophetic, Spirit-filled community of faith. The age of the Church is led by God's spirit and this community is the new people of God.

Luke's world was completely distinct from Roman-occupied Palestine. He was possibly a companion mentioned by Paul, an educated Hellenist, perhaps a physician (see Colossians 4:14). The perspective in his writings reflects a breadth of interests and humanity you would expect from a cosmopolitan person. His Gospel is the first part of a two-volume work completed in The Acts of the Apostles. A separation of the volumes is referred to by Papias during the second century, but the reason for the separation remains unknown. Even so, the greatest numbers of passages in the canonical New Testament are from Luke. As a result, his theology is more available for analysis than any of the other biblical writers.

After presenting the life of Christianity's founder, Luke continues in The Acts of the Apostles to tell how the new faith movement spread from the city of Jerusalem "[to] all Judea and Samaria, and to the ends of the earth" (see Acts 1:8). His account ends with Paul preaching the Gospel in the capital city of imperial Rome: "proclaiming the kingdom of God and teaching about the Lord Jesus Christ with all boldness and without hindrance" (Acts 28:31). The date of composition is thought to be after the fall of Jerusalem in 70 and no later than 85.

SOURCES

Luke's cultural background is revealed in his sensibilities. He is sensitive to the nuances of the relationships between Jesus and his disciples, to the compassion Jesus exhibits for the poor and suffering. It is Luke who depicts kindness as Jesus' motivation to seek out the lost and sinners. He uses the wording found in a number of his sources, including the Gospel of Mark, the Q source of sayings, and other stories. Luke seems to follow Mark's outline and avoids adjustments to the sayings of Jesus. This is evident in his version of the Lord's Prayer. The Aramaic word order used by Jesus is easily reconstructed from Luke's Greek text. In other places, he simply inserts material into Mark's outline from the

Q source of sayings. Luke almost makes it appears as if Mark overlooked or was unaware of the special source.

FOCUS ON THE MARGINALIZED

More than the other evangelists, Luke includes stories involving people in the margins. He is most noted for his inclusion of women. His sensitivity is particularly attractive for modern readers. Contemporary feminist scholars, for example, have evaluated in depth Luke's first-century opinion of women as believers, disciples, and credible preachers of the resurrection. Luke's sensitivity for the marginalized is found with Luke's inclusion of the Samaritans, the remnant of the old northern kingdom. First-century Palestinian Jews despised the Samaritans. Luke's Jesus despises no one. Luke depicts the last days of Jesus in a distinctive way. As noted earlier, he softens some of the horror and violence found in the passion narrative of Matthew. Instead, he emphasizes Jesus' nobility and compassion for others throughout his final ordeal.

JESUS AT PRAYER

Jesus at prayer is noted often by Luke. The evangelist is familiar with Palestinian Jewish practices and locations, and, at times, supplies extra information for his Hellenist readers. He seems to have a deep appreciation for the table fellowship of the Christian community, and a view that the risen Christ continues to be present in the breaking of the bread. Among the stories Luke relates are a few found only in his Gospel, including angels predicting the births of John the Baptist and Jesus, the parable of the Prodigal Son, the way of the cross, and the resurrection appearance on the road to Emmaus.

THE KINGDOM OF GOD

With Luke we have come a long way from the earliest Jerusalem community, who thought that Jesus' resurrection was the "first fruits" of what would prove him to be the messiah when he returned in glory. Luke is definite that the time of the coming reign or kingdom of God is indefinite. He differs from Mark on this point. Luke sometimes omits the urgent phrase "the kingdom of God is at hand." He prefers to say Jesus "sent them to proclaim the kingdom of God and to heal the sick" (see Luke 9:1–6 and compare the passage with Matthew 10:5–15 and Mark 6:7–13). Luke extends expressions concerning false prophets who will rise up and predicts a longer interlude until the final end of the age (compare Luke 21:7–24; Matthew 24:3–28; and Mark 13:3–23).

If Mark presents a Gospel of encouragement to disciples during their final sufferings before the kingdom's arrival, and Matthew offers a reinterpretation of Judaism that is necessary to enter the kingdom when it arrives, it is Luke who comes to terms with the fact that the church community will continue for a long time in history before the last days begin. He emphasizes the church's task in the world, the daily demands of discipleship, and the serenity and joy that even now can be known through knowledge of Jesus and the power of his Holy Spirit. (See the table for a list of the divisions in Luke's writings illustrating his continuous story.)

Divisions in Luke's Scripture Writings

The Gospel According to Luke	Scripture Section
Introduction or prologue	1:1–4
Infancy narrative	1:5—2:52
Ministry preparations	3:1—4:13
Ministry in Galilee	4:14—9:50
Moving to Jerusalem	9:51—19:27
Teaching in Jerusalem	19:28—21:38
The passion of Jesus	22:1—23:56
The resurrection	24:1–53
The Acts of the Apostles	
Spirit and community mission	1:1—2:13
The community in Jerusalem	2:14—8:3
The community mission to Judea and Samaria	8:4—9:43
The community and gentile mission	10:1—15:35
The mission to the world	15:36—28:31

SALVATION HISTORY

It is the historical trajectory and universal impact of the Jesus event that gives Luke's narrative its special character. Unlike the urgent, apocalyptic messenger Jesus is in Mark, or the deliverer of final commandments or covenant as in Matthew, the arrival of Luke's Jesus reconnects to the creation of the world and to Adam. Luke moves across the history of Israel, to the life of Jesus, and then comments on the global spread of the first Christian community after Pentecost. The community ends with a new central location in Rome when Paul, the apostle to the gentiles and the world, arrives in the capital. For Luke, the history of the world has a new horizon in Christ, the Divine Son, who provides a new spirit for people. It is the same spirit who is in the center as the new community organizes, and the church community will endure for all times.

The Holy Spirit and Salvation History

Luke is known by some as the "Gospel of the Holy Spirit." He extends the activity of the spirit backward to some of Jesus' ancestors and relatives. In his infancy narrative, we see that the spirit of God is involved in the announcement of the birth of John the Baptist (see Luke 1:15–17). The same spirit "overshadows" the mother of Jesus (Luke 1:35), and it inspires the old man Simeon in the Jerusalem temple to prophesy the child's destiny as the messiah and "light for revelation to the Gentiles" (Luke 2:25–32). The spirit of God descends on Jesus at his baptism by John (see Luke 3:22) and even leads him out into the wilderness to be tempted (see Luke 4:1–13). The devil disappears from Luke's account until near the end of the story when it "entered into Judas" (Luke 22:3). Jesus returns to Galilee and begins his teaching ministry, and it is the same spirit in the Nazareth synagogue he invokes: "The spirit of the Lord is upon me…" (Luke 4:18–19).

Hymns and Salvation History

So, too, Luke uses themes from Mark and extends them into an account of Jesus' mission that envisions everyone in the world. He adds a number of hymns and narratives to the beginning and end of his accounts. Some of these stories are now deeply embedded in Christian imagination, such as what happened on the road from Jerusalem to Emmaus (see Luke 24:13–35). The Christian liturgy came to include one of his hymns, Mary's Magnificat (see Luke 1:46–55), as a favorite devotion.

The Temple and Salvation History

The background for each narrative in Luke often includes the Temple at Jerusalem. Priests, sacrifices, and worship customs are mentioned. For Luke, the Jerusalem Temple is the most appropriate place for these historic episodes to take place. All the promises to Abraham and their ancestors about the covenant and the salvation of Israel find their fulfillment in Luke's Temple episodes. The story of Abraham, Israel's long history, the Temple, and the city of Jerusalem remains God's story. John and Jesus are linked to them by Luke and connect neatly the Christian revelation, mission, and interpretation of history as other episodes in the story of Israel. For Luke, it is one glorious history of God's interactions with humankind.

Organizing the Narratives According to Salvation History

Luke had to do some editing to connect all of this with the outline he received from Mark. The narrative of John's beheading by Herod, for example, does not fit with Luke's sensibilities. He omits the story. The same is true with the narratives near the end of his Gospel. Jerusalem remains central to the story until forty days after the resurrection at Pentecost. Luke had warned of the eventual replacement of Jerusalem as the center of God's activity (see Luke 19:41–44). When the resurrection takes place, Christ appears in Jerusalem only twice before he leaves, without fanfare, and is "carried up into heaven" (Luke 24:51). As a result, the history of the world has changed. A new community with apostles, Scriptures, the Spirit, salvation for all, and worship centering on baptism and community table fellowship has begun. These are the elements that will define the new church community.

The apostles were passing from history by the time Luke wrote. Luke includes a number of sermons in The Acts of the Apostles, as we have seen earlier, that offer an explanation for the final separation of the movement from Judaism. For Luke, certain developments in each group foster the separation, but Luke continues to associate the prophetic life of Jesus with the promises made long ago by Israel's prophets.

THE BIRTH OF JESUS

Luke includes several special themes in his narratives of the birth of Jesus and resurrection appearances. His additions are more elaborate than those of Matthew. The role of John the Baptist is nuanced in Luke's account, especially compared with those of Mark and Matthew. For Luke, the birth of John is linked to the life of Jesus. Linking events from the Jewish covenant to the new covenant of the Christians is a pattern Luke follows throughout his compositions. For instance, the angel Gabriel gives an auspicious announcement for the upcoming births of John and later Jesus. Luke understands each birth to be a miraculous intervention by God. Each mother responds with initial disbelief, then prayer and awe. The angel explains the significance of each child's life before they are born. This foretelling is accepted by the parents and others with songs of praise to God. John the Baptist will prepare the people for Jesus with a power that resembles the prophet Elijah, who turned people from "the disobedient to the wisdom of the righteous" Luke 1:17). He will "prepare his [the Lord's] ways" (Luke 1:76–79). Jesus is the "son of the Most High" God (1:32), a "mighty savior" (1:69), and "a light for revelation to the Gentiles" (2:32). Males are circumcised according to the Law of Moses and are named as directed or commanded by the angel.

It is unclear why Luke's account of the birth of Jesus remains popular today. In some Christian churches it is the Lucan narrative that is read at worship services on Christmas. The secular environment has eliminated successfully most references to the transcendent. The birth of Christ, the mythic saga of Santa Claus, and winter holiday themes are harmonized into handy props for advertisements urging year-end shopping sprees and seasonal reunions. Whatever the religious significance of Christmas might be, if noted at all, is thought to be a bothersome undertone to festivities. Human ingenuity, among other things, has been at work to accomplish this reality today as it has been known throughout history. For instance, Francis of Assisi combined the narratives of Luke and Matthew into a single Christmas scene for followers in the city of Greccio, Italy, in the thirteenth century. His Christmas depiction gained widespread popularity throughout medieval Europe. The cloying sentimentality well known in contemporary celebrations would not have been denounced by Luke if he wrote today. Instead, Luke would try to reinterpret it.

For little children, Christmas need no proofs, no heady explanations. They simply believe. A mystical being will defy the laws of physics and common sense and shower the planet with gifts.

Some adults find the story and the season something less than sublime. Too exhausted to reject out loud the tidings of great joy, they sit spiritless and annoyed. So much in this season seems a bothersome interruption of real life—a season that is best endured and survived. Those who in principle reject fantasy and illusion inevitably end up having fantastic illusions about themselves.

Christmas is a season of stories of generosity and love. A child believes an energetic old man will enter and exit as he pleases. The only clue of his visit is what he leaves behind. Children know full well that they do not deserve gifts; gifts are by definition undeserved. They also know that gifts are not equal. The friend next door always seem to receive something more interesting, but the white-bearded, jolly gent remains blithely impartial. Faults and mistakes are easily forgiven. Although he knows no favorites, he prefers the company of the generous and the good and all who consider themselves young at heart.

A number of parallels to the birth of Jesus are embodied in a child's story, and many children find the transition from belief in him to belief in the Bethlehem story an easy one.

According to Luke, the birth of Jesus surprised everyone. He came to humanity and not vice versa. The news of his birth was announced to ordinary, lowly types whom the rest of society often overlooks. He did not have to come; his motive was a gift of love. Everything since his birth is a potential repeat performance as he returns to visit God's children offering the gift of his spirit.

Adults might need the story more than children; it keeps us honest. It is a story that reminds us that Christ must be born in us before he can rise in us; that his love given so liberally is in fact the surprising gift of eternal youth. In celebrating his birthday we admit to all the unexpected surprises that love brings into our lives.

When the Christmas carols strike up, we may find ourselves fidgeting a bit, but we never walk out. For in them and in this story we see and hear ourselves, and not just in the sense that through them we remember Christmas past, but in the more profound sense that the Bethlehem story explains the meaning of our own life.

If that view of the Christmas message seems too rosy, remember that it was not pleasant to be without shelter in the night, to have no place to give birth. The stable was smelly and Joseph was worried. But the story says even such grubby realities are always surrounded by light. Even the heartaches, sorrows, loneliness, and injustices we experience or know so well will be transformed.

Celebrating Christmas is not evading reality—much less denying life's messiness—but seeing reality fully. Each year we find ourselves standing before the Bethlehem scene. Held at first by our parents, now years later we stand with our own loved ones and children. Perhaps, we stand alone. Although the scene never changes, we do. And its annual message along the pilgrimage of life is a reminder that we do not roam this world all alone. One night God's Son was born to help us come to understand that we are made in an everlasting way. And when we return again to everyday life, from which we have been seemingly distracted, we may begin to recognize in more mature ways that it is the whole of life that is holy.

INFLUENCE OF GREEK CULTURE ON LUKE

Luke was familiar with the pantheon of Greek divinities. Part of the cultural matrix in which Christianity flourished included Greek polytheism. A short review of the Greek deities and other mystery religions in Luke's time is worthwhile as it forms part of the cultural environment Luke's community and other early Christian communities shared.

Greek Gods

Zeus, who was called Jupiter by the Romans, was the chief Olympian god. He was associated with daylight and destroying his enemies with thunderbolts. His brother, Poseidon, had dominion over the sea and earthquakes. Zeus' other brother, Hades, was known as lord of the underworld and the dead. Zeus had a sister, Demeter, who promoted agricultural fertility and stability of households. Zeus' oldest child, Athene, was honored as the goddess of wisdom. The myth of her creation includes the story of her emerging from Zeus' head. Zeus was Apollo's father. Apollo was the god of self-discipline, good health, and protector of wildlife. Hermes, another of Zeus' children, was the messenger of the gods. Hermes also guided souls to the underworld. Ares was the god of war, while Aphrodite personified beauty and sexual allure. Dionysus was the god of wine and ecstasy.

Dionysus was born a mortal, underwent sufferings, a violent death, and became immortal. The myth of Dionysus predates the Christian movement yet includes parallels to a number of themes emphasized in Luke's theological accounts of Christ. Dionysus has divinities for parents. He suffers a violent death, descends into the underworld, and rises to immortal life and sits near the eternal throne of his father Zeus.

Greek Philosophy

Greek philosophy offered other explanations of forces at work in human life and destiny. Philosophers analyzed observable facts and tried to understand human life and its position in the universe. Plato taught that the human body belongs to two worlds. The "material" portion of our body was believed to change, decay, and die. The unseen spirit world of the eternal and immortal, on the other hand, existed forever in another realm of existence known only by educated humans. Thus education was supposed to help some individuals to understand that the spirit, mind, or soul was superior to bodily limitations. The practice of the virtues was meant to prepare the soul for immortality. Virtues needed to be embraced and were supposed to help the individual and society function.

A belief that reason was the divine principle of the universe characterized Stoic philosophy. A universal mind was considered to be the principle of unity for the world and was intelligible to the human intellect. Stoic teachings emphasized that a person must listen to the inner divine element so that the body and mind could achieve harmony with nature and the universe. One belief emphasized that a true practitioner of Stoicism would be able to endure personal loss or gain without emotion.

Epicureans, on the other hand, believed that the world was physical or material but that all is dissolved into nothingness after death. According to their philosophy, people should create their own purpose in life because the divinities that exist have no interest in the fate of humans. Epicureans believed that mental delights last longer than bodily ones. Epicureans advocate the use of reason to find intellectual pleasures and to live well.

These Hellenistic and philosophical resources, in various forms, were familiar to Luke and his Greek audience. By Luke's time, Palestinian Judaism had been thoroughly reshaped by Greek culture. The Jewish people lived as participants in Jewish and Greek cultures, yet a more thoroughly Greek world was the cultural home of Luke's Christians. They expected philosophies to engage and interpret the fortunes and horrors of everyday life. It would have been as unimaginable for them to understand a God who could be killed as it would be for Jesus' Palestinian contemporaries to understand how God's

Messiah could be captured and eliminated. Luke provides interpretations of Jesus for these cosmopolitan Greek Christians. In Acts 17, Luke has Paul on Mars Hill in Athens speaking with Epicureans and Stoics, yet Paul and Luke never endorse the adequacy of Greek worship or philosophy; Luke is decidedly a more cosmopolitan Hellenist than someone indebted to or limited by a Palestinian Jewish outlook.

LUKE'S USE OF ANCIENT IMAGERY

A number of the ancient images found in Luke, as well as in the other Gospels, fail to have any immediate power for contemporary audiences. A few examples illustrate the point. Remember the Noah story (Genesis 9:8–15)? There are several contradictions and anthropomorphisms that fill the legend of the great flood. The fundamental message of God's love for his creation is symbolized in the image of the rainbow. The rainbow announces like an angel God's peace after the storm. My family had a home on Maui for a number of years, and I have seen many rainbows. I wonder about people who have never seen one. Even so, rainbows have a scientific explanation that is more satisfying than the promise mentioned in Genesis.

So, too, there is an archaic, fragmentary myth included in Genesis 6:1–4 about supernatural beings that lived with earth's women and produced giant offspring. The reader is expected to know these "powers" (also called angels, dominations, and spirits of the air). They are referred to in Ephesians 6:12 and 1 Corinthians 15:24. An ancient legend explains that these powers were no longer able to return to the high heavens and were trapped around the earth, where they continue to cause endless problems and anxieties for people to this day. If we think of the troubles that scare us to death, and then imagine them personified as spirits roaming the world, we would begin to know what a first-century audience felt. For certain, the New Testament's announcement of faith in Jesus Christ includes the message that he has subjected all these "powers and rulers" to himself. And his followers no longer need to fear them. "All things work together for [the] good" (Romans 8:28). Yet talk of the demonic and spiritual forces at work in the world, in many circles, sounds medieval and mythic.

Luke explains that Jesus is tempted in the wilderness before the outset of his adult ministry. Mark's version is short: "And the Spirit immediately drove him out into the wilderness. He was in the wilderness forty days, tempted by Satan; and he was with the wild beasts; and the angels waited on him" (Mark 1:12–13). Luke has Jesus "full of the Holy Spirit" and "led by the Spirit" for forty days (Luke 4:1–2).

One reason we might not feel the power of these images is our distance from the biblical world. A Jewish audience would have been reminded by the desert image of Israel's forty years of testing in the wilderness, and of heroes, like Elijah (1 Kings 19:8), who passed forty days in the desert. They knew passages such as Isaiah 11:6–9 and Psalm 91:11–13 in which wild beasts surround human life.

Wild Beasts

Another reason is the contemporary tendency to be too literal. Passages such as the ones mentioned above, more than most, demand an ability and willingness to explore personal imagination and experience. We have to become aware of our own poetic side, the "wasteland," our "wild beasts," and "angels." The wild animals in these passages are not only the literal ones such as jackals and snakes found in the Palestinian desert; they also live in the shadows and corners of our lives. Like the "powers of the air," they represent the dark side of nature; someone's else's anger, perhaps, or my own. The witches and monsters we feared as children are now the terrorists, bombs, chaos, and poverty lurking in our time. They exist and have power over us, at least, in our imaginations. The New Testament suggests that we face, like Jesus, many shadows in life that terrify us. It is possible to come to peace with them, face them, and recognize that in the end they too will give glory to God.

Prophet

A second image used by Luke, and the other evangelists, is prophet. According to Luke, prophet is a concept that Jesus sometimes used about himself or to explain his mission. His usage is usually in circumstances where Jesus met rejection and the threat of death. Jeremiah, the prophet, said long before, "They will fight against you" (Jeremiah 1:19). The vocation of a prophet inevitably includes threats and opposition from the people God sends the prophet to serve. Sometimes the prophet faces death, as Isaiah chapter 53 suggests. By the time of Jesus the fate of prophets had become well known. According to Luke, the people of Nazareth, his relatives, and closest associates become indignant.

Why do prophets provoke such hostility? Why is it that "no prophet is without honor except in his native place"? (Luke 4:14–30 is his narrative of Jesus' rejection in Nazareth. This explains for Luke why Jesus spent most of his ministry in Capernaum. Mark 6:1–6 and Matthew 13:54–58 have an equivalent story much later in the ministry of Jesus. Luke differs from them by not mentioning Jesus' rejection by family or household members. Luke prefers to emphasize the rage of the crowd goes beyond what they indicate and seems to justify Jesus going to outsiders to preach his message.) First, prophets are often peculiar, angular, and uncomfortable people. People who, especially in the

Old Testament, deal with them sometimes have reason to think that God had nothing to do with their selection. Second, the prophets invite people to experience the uncomfortable process of conversion, to hear more truths than they care to hear, and to be more responsive and generous than they ever thought necessary. Third, even if most people know change is necessary, few are totally prepared to do it. They want to keep change within manageable limits. They are not disinterested in their neighbors' needs, but they do not want to have sole responsibility to fulfill them. We want to be honest, courageous, forgiving, and so forth, and we like to excuse ourselves by saying "we're only human." In other words, even if we avoid admitting it, we have a mixed response to God. We recognize God, worship God, we want God somewhere in our lives, but at the same time God terrifies us. A New York rabbi friend uses an ancient interpretation, likely from the Talmud, to explain it: God is like a blazing fire that may keep us warm as long as we keep a careful distance. And the reason why prophets arouse fierce reactions is that they push us toward the fire.

There are other ways to encourage people to be aware of God and his followers without making everyone angry, but the role of the biblical prophet includes disturbing the ordinary mindset. A biblical prophet reminds people of their shortcomings or points to something more than needs to be accomplished. Biblical prophets love their people, but they feel that the truth, as they understand it, must be spoken. If a prophet simply congratulates and reassures others, they do not fulfill the biblical version of prophecy. "It shall be well with you" is the mark of a false prophet (Jeremiah 23:17).

LOVING OUR NEIGHBOR

Jesus, as presented by Luke, challenges his listeners. One way in which he accomplishes this is to emphasize how Jesus wishes his followers to treat one another and strangers. In other words, there is much in Luke's account that relates to the meaning of "neighbor." I do not recall when or where I heard the following story, but it captures in contemporary language one of Luke's themes.

An elderly man collapsed on the sidewalk of a city street corner. The man was rushed to a hospital where he was diagnosed in grave condition. From a barely legible envelope in his wallet, a nurse was able to read the name and address of a soldier stationed out of state who appeared to be the patient's son. The soldier was contacted and eventually arrived at the hospital. The elderly man was heavily sedated, but responded when told that his son had arrived. The old man reached out his hand, and the soldier took it and held it for the next few hours. As dawn began the old man died. "Who was this man?" the soldier asked a nurse. "Wasn't he

*your father?" she answered with surprise. "No," he said, "I saw that he
needed a son, so I sat with him."*

Something as personal as the title "son" sometimes ought to be borrowed in
the name of compassion. A parallel to the story line is found in Luke's famous
account of the Good Samaritan (see 10:25–37).

The Good Samaritan

The parable of the Good Samaritan is one of the most enigmatic in the Gospels.
There is an unexplained shift in the story line. At first it appears that the story
is about "a certain man" who was beaten and ended up by a roadside where
several people pass him by. The reader spontaneously identifies with a wounded
man. First rejected by a priest and a Levite, along comes a Samaritan, and by
the end the Samaritan becomes the protagonist. He is the one with whom we
are led to identify: "Go and do the same."

Along with the above there is an adjustment in the meaning of the word
neighbor. When the story begins, *neighbor* is understood to mean those people
the reader ordinarily understands to be people one is obliged to love. But it
ends, "Which of these…was a neighbor to the man who fell into the hands of
the robbers?" (v. 36). *Neighbor* is now transferred to the one who offers love,
not one who receives it.

The plot is further complicated by the identities of the three men who pass
by. If the point of the story was to recommend the actions of the third man,
would it have been simpler to leave them anonymous? The fact that they are
identified suggests further definitions of neighbor.

The first to pass by are a priest and a Levite, both members of the special
families who served at the Jerusalem Temple. Is their appearance and reaction
a lesson in anti-establishment commentary? The first two were required by the
Law of Moses to maintain a strict ritual purity, which included avoidance of
contact with the dead. Is this parable a warning to those who are professionally religious, telling them to avoid confusing ritualism and the promptings
of basic humanity? The next to pass by, the Samaritan, suddenly becomes the
lead character in the story. If he were an ordinary Jew, the story would contrast
two hard-hearted professionally religious people with the kindness of an ordinary Jewish person. But Samaritans were outcasts. Jewish in origin, they were
despised by all Jews. Something is being said in the story about moving across
boundaries of race, class, and natural repulsions (in addition to Luke 17:11–19,
see Luke 10:30–37; Acts 10:9–2; 15:5–21; and John 4:1–42).

There is a historical reference that helps to identify the way Luke understands events unfolding in his time. The two Temple clerics represent the Temple

establishment. They reject Jesus' message and have seen their Temple destroyed by the Romans in 70. They have suffered the punishment for their hardness of heart. On the other hand, the role of the Samaritan suggests a special success the Christian preachers found among the Samaritans. It is clear that Samaria holds a special place in Luke's mind, especially from the structure of his second volume (see Acts 1:8).

At least one commentator understands that the Samaritan symbolizes Luke's attitude toward the Law of Moses. The entire parable is offered to answer the question of how to correctly interpret the Law of Moses. This would suggest a question similar to the one raised by Paul: Must members of the new Way obey the Torah? Luke's answer is the same one Paul expresses in Galatians 5:14, "For the whole law is summed up in a single commandment, 'You shall love your neighbor as yourself.'"

There is certainly some emphasis by the lawyer who provoked the parable to attempt to limit the obligation. He prefers a definition of *neighbor* that will set aside some people as having a particular claim on his love and obligations, while others have no such claim. This is also the attitude Paul observed in the Pharisees. It is the desire for a limited number of requirements for a person to fulfill and then have the outlook of having pleased God. The law Christ lays down, according to Luke and Paul, is never fully satisfied. Followers of Christ can never care enough for those who are in need. God's love is not earned.

The central message is not obscure. The passage opens with a lawyer's question to Jesus: "What must I do to inherit eternal life [be saved]?" It ends with Jesus' answer: "Go and do likewise" as the one who showed mercy. The passage consists of an instruction and a parable. Both are given by Jesus to a lawyer who asks, "Teacher, what must I do to inherit everlasting life?" Jesus then asks what is written in the Law of Moses, and how does he understand it. The lawyer responds with a passage from Deuteronomy 6:5 and Leviticus 19:18, which joins the command to love the Lord with one's entire being and the command to love one's neighbor as oneself.

The lawyer is commended for his answer by Jesus, but because he wished to "justify himself," the lawyer asks, "And who is my neighbor?" (v. 29). Then Jesus responds with the parable of the Good Samaritan. It is a story that was once so familiar it needs no retelling or further analysis, yet circumstances today have changed and many do not recall the outline of the story. A passage in the Book of Deuteronomy suggests that people would do well to stop analyzing such lessons and start *living* them. In Deuteronomy 30:10–14, Moses gives his farewell or last testament. He tells the Israelites that the command he has offered them is "not too hard for you, not is it too far away" (v. 11). Rather, it is something near to them, already present in their hearts. "You only have to carry it out," he says (see Galatians 5:14; 6:9–10; see also Matthew 5:43–48; 22:34–39; Mark 12:28–31; and James 2:8–9; 2:14–17).

Moses' blunt advice to the Israelites might resemble Jesus' reaction to the lawyer's second question. Jesus tried to adjust and modify in some ways the commandments, but the lawyer tries to pick apart the language of the relationship between people and God, and Jesus will have none of it. In other words, he tells the lawyer, "Stop tearing people apart into groups of neighbors and foreigners; instead, start to act like a neighbor to everyone."

The parable of the Good Samaritan invites the lawyer and every reader to put themselves into the shoes of the man attacked on the road. The soldier who held the dying man's hand knew that life is too short to avoid an opportunity to comfort someone near the end of life and so much in need. The world is too small for people not to treat others they meet as neighbors.

When the lawyer recognizes the neighbor as the one who treats the victim with compassion, he recognizes that his prejudices do not disprove what his experience knows to be true. What matters most to Jesus, as described by Luke, is not *being* a neighbor but *acting* like one.

Psychologists have names for people who think that they are obligated to take care of everyone who needs them: messiah complex is one. You may have heard of others. If you try to live that way, you may lose your mind. I wonder what the Good Samaritan would have done if he had come upon a second man lying by the roadside, or a third, or a fourth. Of course, there are people who rise to meet the complex challenges and human needs that seem to surround us. The more basic question is "Does God requires this of all of us?" Identifying one's neighbor was a serious challenge for anyone eager about religion, eager to do the will of God, which meant obeying the Law of Moses. The lawyer wanted to know who his neighbor was because if the Torah said he was supposed to care for him, then that is exactly what he would attempt to accomplish. According to this view, the heart of the human relationship with God is obedience to God's instructions. In plain English, a person with this kind of mentality might demand: "Tell me what to do so I may obey."

Jesus never answers the question. In fact, as we have seen, he ends by turning and asking the same question. The man knows the answer, and this is the central point of the passage.

For the most part, Jesus did not teach or offer new rules or a list of stringent ethical standards. The Jewish people were in no need of more laws; they had plenty in their tradition. The Law articulated in the passage is stated by the Pharisee. He quotes the Old Testament. What Jesus tried to teach was an attitude toward rules and the laws of God. Commentators speak of it as a change of heart, a conversion. Jesus does not spell out what the details of conversion entail. He invites people to discover a new motive or power for behavior: discovering the love God has for us. Jesus leaves it to his listeners to figure out how best to live it out.

Biblical passages such as the Good Samaritan and the Sermon on the Mount provide no precise stipulations to be fulfilled. Instead, they give illustrations of certain types of concern and orientation. To answer the question about what exactly God expects of us is simply a call to discover God's love and then try, with all our hearts, to share it. We are not infinite, we cannot take on every problem, but we can be attentive and thoughtful to those who fill our corner of the cosmos.

Some people object to this commentary, saying, "It's too vague, too heady. Pious platitudes don't help us to live in the real world. All this talk of love—we want rules to follow." Addressing these understandable objections is complicated. People need specific instructions when they start out on the spiritual journey. This is why Christians have kept the Old Testament as a preamble for the New.

The Rich Man and Lazarus

The story of the rich man and Lazarus has some peculiar elements (see Luke 16:19–31). Ancient history provides a clue of its popularity. It seems the story of a rich man and a poor beggar is well known in many religious traditions. The description of the two places with a "great abyss" between them could be found by simply substituting "Father Abraham" for any local deity. It seems that at least the first eight verses of the passage are a popular retelling of a simple folk story. There is nothing complicated about it. The rich man has been cruel and unfeeling, and now he receives what he deserves.

On some levels, readers may feel sorry for the rich man. Is this the lesson? The rich man could be me, if I am unresponsive in life to those in need. But the story includes something more than that idea. The rich man's desire to help his five brothers stay out of hell seems to suggest that the man is not entirely evil. Only thoroughly wicked people hope others will be as miserable as they are.

A more sophisticated lesson unfolds in the next four verses. Imagine a situation in which comfortable, wealthy Palestinians give no attention to the moral traditions of Judaism in which they were raised. Is there any event or experience that will make them change and begin to observe those laws again? The answer, as the story has it, is that they already have what they need in the Scriptures. If they do not care about Moses and the prophets, then not even a dramatic sign from God will move them to change.

It was not uncommon for Jesus to take a popular story and reverse the conclusion or add a new twist to it. Jesus used the finished story to describe the upper-class Jewish leaders who without any seriousness kept asking him for signs and wonders. In a similar situation, Jesus says: "An evil and adulterous generation asks for a sign" (Matthew 12:39), "but no sign will be given."

As mentioned earlier, Luke shows Jesus demonstrating patience, friendliness, and gratitude to Samaritans. In first-century Palestine, the expression "You are a Samaritan" was the worst insult anyone could use. In chapter 17 (vv. 11–19), Luke reports that a Samaritan is cured of leprosy by Jesus and runs back to his people shouting praises to God. When he finds Jesus, he throws himself on the ground in grateful acknowledgment. Luke points out that there are other ways to show gratitude. On the eve of his death Jesus took bread, broke it, and gave thanks. Christianity sees this gesture as a sacramental sign that is a summation of the entire meaning of Jesus' life. *Eucharist* comes from the Greek word for thanksgiving. And when Jesus said, "do this in memory of me," he was not encouraging the repetition of a ritual; he recommends living as he did: giving thanks.

The form of thanksgiving that I am suggesting is difficult to capture in words. It is not simple gratitude for this or that good thing. Jesus was able to give thanks even as he went to his death. At the same time tangible blessings are part of it: they anticipate a future fulfillment when every good thing will somehow be ours. And in the light of that hope, it sees even now the anticipation of infinite love in the ordinary moments of daily life.

People with concrete religious sensibilities who prefer black-and-white answers probably think that much of the above is dreamy and abstract. To them there is no sense of cosmic adventure, awe, or mystery. Life is nothing more than meets the eye—what you see is what you get. Perhaps they are afraid of being duped. Some people seem more comfortable with observance of religious regulations and recitation of prescribed formulas.

CONVERSION

The story of Zacchaeus, chief tax collector of Jericho, is an example of Luke's idea that conversion to the way of Jesus is a process, not automatic or uniform (see Luke 19:1–10). Zacchaeus turns away from the fraud and the extortion that made him wealthy and vows to make restitution. He pledges half his income to the poor. The story outlines the pathway to conversion. The story of Zacchaeus is nearly a case study in conversion. The story line includes the first stirrings of personal dissatisfaction with his existence, a willingness to step away from familiar patterns of living with hope that something more may be experienced, a personal call from Jesus, and finally the outline for a new way of life.

Without diminishing Luke's version of the story, some people might judge his ending a bit too definite. One wonders: What happened after Jesus moved away? How did Zacchaeus and his family endure a radically new lifestyle? What happened to him when the enthusiasm for his new way of life began to fade?

Luke does not provide any answers. There is hope he is not the person Jesus had in mind when he speaks about the man whose last state becomes worse than the first (Luke 11:26). The entire passage (Luke 11:14–26) interrupts Luke's genial instructions to his disciples with a controversy and sayings involving unclean evil spirits. There is no need to study in depth the allegorical implications of the passage. It is more important to remember that Luke offers the image of a struggle between the powerful Beelzebul and the more powerful Jesus in order to prepare the reader for what is to take place in Jerusalem during Jesus' last days. The issue is one that Luke's community knows well.

Conversion and the Second Coming

The Acts of the Apostles describes the initial fervor or enthusiasm of the first converts to the way of Jesus. They sold their houses and belongings in order to establish a common fund. Distribution of proceeds would ensure that there "was not a needy person among them" (Acts 4:34). A special kind of dedication and commitment was at work in this early group, but it does not endure. Once the idea of a delay in the return of the triumphant and risen Christ begins to take hold, the group abandons its earliest form of organization, if not enthusiasm. If someone thinks the end is near, it is less difficult to give away their choicest possessions.

Ordinary divisions in the group asserted themselves, straining their unity. People soon quarreled over the common fund (see Acts 6:1). The ordinary demands of living in this world, with certain responsibilities, demands, and problems, once again had to be undertaken. A number of people drifted away from the community.

The same challenge confronted Paul and is evident in some of his writings (see 2 Thessalonians 3:11–15). Paul continues to believe that the second coming of Christ will occur in the near future. "We who are alive, who are left until the coming of the Lord" is the phrase used in 1 Thessalonians 4:15. Yet to remain idle looking up to heaven with hope of Jesus' second coming is no longer a reasonable behavior. "[I] hear that some of you are living in idleness, mere busybodies, not doing any work" (2 Thessalonians 3:11). Paul challenges his audience not to be agitated or terrified by rumors or visions (see 2 Thessalonians 1:6) but to serve God serenely, to stand firm in hardships, to return only good for evil. In other words, Christians need to grow from an initial, enthusiastic conversion into people who tend to the ordinary details of living in this world.

A Life of Gradual Conversion

Not everyone in the first Christian communities had such powerful transformations as reported by Zacchaeus and Paul. A conversion may also consist of a series of small adjustments. Zacchaeus and Paul report that their conversions happened forcefully and suddenly. Either way, according to Luke, the crucial test of a conversion comes with living life in light of the experience. Even the most dramatic "rebirth" imaginable is only the first step in a new life in Christ. The daily struggles with responsibilities are not obstacles or tests to be endured. They are the substance of living faithfully. Anyone who manages to set all worldly cares aside, according to Luke, must continue to learn the many facets of God's offer of spirit and love.

Some years ago a nurse at one of our local hospitals shared the following with me. She works the night shift. All her patients had some form of terminal cancer. Two older men shared a room. She heard their friendly jabbering and was pleased they seemed compatible.

About three in the morning, she found one of them in the hallway reading his book. She smiled and said, "Can't sleep tonight?" He nodded. "Yes, and I don't want to disturb my roommate. So, I came out here for a little while. You don't mind, do you?" She nodded and then asked, "Tell me, what's really troubling you?" He looked up and said, "You know I grew up in Europe. When I was a boy of twelve, you Americans bombed my city. The machine in my room makes a click, click, click sound that reminds me of the ones we counted before the bombs hit. We all survived. That's long ago, but tonight the clicking for some reason brought it all back. Funny thing is that my friend in the other bed was a pilot back then and flew dozens of missions over my country. We're friends, but I can't sleep, so I came out here so as not to disturb him." The nurse looked at the man and whispered, "How civilized you both have become."

After sixty years, war memories may mellow, even if they never completely fade away. Does it take sixty years to stop seeking vengeance? The most vexing teaching of Jesus is his call to imitate his way of forgiveness. For some reason, deep inside there seems an endless desire to punish those who hurt me. Even if I am able to forgive, the best I sometimes can muster is to never speak to the person again. Silence is the only resolution for some disagreements and bitter hurts. Is the example of the man in the hallway of a cancer unit common or an exception to the rule? Is he sensible or foolish to forgive? Is forgiveness multifaceted and, at times, not advisable?

Conversion for All

In Luke's writings the Pharisees continue to be the target of Jesus' preaching, but it is most clear from Luke that Jesus loved the Pharisees deeply (see Luke 18:9–14). The story describes two men praying in the Jerusalem Temple: a Pharisee and a publican. A publican was one who collected taxes for the occupiers, the Romans. They were universally despised by the Jewish people, for their power and wealth came from cooperation with the enemy. When Jesus says in the passage that the prayer of a publican is more acceptable to God that the one prayed by the Pharisee, he is deliberately trying to provoke his audience.

Publicans were not only the epitome of moral worthlessness, but the Pharisees were precisely their opposite. The misimpression that some people have when they read the New Testament is that the Pharisees were nothing but hypocrites and frauds. To a large extent such an attitude reflects an animosity that developed late in the first century when Christians discontinued observance of the Jewish laws and customs. We need to remember Luke's idyllic scene of communal life in Acts 2:37–47 in which a Levite is honored. So, too, the figures of Joseph of Aramathea and Nicodemus, influential and respected Jewish leaders, are identified with admiration in several other places in the New Testament (for Joseph, see Mark 15:43–46; Matthew 27:57–60; Luke 23:50–55; John 19:38–42; and for Nicodemus see John 3:1–17; 7:50; and 19:39) And Paul admits that he was once proud of his devotion as a Pharisee: "Brothers, I am a Pharisee, a son of Pharisees" (Acts 23:6b).

The Pharisees were the most religious people of their times. They tried to live their religion in daily life. The patterns of life and worship they developed were carried over into the Christian churches. The customs derived from the Pharisees include days of fasting, penance practices, readings from the Scriptures that are followed throughout the year, and praying the psalms in a congregational setting. The first part of the Christian liturgy, sometimes called the Liturgy of the Word, is modeled on the synagogue service of readings and psalm responses developed by Pharisee synagogue communities.

Luke and the other Gospel writers make it clear that Jesus never gave up trying to reach the Pharisees with his interpretations. Each of the parables, for example, seems designed to invite, challenge, coax, or even threaten them into accepting his message. Of course, his efforts failed. Those who flocked to hear Jesus were those who had economic needs, moral weaknesses, and unobservant people who lived at the fringe of Jewish life. "Sinners" loved the Nazarene preacher, but Jesus told the parable of the publican and the Pharisee at prayer—not to sinners and publicans but to the Pharisees. Why? He never gave up trying to convince them.

THE ROLE OF WOMEN

Even as contemporary culture continues to eliminate certain stereotypes, the world of first-century Palestinian culture had a number that remained unchallenged. Women were considered more subjective, sensitive, self-effacing, and cautious than first-century men. A few choice adjectives such as vain, venal, sensual, superstitious, and empty-headed were used in their stories and commentaries about women. Men, in the Palestinian view, were their opposite.

The culture Jesus shared did not consider women to be persons in their own right. They were minors and their civil rights were few. A man could divorce his wife for just about any reason; a woman could not divorce her husband. A woman was not permitted a role in synagogue services; she would be relegated to a separate area behind a screen. Even when they traveled in large groups, men walked in groups while the women and children walked together in a separate group. Like slaves or children, women were not held responsible for the full observance of the Law of Moses.

The cultural context makes the visit of Jesus to the home of Martha and Mary a special place to observe his views (see Luke 10:38–42). Martha behaved in the customary ways of first-century Palestinian women. She stayed behind the scenes and waited on the men. The example of Abraham's wife Sarah was a rich image in the Palestinian culture. Sarah was not permitted to be seen by Abraham's visitors; she remains in another room and bakes bread. In Luke's scene, Martha's sister Mary is seated with the men, listening to Jesus and discussion religion, something unheard of in the culture of that time.

In Luke's account, Jesus encourages a woman to think she has the same right as a man to learn about God. Martha is not necessarily shocked by the behavior, as she too was participating in a minor scandal. It may have been unseemly, at least, for Jesus to spend time in the home of two single women.

The New Testament accustoms its readers with stories and ideas that Jesus violated established customs. Contemporary readers usually do not think of women as belonging to the same category as publicans, sinners, and Samaritans. Contemporary people do not know the ancient culture.

Readers often take the scene of Martha, Mary, and Jesus as an allegory, making the two women symbols of larger issues. Martha represents the practical concerns of daily life while Mary symbolizes attentiveness to the Word of God. These symbolic interpretations are legitimate, but they come from later meditations of the Christmas in the more "liberated" Greek-speaking world. It was soon forgotten that Jesus once raised eyebrows of his listeners by insisting that a woman was more in God's eye than one who bears children, "Blessed is the womb that bore you and the breasts that nursed you!" (Luke 11:27). Jesus responds, "Blessed rather are those who hear the word of God and obey it!"

(v. 28). Jesus insists on the revolutionary truth that women are as qualified as men to know, love, and serve God. Both are created equally, created in the image and likeness of God.

READING LUKE TODAY

Comments about living today in a time of great crisis are widespread. We are told that many people are worried; most of the twentieth-century cultural bragging, easy certitudes, and securities are either gone or on their way out. What is ahead of us, some Americans say, only God knows. A number of people in our time seem to have rediscovered the apocalypse.

What exactly has gone wrong? Perhaps the real problem is that few of us know. Is it worldwide terrorism, diminishing resources, polluted water, and pandemics? Is it the loss of will, confusion of moral values, apathy, and overindulgence? Is it all of the above?

For a long time we were blessed with rich harvests, with prosperity like nothing ever experienced before in human history. A multinational corporation once advertised the hope of a generation with its slogan, "Progress is our middle name." It seems we gathered up great stockpiles and then congratulated ourselves. We thought we could rest secure for many years. Let us relax, eat our fill, and drink well. But something has gone wrong. We have begun to hear an unfamiliar voice. It whispers, "You fool! This night all will be taken from you." Luke concludes, "So it is with those who store up treasures for themselves but are not rich toward God" (12:21). The diagnosis and remedy of the contemporary malaise is found in that sentence. Is it possible that we will hear its message in time and take it to heart?

METANOIA

The Greek word for the change Jesus desires is *metanoia*. The translation "reform your lives" is not its entire meaning. The Greek term is built from the word for mind and thought, and it refers not only to external change but primarily to an interior reversal. Acts 2:38 states, "Peter said to them, 'Repent, and be baptized every one of you in the name of Jesus Christ so that your sins may be forgiven; and you will receive the gift of the Holy Spirit.'" Once again, *penance* is derived from a root that means to punish. Penance has something to do with interior remorse or regret, even a firm purpose of amendment or change, but *metanoia* includes something more.

Metanoia indicates a type of inner adjustment, a transformation of awareness, a new way of interacting with the world. The experience of the closest followers of Jesus when they met the risen Jesus is a perfect example of the full meaning of the word. Luke claims that the death of Jesus turned the followers into defeated people, feeling deluded in what they had believed about their leader (see Luke 24:21). They felt guilty for abandoning him, and they were frightened that what happened to him might befall them too. With the experience of meeting the risen Christ, they changed into courageous leaders of a movement that swept the ancient world.

Luke explains the outlines of this transformation in several places (see especially Luke 24:36). There are five stages to the transformation he identifies. First, the apostles and disciples hear from the women who had found the empty tomb and others that Jesus had conquered death, but they remain skeptical. Second, Jesus presents himself to the group; their reaction is one of panic and fright. Third, Jesus reassures them, saying, "Peace be with you." Fourth, slowly their fear gives way to another view or possibility. They become incredulous with joy and wonder. They are dazzled by the transformed Christ who stands before them as it is greater than anything they have ever dreamed. Finally, the Risen One leads them to a certain understanding of what has taken place. Jesus explains how the Jewish Scriptures had predicted his resurrection from the dead.

It is the final step Luke identifies that provides another way of using the process I have identified. We can be misled by the expressions in Luke and Acts, which seem to say that everything about Jesus was described ahead of time in the Old Testament. In fact, there is nothing in the Old Testament that says that the Messiah will be put to death or rise again on the third day. There are only scattered clues that those who serve God most faithfully often must suffer for it at the hands of God's people. To go from an Old Testament to a Christian mentality is not an exercise in deductive logic. It requires that everything we once knew or thought we knew be rearranged to make room for a new realization. Everything from before remains, but we gain a new perspective, a new outlook.

In this regard, Luke often connects the idea of *metanoia* with forgiveness of sins, but if we have a naïve understanding of God's forgiveness, we miss other aspects *metanoia* implies. Too many people continue to think of forgiveness as depending or relating primarily to someone's external statements, and they overlook the interior transformation or renewal of heart and mind within themselves. The inner transformation from self-absorption to generosity, from emptiness to you, from a bleak and uncertain world to one full of God's love, is the same *metanoia* experienced by the apostles.

There is the final matter of announcements. We might think that since *metanoia* is interior, it must be thoroughly private. Those who experience *metanoia* are sent out as witnesses, to share with others the transformation that Christ has made possible in them. This became the mission of not only the apostles but also all Christians. People hunger for this message; they want to believe more is possible, that life has a purpose, that their lives are precision to a God who loves them. They will be skeptical at first, they may be frightened by the enormous risks faith implies. Even the messengers may not always give them reasons to believe, but those who claim to believe in Christ have no alternative. They must share what they have become. They must be the Lord's witnesses.

REVIEW QUESTIONS

1. List five special characteristics of Luke's Gospel. Why did you select each?
2. The figure of Jesus seems more cosmopolitan as presented by Luke compared to the depictions in Mark and Matthew. Does this universal or cosmopolitan focus give us a clue as to Luke's mindset? If so, describe the world Luke inhabited compared to the world of James in Jerusalem.
3. In your own words, explain the parable of the Prodigal Son. What is the image of God that Jesus, according to Luke, tries to teach in this parable? What does this parable say about the power of jealousy and the inability to forgive?

FOR FURTHER STUDY

1. O'Collins, Gerald, S.J. *Easter Faith: Believing in the Risen Jesus* (Mahwah, NJ: Paulist Press, 2003); and *Interpreting the Resurrection* (Mahwah, NJ: Paulist Press, 1988). Each volume is helpful for the beginner to appreciate the varieties of meanings of resurrection. Written with a keen eye to scholarship and the needs of the reader.
2. Fitzmyer, Joseph, S.J. *The Gospel According to Luke* (Anchor Bible; New York: Doubleday, 1985). Clearly written with a deep commitment to the historical critical method.
3. Levine, A. J. *A Feminist Companion to Luke* (Sheffield, England: Sheffield Academic Press, 2002). Raises the major concerns and questions from a variety of scholars in the feminist critique.
4. Green, Joel. *The Gospel of Luke* (New International Commentary on the New Testament; Grand Rapids, MI: Eerdmans, 1997). Green accepts that Luke was the author of one long narrative that includes The Acts of the Apostles. His presentation resounds with Evangelical sensitivities and methods.
5. Neyrey, Jerome H., editor. *The Social World of Luke-Acts: Models for Interpretation* (Peabody, MA: Hendrickson, 1999). Essays by well-known biblical scholars from the social science interpretative school are filled with tidbits of social and culture facts from the first-century world Luke

shared. Scholarly language throughout may be difficult for beginners, yet those interested in learning more of the cultural milieu in Luke's time will be pleased.

6. Johnson, Luke T. *The Acts of the Apostles, The Gospel of Luke* (Collegeville, MN: Liturgical Press, 2006). Johnson sees Luke's use of literary techniques as a clear example of Christian apologetics not unlike ancient historiography and biography.

7. Winter, Bruce W., and Andrew D. Clarke (eds.). *The Book of Acts in Its First Century Setting* (Grand Rapids, MI: Eerdmans, 1993). Scholarly essays in six volumes that evaluate one book: Acts.

8. Brown, Raymond E. *Once and Coming Spirit at Pentecost* (Collegeville, MN: Liturgical Press, 1993). A brief commentary.

9

The Gospel According to John

Special Elements in John's Gospel

1. John's account has no infancy narrative. He begins with the preexistence of the *Logos,* God's Word and Son, who came into the world, and other themes that will be developed in his narrative.

2. There are no exorcisms or demonic possessions in John's account, and he mentions the "kingdom" only once (see John 3:3).

3. John offers seven "signs" performed by Jesus, and he avoids the term *miracle.* These wondrous deeds are interpreted for the reader by John's reflections, narrative, and discourses. The first sign is changing water into wine; the second sign is the cure of a royal official's son (John 4:46-54); the third sign is the cure of a paralytic (John 5:1-15); the fourth sign is the feeding of the 5,000 (John 6:1-14); fifth is Jesus walking on the water (6:15-25); the sixth is the healing of the man born blind (John 9:1-8); and the seventh is the raising of Lazarus from the dead (John 11:1-45).

4. Jesus describes himself as *"I am"* several times that seem related to the seven signs: "I am the bread of life" (John 6:35); "I am the light of the world" (John 8:12); "I am the gate" (John 10:9; "I am the good shepherd" (John 10:11); "I am the resurrection and the life" (John 11:25); "I am the way, and the truth, and the life" (John 14:6); and "I am the true vine" (John 15:1).

5. Some scholars identify Gnostic themes in John's writings. Gnosticism is a later development and includes the idea that special or secret knowledge is needed for salvation.

6. John offers several metaphors such as the Vine and the Branches and the Good Shepherd. These stories do not follow the parable form in the synoptic accounts.

7. John includes the washing of the disciples' feet at the Last Supper, but does not record any words of Jesus over the bread and the cup (see John 13:1-20). He does have a long meditation in 6:22-59 on the nature of "bread."

8. John indicates that the final meal and death of Jesus occur a day earlier than recorded by other evangelists.
9. Mary Magdalene visits the tomb of Jesus twice. On the first visit, she runs away thinking the body has been stolen. The theme of disbelief in the resurrection runs throughout the Gospel. After the resurrection, the apostle Thomas has his doubts and will not trust the word of faith given by the other disciples that Jesus is alive (see John 20:24–29).
10. The "beloved disciple" is never identified.
11. Jesus' ministry takes place in Jerusalem. He chased the money changers from the temple precincts at the beginning of his ministry. In the synoptic narratives, he overturns tables during the final days of his life.
12. Jesus carries his cross to Calvary. Simon from Cyrene is not mentioned.

There are several differences in the language, style, and content in John's Gospel compared with the other Gospels.

LIMITED USE OF THE KINGDOM OF GOD

As we have seen, one major theme in Mark's account, for example, is the dawning of the kingdom of God at the outset of Jesus' ministry. According to Mark, it is essential for Jesus' disciples, and all who call themselves followers, to integrate the meaning and centrality of the Lord's suffering and cross in their lives. In Matthew's Sermon on the Mount, Jesus proclaims the kingdom of heaven, teaches a prayer for its arrival, and recounts its mysterious qualities in the parables. In Luke's narrative. we meet a serene, at times joyful, prophet of God as he travels and offers an appealing message of universal importance. The kingdom continues to be central in Luke's summary even as he adjusts the earlier Pauline timeline that had anticipated an imminent and triumphant return of the risen Christ. According to Luke, the kingdom begins to be experienced in the everyday life of the church community. No one knows when the promised return of the Lord will take place. Now is the age of the church community. It is the church community where the kingdom is found under way.

John uses the expression *kingdom of God* only twice (see John 3:3, 5). He includes no parables taught by Jesus. Instead, his narrative Jesus offers long, circling meditations that return to the same subject: himself.

LOGOS

John summarizes his point of view in an opening hymn or prologue to the Gospel in which he offers a poetic outline of the history of God's existence and intimate communication to the world. We learn that God's *Logos* is present at the beginning of creation and helps to turn darkness into day. *Logos* has a number of possible meanings. It is usually translated into English as "the Word." In April 2005, Pope Benedict XVI (then Joseph Cardinal Ratzinger) wrote, "From the beginning, Christianity has understood itself as the religion of the *Logos,* as the religion according to reason." It seems that the term originally provided an answer for Greek philosophers who noticed the disparity between this finite world of ours and the infinitely perfectly eternal world imagined by Plato and others. At the time of Jesus, many Greek Jews were familiar with the Septuagint translation of the Bible. In fact, Philo (ca. 20–42 BCE) found the Jewish Scriptures to be in harmony with the best insights from Plato and the Stoics. Several biblical scholars contend that John uses multiple meanings of the term *Logos* as he writes to Greek Jews, Hellenists, and Greek Christians. Each group has its special familiarity with the term and would understand his usage according to their preference. John extends the usual Greek meaning of the term when he proclaims: "And the Word *[Logos]* became flesh and lived among us" (John 1:14). This usage of *Logos* would be meaningful to a variety of audiences.

John's other images would be understandable too. A world without God is lost in darkness, but God has sent his Word to be humanity's light and life. There is a new community of life and a spirit that the Word has given to the world is recognizable to all who choose to believe. Those who believe will have "truth," and the truth will set them free.

GNOSTICISM

John's language anticipates some of the teachings associated with later Gnosticism, a second- and third-century movement and heresy. *Gnosticism* is derived from the Greek word for knowledge, *gnosis.* It includes the idea that the world is evil and powerful. The power of this world can be overcome by learning the secret truths about a more perfect, eternal realm. Gnosticism is a current in second- and third-century Greek thinking that centers on knowledge of God and human salvation. They emphasize the transcendent life of God and how human salvation is possible is described in their later writings and myths. Humans alive now in the world are polarized from the transcendent God. The knowledge of God is a special gift or possession for their group alone. The New Testament writers have a different concept of redemption and salvation. Gnostic writers do not conceive of God as the creator of the material world. Creation is the work of an evil demiurge. The inner light in people that allows them to respond to the special Gnostic teachings is not part of the material world. Gnostic texts that include these themes were developed late in the second century, long after the time of John's Gospel.

The symbols found in John's Gospel were readily understood by the people of his time. The Jewish Greek writer Philo of Alexandria (ca. 20 BCE–50 CE) wrote extensively using what might be termed *early Gnostic* symbolism. For example, Philo made extensive us of dualistic images in his writings, such as light and darkness, good and evil, life and death. Therefore, it seems likely that certain themes John used were familiar to his community. They were part of the literary and cultural atmosphere, yet John's usage is not identical to that of second-century Gnosticism.

The central themes of John's Gospel are not Gnostic. John's Gospel insists that the truth Jesus brings is not just something to know but something to be lived and obeyed, "Just as I have loved you, you should love one another" (John 13:34). Gnostic ideas deny such possibilities. John's Jesus does not proclaim that the world is evil as the Gnostics do. Even though evil seems today to have its way, God continues to love the world and wills to save it (see John 3:16–17). God demonstrates this love even to the point of becoming one with the world (see John 1:14). He sends his son into the world. This type of thinking was known in the first-century Hellenistic world, but it is not yet Gnosticism. A more balanced view of John's writings may include antecedents to later Gnosticism and recognize that the later Christian communities would find in John's outlook and presentation.

There is a warning in John's narrative that those who shrink away from death and try to cling to life are headed for destruction (see John 12:20–33). "Those who hate their life in this world" are praised by the author. Is this an example of fully developed Gnosticism? The passage from John, taken by itself, could suggest the advantage of morbid rituals of self-punishment and vigils in gloomy cemeteries.

THE JESUS OF FAITH, NOT HISTORY

Some scholars claim that John developed an entirely different theological interpretation of Jesus than the ones found in the synoptic Gospels. As a result, the historical picture of Jesus that is recognizable in Mark, Matthew, and Luke is thought to be closer to the historical Jesus than the material provided in John. In other words, John's Gospel is a theological narrative written long after the historical beginnings of the Christian movement. He has fewer links to the original eyewitnesses and disciples of Jesus.

DATE OF THE GOSPEL ACCORDING TO JOHN

A second-century dating of John's material was often given based on the analyses mentioned previously; however, contemporary interpretations have been revised due to the discovery, among other things, of a papyrus fragment of John's eighteenth chapter. The fragment dates no later than the early 100s. It is more often recognized today that some of the historical details in John's writings have substantially as much claim to historical accuracy as what is found in the other canonical Gospels. For instance, the pool with five porches/porticoes in John 5:2 had been thought to be symbolic. Excavations at the site in Jerusalem during the twentieth century now confirm John's historical accuracy. It seems reasonable to assert that a number of John's special themes developed within a distinct community of believers, and the Gospel dates no later than the years AD 90–95. His community developed several local customs and opinions yet was aware of other communities.

THE WORDS OF JESUS

Even with the above facts in mind, there is no denial that the synoptic Gospels record the words of Jesus more literally than John. Certainly, the Gospel writers and editors felt free to adjust or modify the words of Jesus to teach their particular theological interpretations. It seems sensible and more accurate to interpret the fourth Gospel as a translation of Jesus' original message into an entirely new pattern of thinking that was familiar in John's early Christian community.

John makes a number of adjustments to themes developed by the synoptic writers. Instead of the kingdom of God, John has Jesus speak more often about "eternal life." Instead of exorcisms, or the defeat of demons by stupendous acts that illustrate God's mighty and dynamic powers, John has Jesus perform several "signs" in which the power, love, and glory of God are revealed so that the world may come to believe. Instead of warning people to prepare for an impending judgment, the fourth Gospel challenges people to decide now to live in the light of the truths Jesus offers the world. Even if the world seems filled with illusion and darkness, whoever chooses the light has already passed over from death into new life, and whoever chooses the darkness over the light is already judged and lost.

LIFE ON EARTH VERSUS ETERNAL LIFE

Even if Christians distort the message of Jesus and behave like unbelievers, most are aware that Jesus did not walk among us to reward people with riches and fame. One persistent undercurrent in Western Christianity has been a pessimism regarding life in this world. Certain extremes, such as medieval monks who slept in coffins at night so as to better imagine their eventual deaths, or Calvinist efforts to prohibit every kind of human pleasure, are documented and well known. There is also the more subtle disdain that some Christians advocate for ordinary concerns such as the environment, health, and equitable political systems and activities. Others prefer to think "religion" belongs only in church and not in the public square. Some of these people claim that they are more concerned about the eternal life, or heaven. In the meantime, other Christians warn that we should "be in the world, but not of it." They quote John's passage about "hating one's life." They are unaware of the peculiarity of Semite grammar and its limited ability to express comparative forms.

Jesus' demand, according to John, is that people come to recognize that life on earth is only a relative good, not an absolute one. There is nothing in the New Testament that would justify the literal hating of our lives in this world. Jesus did not accept death on the cross because he was disgusted with life. The cross of Jesus is the symbol of the only way to love authentically.

As we have seen, John makes it clear that humans are creatures made to share in God's own life. It is for this reason that we are strangely torn as we try to live in this world. On the one hand, we have endless desires, and on the other hand we have endless limitations. We desire much, yet even our finest achievements fall short of the endless life for which we are made. The result is that too often we either congratulate ourselves on the life we have achieved, and pretend that it is perfect as we cling to it, or we give up on life, deny it, or try to blot it out. Some of us even manage to do both at once, worshipping the little bit of the world we can control and despising the rest of it. According to John, the only one who can love life correctly is the one who, when the time comes, can let go of it and trust God to provide even more life. "Those who love their life [as if this life is all there is] lose it" (John 12:25; see also Mark 8:35; Luke 17:33). But those who hate [yield over] their lives as they know them in this world, will find life given to them in a new way.

Divisions in John's Gospel

Section	Theme	Scripture Passage
1	John's prologue hymn	1:1–18
2	Seven signs given by Jesus	1:19—12:50
3	Passion and entrance into glory	13:1—20:31
4	The Risen One appears in Galilee	21:1–25

JOHN'S PRIMARY CAST OF CHARACTERS

As we have seen, even if the New Testament authors were inspired, it is important to remember that the description of inspiration we favor does not prevent them from developing their own interpretations, imagery, and tone throughout their writings. When authors borrow images and passages from the Old Testament, they borrow selectively. The Old Testament, as we have seen, also includes a spectrum of styles, expressions, and cadences. The source of borrowed Old Testament passages and favorite images also reveals something about the author who borrows them. If theology includes a personal appropriation of various understandings of religious faith, then it is no surprise that the New Testament includes a spectrum of styles and theological viewpoints.

The issue of personal preferences runs deeper than any one image a writer favors. Preference reveals the person. As a result, contemporary readers may have as many likes and dislikes for individual books of the Bible as they have for other types of literature. For instance, the picture of Jesus John presents is someone very much in full self-possession. Jesus is serene, one step ahead of others. John gives the impression that Jesus is omniscient. This picture of Jesus may not be preferred by every reader.

A further question suggests itself: how much preference is legitimate? Religious leaders, at times, fear that ordinary believers will be too selective in their preferences for one book of the Bible. It is the same with contemporary readers, who prefer to think that Jesus never showed any preferences. If we deny that Jesus did so, we might deny that preference has anything to do with the reality of human love. Is it love when everyone is liked equally? Is it love when we never care to be reminded of differences in talent, whim, and sensibility?

Without going to extremes on the topic, there does seem to be room for individual tastes and preferences, at least, when the issue is a reader's preference for other Gospels or John's selective use of other New Testament writers.

The Role of the Apostle John

This seems true not only when the question is reading the Bible, but in spirituality in general. The curious fact offered in John's Gospel is that some disciples are more beloved than others. It seems the variety of styles of discipleship and prayer never denies that it is the same for God. God may have favorites, but this is not the same thing as saying God *plays* favorites. For example, there is something entertaining in the way John presents the relationship between Peter and John in his Gospel. In the other three Gospels, Peter and Andrew are the first to be called as disciples (see Matthew 4:18), but in John's Gospel it is John and Andrew (John 1:35–42).

"The disciple Jesus loved" sits closest to Jesus at the Last Supper, and when Peter has a particularly difficult question for Jesus, he has John to ask it for him (see John 13:24). Following the arrest of Jesus, John arranges for Peter to get into the high priest's courtyard (see John 18:16). After all the other disciples flee, John remains close throughout Jesus' final ordeal. In fact, John—and no other disciple—takes Jesus' mother into his home. When "on the third day" John and Peter run to the tomb after they hear Mary Magdalene's report, John runs faster. John reaches the tomb first and waits for Peter. Peter is the first to go inside the tomb, but John is the first to appreciate what has taken place:

"Then the other disciple, who reached the tomb first, also went in, and he saw and believed" (John 20:8).

Later in the text, there is a story of the "beloved disciple," who is the first one to recognize the stranger on the beach is Jesus. He calls to Peter who immediately shouts: "It is the Lord!" (John 21:1–19). And a few passages later, we find Peter walking with Jesus only to turn and see John following closely behind. "Lord, what about him?" Peter asks, and receives a sharp response from Jesus: "If it is my will that he remain until I come, what is that to you?" (John 21:21–22).

None of the above scenes is found in any other Gospel. One reason they are included in the fourth gospel is related to the special context or situation of John's followers in the early church. The people who edited the final version of the gospel, the "we" in the last statement of the gospel narrative, had their own way of discipleship. "This is the disciple who is testifying to these things and has written them, and we know that his testimony is true" (John 21:24). This community differs from other churches in theology and organizational structure. It seems clear enough that John's followers are making a claim that they too follow an apostle as good as Peter; that their brand of Christianity is as legitimate as others.

The Role of the Apostle Peter

Even as John's community insists on the special character and place of their namesake, they acknowledge the esteem and special place Peter occupies. In a number of crucial moments throughout John's narrative, Peter is the spokesman for the other apostles and followers. The New Testament suggests Peter's special place in the early church in many scenes. For instance, Peter is shown as the chief fisherman (see Luke 5:10). He is the missionary who draws in a variety of people and brings them safely in without breaking the net or unity of the church. It is Peter who is given the role of shepherd, leader, and guide. Peter finds pasture for the church flock. Peter protects them from harm and rescues those who stray. Like Jesus, Peter is recognized as an ideal shepherd (see John 10:11) and must be willing to lay down his life for the flock.

The fourth Gospel tries to highlight the importance of John, yet permits the personality of Peter to emerge clearly. For all that is suggested in the text that John is "the one Jesus loved," it is Peter who seems more likable. The one Jesus loved seems innocent, while Peter is a sinner. The redeeming part of Peter's character centers on his recognition that he is a sinner. Where John seems never at a loss, Peter is willing to ask for help. Where John seems intuitive and certain in his faith, Peter takes risks and vacillates in faith.

THE ROLE OF JESUS

We must not overlook the most important figure whom the fourth Gospel depicts—Jesus. How does John's Gospel understand someone like Jesus, who is also proclaimed to be God? From the outset we read in John's narrative that Jesus is someone totally joined to God. He says, "The Father and I are one" (10:30). Joined as he is to God, he "know[s] all things" (6:30); as he moves through his life he meets no surprises, and when he asks a question he seems to already know the answer (see John 6:5). There is never a question that he raises about what decision he will make. He seems to know in advance every outcome. It is difficult to imagine such a person ever facing temptations. In fact, John omits the story of the wilderness temptations from his narrative. So, too, the episode of the agony in the garden is omitted. The closest passage to it is John 12:27 where Jesus asks a rhetorical question: "What should I say—'Father save me from this hour?' No, it is for this reason that I have come to this hour."

Alongside this picture there is the familiar one that we noticed in Mark's narrative, for example, where Jesus is quoted as saying: "Why do you call me good? No one is good but God alone" (Mark 10:18). Mark shows Jesus asking questions and waiting for the answers. Jesus' ignorance extends to ordinary items such as the time of the last day (see Mark 13:32). The Letter to the Hebrews joins with Mark, Matthew, and Luke to insist that Jesus was truly tempted as ordinary people experience temptation (see Hebrews 4:15; 2:17–18; see also 2 Corinthians 5:21; Matthew 8:16–17; Luke 4:2, 22:8; John 8:46; 1 Peter 2:22; 1 John 3:5), and the account of the agony in the garden includes Jesus pleading with the Father for some other end to unfold.

Fully Human and Fully Divine

How then can two such opposite biblical pictures of Jesus be reconciled? The easiest solution might be to ignore one of them, and various Christian heresies in history have done so. But the Christian church has always been more patient with the mystery of Jesus Christ. The church Council of Chalcedon in 451 articulated what has come to be known as the central Christian position by stating that Christians live with both interpretations: "We teach one and the same Lord Jesus Christ…at once truly human, complete in manhood, like us in all respects apart from sin…and also truly divine, of one being with the Father as regards his Godhead…the characteristics of each nature being fully preserved, not confused or altered."

This means that when we ask a question about Jesus' experience, we ask first whether our question involves the human experience or his divine experience. Human awareness, human knowing, and choice are not to be confused with those of divine awareness. Does the eternal, divine Word know all things? The

Church teaches, "yes." Did Jesus of Nazareth, in his human awareness know all things? The Church teaches, "no." Did the divine *Logos* have to "learn obedience through what he suffered" (Hebrews 5:8)? Again, the Church teaches, "no." Did Jesus of Nazareth face temptation, struggle to find and do what was good, and trust that the Father was with him despite apparent abandonment? The Church teaches, "yes."

In other words, contrary to what we may first imagine, Christianity affirms that both perspectives are aspects of the one truth that is Jesus Christ. When we consider the human side of Jesus, we see someone who faced all the difficulties that people face, but he faced them more heroically. The second statement that he is truly God does not alter the image of his humanity. Jesus is not a split personality. He could not escape to his divine zone so as to take rest from his humanity.

Yet Christians profess that in this one man people meet God himself; a God who does not hold back from his creatures but gives himself completely as he becomes one of them. He became one of us, not some imaginary superhuman being. His sufferings constitute the very incarnation of God's unspeakable love for us.

This becomes clear when you read John 11:1–44. In the account of Lazarus, John describes Jesus as having very strong emotions. The narrative states that Jesus felt indignant. The word expresses a type of inner anger people feel when they confront a situation that simply should not exist. John says that Jesus was "greatly disturbed." Jesus then sobs, is again indignant, and, near the climax of the story, "cried with a loud voice." In light of our contemporary awareness of emotions, John's Gospel includes understandable commentary on what Jesus may have felt.

Scholars offer a series of interpretations. Is Jesus angry at the crowds? Is their mourning a sign of disbelief? If so, why does Jesus too begin to weep? Other translators slant the meaning of the passage away from anger in the direction of grief, but the intensity of Jesus' feelings continues to need explanation. One clue comes from the language used in other places to describe Jesus' feelings about his approaching death. Mark 14:33 recounts that in the Garden of Gethsemane Jesus became distressed and troubled, and Hebrews 5:7 seems to have the same passage in mind when it says: "Jesus offered up prayers and supplications with loud cries and tears to the one who was able to save him from death."

John omits any mention of these reactions. He is more interested in reporting that Jesus was totally at one with God. There is no agony in the garden in John's Gospel. He omits the earlier temptation in the wilderness, perhaps for the same reason. "My food is to do the will of him who sent me" (John 4:34).

"The Son can do nothing on his own, but only what he sees the Father doing" (John 5:19). "I have come...not do to my own will, but the will of him who sent me" (John 6:38). These themes are repeated several times by John in 8:29, 10:27, and 10:30. The only mention of struggle in John's narrative is one scene, and it reads almost as a denial of the Gethsemane account: "Now my soul is troubled;. And what should I say—'Father, save me from this hour'? No, it is for this reason that I have come to this hour" (John 12:27).

The Meaning of Jesus' Death

What Jesus confronted in Gethsemane was not only his death, but all death and everything that it represents. The entire tragedy of evil, sin, and misery in our world is summed up in biblical language or thought as the kingdom or reign of death.

John makes Lazarus, "the one Jesus loves," into a symbol of every person who is threatened by the power of death. He deliberately places Lazarus' rescue near the end of Jesus' ministry and life's work. It is the seventh great sign that Jesus performs.

Why does Jesus show anger? Death is wrong; it should not exist. We are not made for death but for life. Why is Jesus stressed and shaken? Death has a terrible hold on us; it frightens some of us to a point where we hardly dare to live. To live with the fearless, generous, and large-hearted way Jesus suggests requires a slow process of integration. Discipleship is not instantaneous.

Why does Jesus shout as he calls Lazarus from the tomb? It is similar to the same one that the other evangelists place in Jesus' mouth at the moment of his own death (Mark 15:37; Matthew 27:50). It is a shout not of anguish, but victory. It is the shout of one of God's heroes, as in Joshua 6:16, whereby Jesus' death also marks the moment he conquers death and sets us free to live.

Jesus, the Gate

John refers to Jesus as a gate that leads into the place where sheep are kept. It is a controversial image. On the positive side, a gate gives access; it may even be a sign of welcome. A gate often gives some view of what is within; it may make people curious. On the negative side, a gate makes a claim. A gate may be a checkpoint, where selectivity and searches take place. A gate keeps strangers out. In fact, the picture that emerges of Jesus is someone who is special by being most human. Jesus is the gate that defends people from marauders and thieves who invite everyone to the wrong expectations about life and humanity. Thieves and marauders beckon others to live in the shadows. They steal from us our hopes to cope with the frailty we see in and around us. These people are strangers to our humanity. Jesus, according to John, is not.

Jesus Carries Our Burdens

John proclaims that Jesus carries many burdens that are not his own. This is a common human experience. Nowhere do feelings of unfairness well up more powerfully than when someone feels that they are being "dumped on" indiscriminately by others. Some people carry the weight of the world on their shoulders without knowing how it got there. They become hypnotized by their undeserved pain. They fail to realize that it is other people who are heaping the weight on them. John's Jesus knew why. According to the Gospel, Jesus carries around the sins of others in his own person. He shoulders the emotional burdens of strained, broken, or nonexistent problems. He takes it on as God's son. In turn, he receives the same accusations, curses, and indifference that God receives.

Jesus' Trust in God

In John's narrative Jesus does not vent his anger on others. There is more to this behavior than first meets the eye. We know how people commonly harp on their fate, resenting this or that turn in their fortunes. Some of the greatest problems we find ourselves in are those in which our integrity, sincerity, or competence are at stake. We recite past hurts as if we have them itemized and tallied. We relive quarrels, rehash sequences, and convince others to agree with our summation. In a way, we become lawyers. Yet the attitude of Jesus is free of litigation. The most solid insight into humans begins with a conviction that knows people are complex. All else is excuses. Within the actual limitations, adventures, and disasters that happen in our lives, a great deal of trust needs to be exercised that God remains in charge of our destiny. And Jesus, according to John, embodies trust.

To imagine Jesus with this kind of faith is not what some people anticipate. They prefer to imagine Jesus as so much in charge of every event he experiences that he never has to surrender and throw the whole thing over to his Father. John is clear when he reports that Jesus says, "But now I am coming to you, and I speak these things in the world so that they may have my joy made complete in themselves. I have given them your word, and the world has hated them because they do not belong to the world, just as I do not belong to the world. I am not asking you to take them out of the world, but I ask you to protect them from the evil one" (John 17:13–15).

Jesus the Shepherd

The image of the shepherd invokes the idea of speech. "The sheep follow him, because they know his voice. They will not follow a stranger…because they do not know the voice of strangers" (John 10:4–5). A number of Christians find solace in John's description of Jesus as the Good Shepherd. As we have seen, the other Gospel writers use the image in parable forms. The logic of John's version carries the reader into a deeper insight. John prefers allegorical figures with no story. For instance, in John 10:11–18, we are presented with the image of a flock of sheep. They move out of the gate into a pasture and are tended by a faithful shepherd. There is no plot to the story. One might ask, What is the point of the comparison? For sure, Jesus is intended to be understood as the shepherd (see John 10:7). So, too, Jesus is also the gate through which the sheep pass on their way to a perfect pasture. Even more, it is implied that Jesus is the pasture or true food for the sheep. He is also the pathway to eternal life. There is no one focus to the story, and this is John's intention. He deliberately offers disintegrating pictures to force the reader to move beyond superficial points in order to reach the level of "truth."

The "truth" is Jesus. The image of sheep and shepherd is one more way to meditate on the eternal relationship that Jesus has with his community. They find safety, confidence, and eternal life (see John 10:28) as members of the one community that Jesus protects, guides, and leads.

JOHN'S USE OF THE WORD *KNOW*

Related to John's interest in the "truth" is his fascination with the word *know*. John composes, especially in chapter 10, in such a way as to continuously return to it (see John 10:4, 5, 14, 15, 27, 38). "I know my own [sheep] and my own know me." *Know* is a key word throughout the entire Gospel. "[T]his is eternal life, that they may know you, the only true God, and Jesus Christ whom you have sent" (John 17:3; see also John 3:14, 16; John 6:40, 47, 58; John 10:28; John 11:26; John 12:25; and 1 John 2:25; 5:11–13).

As discussed earlier, the Christian church confronted Gnosticism, a sect devoted to secret "knowledge," during the second and third centuries. They insisted that the core of Christianity was "to know" God in a rather narrowly intellectual way, and they used John's wording to justify their position. But John originally intended for his listeners to understand the term with a deeper meaning. For John, people *know* the truth if they come out from the darkness of human control and embrace the light of God. Those who are truly *in the know* recognize in Jesus "the light of the world," the true revelation of God. And they live by his light, not their own.

OUR BROKENNESS LEADS TO LIGHT

People will come to know God by coming to know Jesus (see John 12:45). The mission of Jesus and his teachings, as John organizes them, reveals how true knowledge of God is found. For John, it is the cross where Jesus most completely reveals the truth of God as he lays down his life (see John 10:17). When does he come closest to revealing the ultimate meaning of everything? It is in John's picture of the free acceptance by Jesus of what this unfinished world promises. "No one takes [my life] from me, but I lay it down of my own accord" (John 10:18). The truth is that the terrible and inevitable brokenness of human existence does appear to win. The wolf does get us, all of us, one way or another. And it is precisely there, in our confrontation of this fact, that we make a choice between light and darkness, between the truths revealed by Jesus that will set us free from the futility of falsehood. It is an odd sense of security that this Shepherd offers.

How do we know that we are living with this type of security and knowledge? In John 15:1–17, Jesus says, "I am the true vine, and my Father is the vinegrower...you are the branches. Those who abide in me and I in them bear much fruit." According to John, if we make Jesus the root and center of our existence, then we will share in his eternal life and relationship with God. Even so, the question is not easily answered. Even though John insists that no branch will live broken off from the vine, that apart from Jesus there is only futility, there are those who remain apart from the vine, or, as we saw above, other sheep not of his fold. Apparently it is possible for some people to be in touch with God, according to John, even though they may never hear Jesus' voice. The New Testament does not explore this idea in great depth because its interest is missionary, but the point of other ways to God is admitted in a few places (as in 1 Timothy 2:3–7 and Acts 17:25–28).

TO ABIDE IN JESUS

Another question is: Is it possible for someone to say, "Lord, Lord" and be deceived? Is it possible to belong to the community of eternal life and not share in the life of Jesus? These kinds of questions are of interest to the New Testament writers. From the beginning it was clear that there were some members who had begun to follow with the Christian community who had stepped away from the group in one way or another. For example, the First Letter of John is specifically written to address this situation. The author tries to spell out exactly what to "abide in Jesus" means. The letter suggests several indicators. First, there is attention given to mutual love. The epistle of John specifies "love in truth and action," (1 John 3:18), a theme found also in the Gospel of John. This is a principle based on Jesus' criterion: "By their fruits you will know them" (1 John 3:18; see also 3 John 1:1; John 15:13; see also James 1:14–17). A life centered in God through Jesus will be signified in a practical and genuine love and care offered to others. John also suggests, "How does God's love abide in anyone who has the world's goods and sees a brother or sister in need and yet refuses help? (1 John 3:17). So, too, if we are willing to surrender what we possess for the sake of others, then we are in communion with God who gave his own Son (1 John 4:10) and the son who surrendered his own life for our sake (3 John 1:1).

PEACEFUL CONSCIENCE

A second point in John's epistle speaks of a peaceful existence. This does not mean that people will always avoid evil actions (1 John 2:1), but that when they do they may turn back, knowing they are loved by God. If sin is produced by fear, it is love that casts out fear (1 John 4:10). The Christian is to stand with confidence (1 John 2:2-5; see also John 13:35). Confidence in the original Greek language described the experience citizens of the free city states shared.

THE POWER OF PRAYER

John also reports that people will receive everything they need when they ask for it in prayer. If answered prayers were the essential indicator of God's presence, most people would walk away. In fact, the excerpt is expressed using the future, not the present, tense of the verb. We *will* receive all that we ask, in the end. We *will* receive because what we ask is precisely that God's will be done or accomplished, that God's name be praised. The sign of all this in the present hour is an inner peace, or sense of security that what we most desire *will*, in fact, take place by the power of God's love.

"And by this we know that he abides in us, by the Spirit that he has given us" (1 John 3:24). But how do we know God's Spirit? John answers this question with a teaching about the fact that God's Son has come to the earth, lived with us, and is not distant but intimate with us. And within the human conditions of life, the Son has opened up for us a way to God. Acceptance and contemplation of God's love for is the source and content of discipleship.

GOD IS LOVE

What, then, is God's love? One familiar Christian formula—"God is love"—comes from John's Gospel, but the love John has in mind is not limited to what we find comfortable; our understanding is not the measure of what this love may be. On the contrary, it is we who are measured by what we can grasp of this kind of love, who is God. "In this is love, not that we loved God but that he loved us and sent his Son to be the atoning sacrifice for our sins" (1 John 4:10). This is not to say that love and, for example, cruelty are one and the same, that there is no such thing as evil in the world. The statement "God is love" is incomplete without the remainder of John's thought, "And he sent his son" (1 John 4:10; see also John 1:34; John 5:37) to share our human condition, to be one with us, to know, as we do, the pointless sufferings innocents face all around us. God does not remain high above us, aloof, in heaven commanding and sending evils that leave him untouched. If we suffer, so does God. If we are to bear with evil and forgive, so does God. If we face death, so does God.

The perspective that John affirms does not pretend to tell us why innocent people suffer, why our best efforts so often end in ambiguity, or why all of us will die. Once John's premise is accepted, there is some limited glimpse of a higher meaning, the greater value to be found in waiting for the conversion of evil people than in destroying them, the superiority of patience and forgiveness to vengeance. Even so, our questions always go further than our answers. What we are offered, according to John, is a love beyond comprehension, a light shining in the darkness. We are not given explanations, but presence.

LIVING UP TO THE STANDARD OF JESUS

Critics maintain that the Christian church has fallen away, even as early as New Testament times, from the difficult ideals that were set forth by Jesus. Christians made them over into formulas that are easy to observe. Jesus gave a commandment to love, which does not end with caring for those normally regarded as neighbors but extends even to strangers, despised people, anyone in need, to one's enemies, to everyone without qualification.

When we analyze the early Christian churches, what do we notice? In the First Letter of John (3:11) we read, "For this is the message you have heard from the beginning, that we should love one another." There is no emphasis on outsiders or despised enemies. "Beloved, let us love one another, because love is from God; everyone who loves is born of God and knows God. Whoever does not love does not know God, for God is love" (1 John 4:7–8). The concern in this passage is entirely with one's own people. The same is noticeable when look at the community described in The Acts of the Apostles: "There was not a needy person among them" (see 4:32–35). In other words, the community took care of their members, but is this all that Jesus demanded?

Jesus commanded a love of staggering, even frightening scope. "If you love those who love, what credit is that to you?" (Luke 6:32; see also Matthew 5:46). Yet the love for one's own, for those who love us in return that we find in the church of the New Testament, is not an inferior substitute. It is a foundation, an essential first step in the journey of Christian discipleship.

It seems the church or community of believers in Christ exists in order to become the visible presence of Christ in the world, to embody his love and concern for the needy, to be a sign of his willingness even to forgive his enemies, yet in order to do this, the internal life of the community must first be based on that same type of selfless love. Unless the miracle of loving forgiveness, the power of the Spirit, that overcomes natural self-interest, is evident in the way we live and relate together, the world will never know God's love. John seems to suggest that instead of "see my hands and my feet," Christ points to the body of his church, and says, "By this everyone will know that you are my disciples, if you have love for one another" (John 13:35).

Luke also suggests an equivalent meaning, especially where he mentions in The Acts of the Apostles that it is because of the presence of the Spirit in the community that "…day by day the Lord added to their number those who were being saved" (Acts 2:47). No one is expected to imitate the earliest believers. We know that many sold their property and lived communally. There were special circumstances that necessitated such an arrangement. The nucleus of the first Christian community was made up of people from northern Galilee, who had to sell their property to relocate in Jerusalem. In any case, they firmly expected the return of the risen Lord to occur soon. There was no reason to hold on to material possessions. When Luke composed his narratives some fifty years later, it was a very different time from the one lived by the earliest followers.

Even if we are not expected to renounce all private ownership, Jesus does expect us, according to John, to understand that our church community must be a place where people are aware of others' needs. The community imagined by John is to be a place of reconciliation, where natural differences are overcome and offenses forgiven. John expects that his community will know that the "peace of Christ" is more than a place for the repetition of rituals, or sharing only community concerns. Charity may begin at home, but it does not end there. The charter, the reason for the existence of the community, according to John, remains to carry on Jesus' mission to the world, to outsiders. "As the Father has sent me, so I send you" (John 20:21).

John describes the mission of Jesus as one to "take away the sin of the world" (John 1:29). Jesus is the "true light" of God, who makes known the mystery of God: "No one has ever seen God. It is God the only Son…who has made Him known" (John 1:18, also 14:9). Jesus is sent by the Father so that this light may shine throughout the world, and the world may come to believe. Yet God's light can produce two effects. When people see it, some choose to come forward, into the light (see John 3:21). These are those who are open to the stirrings of the Spirit of God that is in their hearts. Others, however, flee from the light, unwilling to consider Jesus' meaning for their lives. They love the darkness more than the light (see John 3:19 and 9:9). The mission of Jesus only confirms them in their choice.

Following the resurrection, Jesus entrusts his mission to his closest followers. It is the community, the church that is to bring his knowledge of God to a darkened world (see John 17:3, 26). It is this knowledge that will give the world eternal life. As he gives his disciples the command to go forth into the world, Jesus breathes on them and says, "Receive the Holy Spirit" (John 20:21–23; see also Acts 19:2; Luke 24:49). This action is deliberately intended to remind the reader of the account in Genesis 2:7, where God breathes his own life into Adam. Creation has reached a new beginning, a new genesis. Jesus' disciples are "born of God," knowing and sharing the very life of God.

TO BELIEVE IN GOD

What is the life of God? According to John it is love, forgiveness, and the willingness to surrender oneself for others: "God is love" (1 John 4:16). "Everyone who loves is born of God and knows God" (1 John 4:7). The followers of Jesus are charged to make God's love and mercy known in the world. Some people will see the light of truth and come forward into the light. They will turn away from evil and experience peace and joy. Others will turn away into the darkness and unbelief.

There is an old Latin expression, *fides quae creditur*, that refers to the objective truth of the statements of faith, or literally "the faith that is believed." In other words, you cannot believe without believing something to be true. If we are not merely deluded, it is essential that the something believed actually is true. As Paul, for one, said, "If Christ has not been raised…your faith has been in vain" (1 Corinthians 15:14). In this sense, to *believe* means to assent, for example, to the resurrection as a fact: "I *believe* that Jesus was raised from the dead on the third day." By itself this sense of the word *believe* implies nothing about one's personal disposition or feeling. I might believe that Jesus rose from the dead, or I might be curious about it, or even astonished. I might be the worst type of sinner possible. It was James who wrote, "Even the demons believe" (John 2:19).

The above is clearly not what Jesus had in mind when he gives a promise as recorded by John, "Blessed are those who have not seen and yet have come to believe" (John 20:29b). The faith that makes us "blessed" includes faith in the other sense, *fides qua creditur*, "the faith by which something is believed." In others words, this second sense refers to the interior decision or action in which I give over my existence into God's care. It implies not only the objective truth that there is a God who raised Jesus from the dead, but also that I as an individual have taken him as my God in whom I place my hope and trust.

John's Gospel gives further support to this insight by using words, such as "follow" and "obey." These are synonyms for *believe* (see John 3:36; 10:25–27 12:46–48). "Those who have believed" must be interpreted as those who have freely chosen to submit their lives to God as revealed in Jesus. According to

John, belief in the resurrection then means much more than affirming the resurrection intellectually. It means opening one's heart to the possibility of a further mode of life; it means discovering the person God desires me to be; it means trusting that the project of my life is secure no matter what happens. "Blessed are those who…have come to believe" (John 20:29b). To believe in this sense is to enter into an intimacy with God during life on earth. Of course, we might demand with Thomas to see with our eyes before we believe (John 20:27) rather than with the father of a convulsing boy who begs, "I believe; help my unbelief!" (Mark 9:24).

PEACE

The heart of John's Gospel is this: to become a believer in Jesus' resurrection is to receive the Spirit. To be "reborn" is to be born again of the Spirit, to become a child of God, and to share in divine life. These different phrases describe the same thing. One of John's favorite expressions concerns the final destiny God imagines for people, and John calls it *peace*. When people experience this type of peace, there will be great rejoicing and a responsibility to share the experience with others. In some cases, this can involve explicit missionary work, but it also refers to the kind of contagious love Luke describes in Acts 2:42–47. This contagious love won "the good will of all the people. And day by day the Lord added to their number those who were being saved" (Acts 2:47–48). Forgiveness of sins is another idea that is extended to be included by every believer; they are to become forgivers, peacemakers, demonstrating God's own mercy in the world around them. John sums up with the word *life*. As he tells us in the narrative, his goal is that we too might believe in the risen Lord, and "believing you may have *life* in his name" (John 20:31, emphasis added).

THE SPIRIT

The New Testament has several ways in which it describes the Spirit. On the most public level, the Spirit is the creative power of God that brings the community into existence (see Acts 2:1–4). Led by this Spirit, people go out as missionaries to the ends of the empire. A few Palestinian fishermen become the foundation of a worldwide community. The New Testament stories chronicle many of the events the earliest communities endure as they grow, strengthen, and face new challenges.

There are stirrings of the Spirit in individuals as well as the community. A community comes into existence because of the free, personal actions of the people involved. And the New Testament reports on the Spirit's work in the specific insights, choices, and concerns of particular individuals. Courage, patience, faith, wisdom—whatever moves a person beyond their personal concerns—is thought to be the stirrings of God's Spirit within them. There is a more profound experience described by Christian spiritual writers and mystics whereby that experience can almost be called a direct contact with God in the depths of an individual. If we are able to be aware of something more than the ordinary round of daily survival, and go deeper than even the deeper commitments and values that underlie these activities; if we go down to the most fundamental level of our lives, what do we discover? What are we? Some people call it a hunger, a question, a mystery. At the very core of our intelligence and affectivity, we find ourselves restless. Restless for what?

According to John, the answer is God. What we have deep within us is a question. And for the Christian the question has a divine answer. We would not be restless unless we somehow knew, or somehow could anticipate the destiny for which we long. We would not reach out for God unless he had first reached out to us. This is what Paul, among others, refers to when he says in Romans 8:15 that we experience a "[longing] too deep for words" (Romans 8:26–28). When we reach that level of awareness, we experience God's own Spirit and life (see John 20:19–23).

THE DEVELOPMENT OF THE EUCHARIST

The sixth chapter of John's Gospel continues to disconcert those who insist that a sacramental or eucharistic doctrine is a late development in church life. There is less argument regarding the final section of the chapter (see John 6:51–58); it describes not only an editor's hand but also an early community practice. So, too, it is clear that John's interpretation and theology is linked with his subtle and complex assessment of Jesus and what believers ought to share. As we have seen, his narrative offers dramatic interplays of dialogue, misunderstandings, refusals, and a final choice between belief and unbelief. This seems to form for John a timeless dialectic that is at the heart of the original disputes Jesus confronted between himself and the world, between light and darkness. It is a dialectic that continues today.

Unlike Paul and the synoptic accounts, John presents no recognizable scene where the Eucharist is instituted. He seems familiar with those other traditions, especially with Mark. John is the only Gospel writer who inserts a special episode, the washing of the disciples' feet, into the final meal (see John 13:1–20). Earlier in the narrative John identifies Judas' intentions to betray Jesus (see John 6:70–71 and 12:4–8). The reader learns of Judas' intent to betray Jesus following the discourse on the "bread of life." Then at dinner in the Bethany home of Lazarus, Judas speaks against anointing Jesus with expensive oil. During the final meal, after the foot washing, Jesus identifies his betrayer, gives Judas a morsel of bread, Satan enters Judas, he walks out, while the others misunderstand what is transpiring (see John 13:26-29). The reader does understand. John concludes the scene with a dramatic reminder: "And it was night" (John 13:30).

Judas' betrayal is not the only one John mentions after the foot washing scene. Peter's denial is predicted (John 13:36–38). John inserts the foot washing scene where the synoptics recall Jesus' words over the bread and cup of wine. Jesus answers Peter objections to the washing (John 13:6–11). After the explanation, Peter concedes and Jesus gives a mandate to imitate his gesture. The usual social behavior of the times is reversed by John. The foot washing gesture symbolizes how Jesus' closest followers are to serve.

The so-called bread of life discourse John locates earlier in his narrative is offered during the public ministry of Jesus in chapter 6. John seems to share Paul's interpretation and theology of baptism as a sharing in the death of Christ. His special phrase, "Those who eat my flesh and drink my blood" (John 6:54), has become one starting point for later theological understandings and disagreements regarding the meaning of the Christian Eucharist.

John uses a shocking and realistic vocabulary. The bread is literally to be "chewed" and the wine is "blood to drink." The bread is "true food" and the blood is "true drink" (see John 6:55). Jesus further describes the bread as his own flesh given for the life of the world (see John 6:51). He adds to an earlier statement, "I am the bread of life" (John 6:35), and has Jesus claim, "This is the bread that came down from heaven" (John 6:58). At this point, John seems to parallel Paul's report from the Last Supper in which Jesus says, "this is my body" (1 Corinthians 11:24).

It seems that John differs from Paul and the synoptic traditions in other ways. They emphasize the repetition of the Last Supper as a memorial of the death and resurrection of the Lord. It is part of an expectation of a final kingdom that will unfold when Christ returns in glory. John offers no kingdom imagery, nor any of Paul's admonitions concerning proper etiquette at community gatherings.

The Eucharist in John's portrayal is, among other things, a time when the community of believers remembers. They are to recall the life and teachings of Jesus, his resurrection, his words and wisdom. As followers they understand that their lives are to be understood as living out the death and resurrection of the Lord.

THE PARADOX OF KNOWING GOD

At the very heart of John's interpretation of the Christian religious experience is a paradox that may not be avoided. The paradox brings believers into the presence of the One whom Jesus named Father. For John, indeed for all

Christians, the religious experience of God is identical with human experience even as God's mysterious totality remains beyond complete human fathoming. In John's view, the human experience of God never requires an escape or movement away from human experience. Within each person dwells the beckoning presence of the Creator. As a result, when we find ourselves moving either in a personal search or moved by the apparently accidental situations in which we find ourselves, or to use an imaginative expression, when we move toward "the face of God," what we will see, according to John, is another human face. For John when you are most in the presence of God, you will find yourself deeply connected to humanity.

This paradox is part of a theological term developed later than the first century known as the *incarnation*. God enters human life and does not destroy the human situation. What it means to be alive is now further understood in a revelation given by God. And this revelation is meant to be a wisdom that Christ's disciples share with others.

THE WISDOM OF GOD

The theme of wisdom reappears throughout the Bible. At times the eternal wisdom of God is depicted as the one who is the architect of all creation. It is a majestic wisdom who conjures up the continents from the chaotic water, sets the firmament of the sky and stars, and fills the earthy landscape with glorious works of natural beauty. According to the Book of Wisdom, wisdom grows weary of its clouds and ocean depths. It longs to come down from the heavens and reside in people. "Although she is but one, / she can do all things, / and while remaining in herself, / she renews all things; / in every generation she passes / into holy souls / and makes them friends of God, / and prophets (Wisdom 7:27).

Not every ancient tradition explains the world this way. Sometimes wisdom descends to the world, and in the words of mythology, takes a look around and wisely rushes away. The Hebrew view describes wisdom as a sojourner. In some places wisdom is found in Jewish religious shrines, the Temple at Jerusalem, in the Law of Moses, or in pious customs. By the time the author of Sirach preached during the early second century before Jesus, there was little that seemed glorious in the life of Palestinian Jews. The many enmities between members of the old northern kingdom with their shrines and the southern kingdom people with their loyalty to the Jerusalem Temple were exhausted. Occupation by foreign rulers fueled new despair. People discovered a link between wisdom and hope during this period. Without hope, wisdom is foolish.

Wisdom is an obscure theme. A wise judge is not the same as a wise politician. The wisdom needed to rear a child is not quite the wisdom of a senior citizen. Wisdom comes to some people through suffering and to others when they decide to suffer no longer. Wisdom is sometimes equated with common sense, yet common sense, at times, is the enemy of wisdom. Wisdom may be expressed in silence, or in carefully chosen words. Wisdom is said not known, and at other times to know in depth. In some works of literature or on the stage, wisdom is played by fools.

Wisdom in John's narrative is personified in God's Son. His teachings enlighten and provide spirit to his friends as they live in this wonderful, yet unfinished world. A directive intoned during the liturgy in some Christian churches immediately before the Gospel text is proclaimed states, "Pay attention to the wisdom of Jesus Christ." John's community would agree.

REVIEW QUESTIONS

1. John has a special interpretation of Jesus. Describe several special characteristics of his interpretation.
2. A central theme of John's presentation is that Jesus is "the bread of life" and the one who has come into the world to give "eternal life." Explain each of these concepts.
3. Thomas reveals the difficulty some people have with belief in survival after death. He comes to believe in Jesus in a direct experience of meeting the risen Christ. The text honors those who have not seen, yet believe. Offer your comments on various ways people come to believe in the risen Christ.

FOR FURTHER STUDY

1. Brown, Raymond, and Francis Maloney. *An Introduction to the Gospel of John* (New York: Doubleday, 2003). See also Brown's article "The Gospel According to John" in *An Introduction to the New Testament* (New York: Doubleday, 1997), pp. 333–382.
2. Bauckham, Richard. *The Testimony of the Beloved Disciple: Narrative History and Theology* (Grand Rapids, MI: Baker Academic, 2007). Twelve essays rooted in evangelical claims that the Gospels are reliable and historical and other sensitivities.
3. Schneiders, Sandra. *Written That You May Believe: Encountering Jesus in the Fourth Gospel* (New York: Herder & Herder, 2007), revised and expanded). After reading Bauckham, try Professor Schneider. She offers a spiritual call to meet Jesus in John's texts as an extension of her multidisciplinary scholarship. An excellent survey of feminist scholarly questions and possible applications to the spiritual life of the reader.

4. Koester, Craig G. *Symbolism in the Fourth Gospel* (Minneapolis, MN: Augsburg Fortress, 2003, revised and updated). Koester, a Lutheran scholar, sees much in John's text that is historical (there was a wedding at Cana, there were miracles, and so on). Even more, there are numerous references in John to community rituals (sacraments), especially the Eucharist. His discussion of the multiple meanings for symbolism is intelligible for all readers.

5. Martyn, J. Louis. *History and Theology in the Fourth Gospel* (Louisville, KY: Westminster, 2003, revised third edition). Martyn was a trailblazer in the critical study of John. His analysis is a resource for many biblical scholars. This is an excellent tool to use to learn of the groundbreaking theses a scholar first proposed four decades ago about John and his church community.

6. Barton, John. *The Nature of Biblical Criticism* (Louisville, KY: Westminster, 2007). A clear survey of fresh developments and divergent methods in the field. Barton contends there is more unity of usage by scholars than sometimes admitted.

7. Dennis, John A. *Jesus' Death and the Gathering of True Israel: The Johannine Appropriation of Restoration Theology in the Light of John 11:47–52* (Tubingen, Germany: Mohr Siebeck, 2006). A revised doctoral thesis in which the author uses an interpretative method that combines narrative-critical and historical-contextual approaches. He claims his method offers a sensible dialectical connection with others who are interested in John's restoration theology as found in 11:47–52. The volume is for students who seek an exhaustive bibliography of recent scholarship and lengthy footnotes.

8. Many professional societies offer annual reports on recently published scholarly works. *The Journal of Biblical Literature,* The College Theology Society, and The Catholic Theological Society of America (among others) offer book reviews as do professional journals, such as *Theological Studies and Theology Today.* The student who "falls in love" with the wisdom of the New Testament may find in these resources helpful guides for further reading and study.

Epilogue

We began our study of the New Testament with a consideration of Benedict XVI's assessment of the importance of biblical theology in the life and devotion of individual Christians and the universal church community. His call for a renewed spiritual exegesis in which the work of biblical scholars continues to inform the worship and devotion of believers hinges on a clearly articulated concern that certain presuppositions in scholarly methods today are detached or indifferent to the liturgy of the church and the spiritual journeys of its members.

Spiritual exegesis has taken a number of forms in the history of Christianity. The earliest Christians, especially those who first recorded remembrances of Jesus' teachings, used a particular form of spiritual exegesis. They searched Hebrew and Greek Jewish Scriptures to explain and to justify not only their favorite proclamations about Jesus, but also to give answers to their associates and opponents for the special kind of hope and spirit that characterized their new way of life. Their testimonies were shared when the community gathered for prayer and worship.

As a result, the New Testament is a treasure trove of first attempts by Christian believers to unpack the mysteries of God and his Christ, even as it gives witness to new questions and insights individuals and communities shared and sometimes resolved. As they applied the teachings of Jesus to new circumstances, fresh insights—as well as new uncertainties—developed. Early on they shared a creed, a simple outline of their new beliefs.

Their original stories were resurrection stories. The Risen One was the foundation of their belief, and his revelation rested on the testimony of eyewitnesses and those who had personal conversions to his way of living. As time passed, communities of believers rethought all of the things that had happened between the earliest believers and Jesus and tried to make applications to the new situations they confronted. Slowly they came to realize that some of their earliest formulations could be extended; not everything was revealed during Christ's lifetime or in the experience of the first band of eyewitnesses. The community claimed that it was God's Spirit guiding them from the beginning in a new way of faith.

The "deposit of faith" they offer is not a static, once and for all, expression of static propositions. Faith has several forms, yet what is termed *blind faith* is seldom honored in the New Testament. More often faith in Christ resembles a perspective that is lived and applied as a living creed.

The Gospel writers have a powerful instinct to remember the first events with Jesus as one way to strengthen their faith. This is not unusual. People do this with memories of the early days of love or friendship. They go back to the beginnings of it; they remember and share in the present time their memories from long ago. They report what it was like when they first began as students or when they started anything. People want to retouch the power and freshness and upsurge of what they now have become. Some memories are pleasing; others are less so.

The New Testament is not embarrassed to report that from the beginning some of the closest friends of Jesus failed to understand him. More than a few of them walked away disappointed. Long before they wrote about Jesus, Christians gathered to pray and share their present-day imitation of his way. Their Eucharist (thanksgiving) was a communal expression of personal and shared faith in the One who reveals yet remains mysterious.

For some contemporary people faith has been reduced to an emotional and private preference. Others regard religious faith as wishful or magical thinking. Still others consider religious faith a dangerous delusion. The Gospel writers were aware of ancient equivalents of these viewpoints and admit to memories of misunderstandings, betrayals, and failures while Jesus was with them. They are not ashamed to admit that the way of Christ is not the easiest path in life to follow, especially since Christ often recommends a reversal of the ordinary ways in which people evaluate reality or what is important in life.

Jesus desired that his closest followers work quietly to establish God's age or kingdom on earth. He could turn a phrase and make words dance. His closest friends were not to work for wealth or prestige. Instead, they were to work quietly, unnoticed much as a buried seed in the ground grows while people sleep. Like a bit of yeast in a batch of bread dough, they were to bring the lightness and expansiveness of God's presence into this unfinished world. Into whatever darkness they entered, they were to know that they carried within the light of the world. They were to carry God's compassion to those who endure unbearable sufferings, and his closest friends were to become salt of the earth to create a kingdom wherein the world would be renewed by the purity of their motives and the honesty of their friendship.

The Christian imagination is an imagination of promise. It often makes use of Jesus' images for the future as recorded in the Gospels and thereby becomes a language used to interpret each moment in life. For Christians our world is to be transformed by his closest friends into a preview of what the resurrection of Jesus promises awaits us all. It is a perspective that helps us to live and understand that even with a destiny in heaven, our task in the present is to discover a loving presence that is the reason for our hope.

"Give them what you have," and Jesus will take care of the rest.